FOUR
VIEWS
ON **CHRISTIAN SPIRITUALITY**

Books in the Counterpoints Series

Church Life

Bible and Theology

FOUR
VIEWS
ON
CHRISTIAN SPIRITUALITY

Bradley Nassif

Scott Hahn

Joseph D. Driskill

Evan Howard

Stanley N. Gundry, series editor
Bruce Demarest, general editor

ZONDERVAN.com/
AUTHORTRACKER
follow your favorite authors

ZONDERVAN

Four Views on Christian Spirituality
Copyright © 2012 by Bruce Demarest, Bradley Nassif, Scott Hahn, Joseph Driskill, and Evan Howard

This title is also available as a Zondervan ebook. Visit www.zondervan.com/ebooks.

Requests for information should be addressed to:
Zondervan, *Grand Rapids, Michigan* 49530

Library of Congress Cataloging-in-Publication Data

Four views on Christian spirituality / Bradley Nassif . . . [et al.].
    p. cm. — (Counterpoints)
    Includes index.
    ISBN 978-0-310-32928-2 (softcover)
    1. Spirituality. I. Nassif, Bradley.
BV4501.3.F685 2012
248 — dc23   2011051672

Cover design: *Tammy Johnson*
Cover photo: *National Geographic/SuperStock*
Interior design: *Matthew Van Zomeren*

Printed in the United States of America

12 13 14 15 16 17 18 /DCI/ 21 20 19 18 17 16 15 14 13 12 11 10 9 8 7 6 5 4 3 2 1

CONTENTS

FOREWORD

In recent years, we have seen a surge of interest in spirituality among evangelicals that has continued unabated. Most works on spirituality, however, have tended to build on a specific tradition. This is understandable, since spirituality is the lived dimension of the Christian faith, and the faith is always expressed through specific traditioning communities. Sometimes a particular spiritual practice may become closely associated with a particular spiritual tradition. For example, when it comes to spiritual guidance, many modern Christians tend to associate it with the desert fathers and Ignatius Loyola. Similarly, Christians seeking a more intensely personal and "supernaturalistic" form of spirituality have turned to the Pentecostal/charismatic churches. But seldom do we have a book that compares the major Christian spiritual traditions in such a way that their respective contours are sharply defined. The value of this approach is that readers unacquainted with these spiritual traditions are given a faithful and succinct introduction, and those who are more knowledgeable will be able to appreciate the finer nuances.

The contributors are intimately familiar with the spiritual traditions they represent. The essential features of Catholic, Orthodox, evangelical, and mainline Protestant spiritualities are expertly fleshed out and seen at their best. What they have given us are four rather winsome portraits of Christian spiritualities, while the responses to each from the other three enable readers to see where these spiritualities converge and diverge.

The resulting pictures allow us to make comparisons and contrasts in various configurations. For example, if we compare Eastern and Western spiritualities as they are given here, Western Christianity, both Catholic and Protestant, tends to emphasize the salvific work of Christ, while Eastern Orthodoxy sees Christ's work as going beyond restoring what was lost through the fall to include bringing humanity to where it never was before the fall, namely, growth into fuller communion with the triune God. The central motif of Orthodoxy is communion, while the central motif of Western Christianity is salvation.

Again, while both evangelical and Orthodox spiritualities are gospel centered, there are distinct differences in the way each understands the gospel. For the evangelical, the gospel is largely focused on the person of Jesus Christ and his salvific work on the cross, whereas for the Orthodox, Jesus Christ is always seen in relation to the Trinity, and the gospel is about the whole story of Christ from his conception to his second coming. Further, for evangelicals, the Christian life is more about the individual's relationship with God, whereas for the Orthodox and Catholic, it is about life in a community shaped by Scripture and the living tradition expressed supremely in the liturgy.

In Catholic spirituality, the dominant image is the family, and the key figure in the triune family is the Father, who through his Son makes us "sons in the Son." Thus the church is seen as the extension of the Trinitarian family, and the earthly family as imaging the church. In evangelical spirituality, by contrast, the Father is hardly mentioned; rather, the focus is on Jesus and what it means to be personally related to him, especially through his redemptive work on the cross.

Progressive mainline Protestant spirituality stands in an interesting relation to the other three. As Joseph Driskill himself has observed, "Mainline Protestant spirituality seems more vulnerable and more in need of changing course than the other interlocutors because of its enmeshment with the modern worldview." Its main resources for change are social institutions, whereas for the others, the resources are essentially spiritual. In contrast to evangelicalism, which stresses the individual's relationship with God, progressive Protestantism stresses the social and structural dimensions of life. Unlike Catholicism, which also stresses the role of the church in individual and corporate transformation, mainline progressives rely largely on social institutions to do it. And in contrast to Orthodoxy, progressive Protestantism centers the work of the kingdom of God in the created order, whereas Orthodoxy centers it in the ecclesial community.

These few examples give us a hint of what this book seeks to accomplish. But beyond helping us appreciate the similarities and differences, the strengths and weaknesses, the exchanges between the interlocutors also highlight at least three other important implications. First, they show that our common Trinitarian confession has spiritual ramifications too large to be adequately captured by any one spiritual tradition. If that is the case, then, second, the mutual critique and appreciation should lead to self-correction and transformation from within. Third, the awareness of each other's strengths and weaknesses should serve to motivate all toward a more holistic and ecumenical spirituality. Hopefully, evangelicals will come away with a better grasp of Catholic comprehensiveness, Catholics and Orthodox Christians with a fresh injection of evangelical fervor, and mainline Protestants with both.

Simon Chan (PhD, Cambridge) is Earnest Lau professor of systematic theology at Trinity Theological College in Singapore. He is the author of several books, including *Pentecostal Theology and the Christian Spiritual Tradition*, *Spiritual Theology: A Systematic Study of the Christian Life*, and *Liturgical Theology: The Church as Worshiping Community*.

INTRODUCTION

BRUCE DEMAREST

A prominent feature of our times is the robust revival of spirituality, both Christian and non-Christian. Researchers have developed spiritualities of women, men, marriage, children, midlife, the workplace, leisure, suffering, the Eucharist, and so on. Dissatisfaction with materialism and consumerism, as well as with formal institutional religion, have all contributed to this trend. Economic crises, ecological calamities, and worldwide terrorism have intensified the search for ultimate reality, meaning, and security.

Seeking to nurture their souls, many people are attending seminars on life enrichment, gathering in prayer and meditation groups, attending conferences and workshops on the spiritual life, and receiving spiritual direction. A plethora of books and periodicals explore sacred terrain and spiritual experience. Popular works on spirituality are hot-ticket items, outselling most other categories of books. Scholarly organizations such as The Society for the Study of Christian Spirituality and journals such as *Spiritus* and the *Journal of Spiritual Formation and Soul Care* creatively engage spirituality on an academic level. In addition, a growing number of programs in spirituality and formation are offered by colleges and seminaries. Moreover, local and national parachurch organizations have formed around spiritual emphases. Websites devoted to spirituality further fuel interest in the subject.[1] At this writing, an online search of the word *spirituality* yields more than 150 million entries. A defining characteristic of our restless times, then, is that spirituality is back with a vengeance, as fully two-thirds of America's adults regard themselves as "deeply spiritual."[2] The spirituality sprawl evidenced in both the church and the culture has led to a tsunami of options available to seekers of all stripes.

---

1. See Brenda E. Brasher, *Give Me That Online Religion* (San Francisco: Jossey-Bass, 2001).

2. Barna Group, "American Spirituality Gives Way to Simplicity and the Desire to Make a Difference," www.barna.org/faith-spirituality/19-american-spirituality-gives-way-to-simplicity-and-the-desire-to-make-a-difference (accessed February 15, 2011).

A Walmart of Spiritual Options

The superabundance of highly diverse spiritual practices in the market-place challenges classical Christian understanding. Zen meditation groups, parapsychology, Yoga paths, psychic readings, channeling workshops, Wicca (witchcraft *redivivus*), out-of-body experiences, UFO phenomena, and Native American practices are prevalent in our culture.[3] Eclectic movements such as the New Age continue to capture widespread interest today.[4] According to the Pew Foundation, one-quarter of Americans dabble in astrology. Driving such freewheeling forms of spirituality is the human capacity for self-transcendence, the pursuit of human potential, and the quest for meaning and value.

Allowing for flexibility of categories, what might be designated secular or self-styled spirituality constitutes the quest for self-actualization without reference to God or commitment to any religious tradition. Sandra Schneiders describes spirituality generically as "conscious life involvement in the project of life integration through self-transcendence toward the ultimate value one perceives."[5] John Macquarrie envisions spirituality as *"becoming a person in the fullest sense."*[6] In a recent national survey, 24 percent of respondents identified themselves as "spiritual but not religious," meaning that nearly one-quarter of citizens surveyed have "combined diverse beliefs and practices into a personal faith that fits no standard definition."[7] Indeed, the "spiritually inclined" represent one of America's fastest-growing movements. One indicator of this trend is the fact that "in the USA nearly 2.8 million people now identify with dozens of new religious movements, calling themselves Wiccan, pagan, or Spiritualist."[8]

---

3. See Pamela Carswell, *Offbeat Spirituality* (New York: Sheed & Ward, 1961).

4. See Richard Woods, "What Is New Age Spirituality," *The Way* 31 (July 1993): 176–88.

5. Sandra M. Schneiders, "Christian Spirituality: Definition, Methods and Types," in *The New Westminster Dictionary of Christian Spirituality*, ed. Philip Sheldrake (Louisville: Westminster, 2005), 1.

6. John Macquarrie, "Spirit and Spirituality," in *Exploring Christian Spirituality*, ed. Kenneth J. Collins (Grand Rapids: Baker, 2000), 63.

7. Christine Wicker, "How Spiritual Are We?" *Denver Post, PARADE* magazine (October 4, 2009), 4.

8. Cathy Lynn Grossman, "Most Religious Groups in USA Have Lost Ground, Survey Finds," www.usatoday.com/news/religion/2009-03-09-american-religion-ARIS_N.htm (accessed April 27, 2010).

Followers of generic spirituality might be found skydiving from a plane, bungee jumping off a cliff, taking in a rousing rock concert, or pondering a brilliant ocean sunset in quest of a scintillating experience and enhanced self-knowledge. Donald Bloesch maintains that secular spirituality, or what he terms the "new spirituality," embraces the New Age movement, process philosophy, creation spirituality, and postmodernism. The new spirituality, he insists, is promoted by "untrustworthy guides" such as Carl Jung, Matthew Fox, Deepak Chopra, and Joseph Campbell.[9]

Postmodern spirituality, under whose eclectic umbrella can be found the self-help movement, Native American sweat lodges, Taizé communities, and the Mosaic generation, embraces a unique set of common characteristics. These include the limitations of reason and the scientific method, the subject-oriented and culturally conditioned nature of knowledge, rejection of metanarratives and authoritative dogmas, and the conviction that all spiritual quests lead to God. Of particular relevance for postmodern spirituality is concern for spiritual experience and human connectedness, disillusionment with material possessions, and distrust of the institutional church.

Religious spirituality represents a second expression of spirituality, involving pursuit of the Absolute in non-Christian faiths such as Hinduism, Buddhism, Judaism, and Islam. The rise of interest in comparative religions has produced a flood of books depicting the spiritual quest in the world's religions. The monumental series The Classics of Western Spirituality contains volumes devoted to Jewish, Christian, Islamic, and Native American spirituality. Scholar Ewert Cousins expounds a pluriform religious understanding of spirituality in his twenty-five-volume series titled *World Spirituality: An Encyclopedic History of the Religious Quest*. The series devotes extensive attention to the spirituality of the major traditions — Hindu, Buddhist, Taoist, Confucian, Jewish, Islamic, and so forth.[10]

Popular today is the synthesis of world religious perspectives in a common spiritual quest, often referred to as "eclectic" or "hybrid"

---

9. Donald G. Bloesch, *Spirituality Old and New* (Downers Grove, Ill., InterVarsity, 2007), 45–46.

10. Ewert Cousins, ed., *World Spirituality: An Encyclopedic History of the Religious Quest* (New York: Crossroad, 1985–).

spirituality.[11] Wayne Teasdale, former professor at DePaul University and the Catholic Theological Union and principal at the Parliament of Religions, sought to unite Christianity, Hinduism, and Buddhism "in the way of Christian sannyasa" (i.e., unfolding of life within Hindu life stages).[12] Moreover, in his prize-winning book *Care of the Soul*, former Catholic priest and therapist Thomas Moore expounds a pan-religious spirituality that he insists is not specifically Christian. Moore's syncretistic spirituality endorses Greek polytheism, Zen Buddhism, spiritualism, and Native American spirituality.[13] The Pew Forum on Religion and Public Life reported in 2009 that "elements of Eastern faiths and New Age thinking have been widely accepted by 65 percent of U.S. adults, including many who call themselves Protestants and Catholics."[14]

Contemporary culture, then, reflects a tidal wave of spirituality where humans eagerly grasp for personal integration and meaning for their lives. As noted by the secular press, "When it comes to religion, the USA is now land of the freelancers" or "a greenhouse for spiritual sprouts."[15]

The third form of spirituality—Christian spirituality—will be defined below.

Spiritual Hunger in the Culture

The above phenomena reflect deep-seated spiritual restlessness and longing for personal fulfillment and life satisfaction. During the summer of 1999, some forty thousand people gathered in New York's Central Park to hear the Dalai Lama speak. A twenty-four-year-old man reportedly said of his speech, "This shows that people are spiritually starved. I hope some people will hear his message." Centuries ago, Augustine underscored this principle: "I sought for something to love

---

11. See Valerie Lesniak, "Contemporary Spirituality," in *The New Westminster Dictionary of Christian Spirituality*, 10.

12. Frederic and Mary Ann Brussat, "Remembering the Spiritual Masters Project: Wayne Teasdale," www.spiritualityandpractice.com/teachers/teachers.php?id=202&g= (accessed June 25, 2010).

13. See Thomas Moore, *Care of the Soul: A Guide for Cultivating Depth and Sacredness in Everyday Life* (New York: HarperCollins, 1992).

14. Cathy Lynn Grossman, "More U.S. Christians Mix in 'Eastern,' New Age Beliefs," www.usatoday.com/news/religion/2009-12-10-1Amixingbeliefs10_CV_N.htm (accessed April 27, 2010).

15. Grossman, "Most Religious Groups in USA Have Lost Ground."

... There was a hunger within me from a lack of inner food, which is none other than Yourself, my God."[16]

Heightened interest in spirituality in the West is accompanied by growing indifference to Christianity and a decline in traditional religious practices. Many twenty-first-century people are turned off by organized religion, which they perceive to be legalistic and bureaucratic. Research confirms that most American religious denominations have declined numerically since 1990. "The percentage of people who call themselves in some way Christian has dropped more than 11% in a generation."[17] Furthermore, 15 percent of Americans report they don't practice any religion.[18] A Pew Survey concluded that young people as a group were far less likely than those in past generations to affiliate with any religious organization. Thus, 26 percent of Millennials (born 1981–2000)—who value innovation, meaningful pursuits, and social networking—cite no religious affiliation, as is the case with 20 percent of Generation Xers (born 1965–80).[19]

The "Nones"—people who claim no religious identity—have increased significantly in recent years. In 2009, the "Nones" comprised 15 percent of the American population, up from 8 percent in 1990.[20] As an aside, the state with the largest percentage of "Nones" in 2008 was Vermont, with 34 percent declaring no religious affiliation.[21]

But apathy to organized religion in no way implies indifference to spirituality that often is viewed as personally nurturing and life giving. In a survey of twelve hundred eighteen- to twenty-nine-year-olds, Life-Way Research reported that 72 percent are "really more spiritual than religious."[22] Sculpted as *imago Dei*, humans instinctively search for the

---

16. Augustine, *Confessions*, 3.1.

17. Grossman, "Most Religious Groups in USA Have Lost Ground."

18. Cathy Lynn Grossman, "When the Spirit Moves You," *USA Weekend*, www.usaweekend.com/article/20100402/LIVING/100331001/When-spirit-moves-you (accessed July 14, 2011).

19. Cathy Lynn Grossman, "Young Adults 'Less Religious,' Not Necessarily 'More Secular,'" www.usatoday.com/news/religion/2010-02-17-pewyouth17_ST_N.htm (accessed April 27, 2010).

20. Cathy Lynn Grossman, "'Nones' Now 15% of Population," www.usatoday.com/news/religion/2009-03-09-aris-survey-nones_N.htm (accessed April 27, 2010).

21. Grossman, "Most Religious Groups in USA Have Lost Ground."

22. Cathy Lynn Grossman, "Survey: 72% of Millennials 'More Spiritual Than Religious,'" www.usatoday.com/news/religion/2010-04-27-1Amillfaith27_ST_N.htm (accessed April 27, 2010).

transcendent "who" and "why" in a world of the scientific "what" and "how." Endowed with undying souls, persons consciously or unconsciously quest for the "tree of life"—for personal, lived experience of the Transcendent that holds out the promise of security and hope for the future.

Spiritual Hunger in the Church

Laypeople testify that the pressures of earning a living in today's competitive world, lack of genuine community, and anxiety about the future often impede relationship with God. Seminarians frequently admit that the intellectual rigors of academic life challenge their spiritual vitality. Many clergy lament that the plethora of ministry responsibilities often presents roadblocks to cultivation of spiritual life, even causing spiritual burnout. A Baptist pastor pursuing a Doctor of Ministry degree related, "Toward the end of seminary, my spiritual life reached an all-time low. Seminary sent my spiritual life into hibernation, and my first church nearly killed it altogether." A Lutheran pastor bemoaned, "I would quit my position tomorrow if it wouldn't screw up my retirement."

Barna research demonstrates that only 52 percent of Christians are making some effort to grow spiritually, and many of these are inconsistent and achieve limited results. As discipleship evangelist Bill Hull points out, "Even more well-intentioned believers drift and find themselves nearly comatose spiritually, numbed by years of religious activity without transformation."[23] Pastor and writer A. W. Tozer observed that "for millions of Christians ... God is no more real than He is to the non-Christian. They go through life trying to love an ideal and be loyal to a mere principle."[24] In his book *The Great Omission*, Dallas Willard quotes Thoreau's famous phrase to illustrate that most Christians "live lives of quiet desperation." I interpret this to mean that Christians read in the Bible about the dynamic and victorious life in Christ but don't know how to get there themselves.[25] The judgment of the apostle Paul remains relevant today: "I could not address you as people who live by

---

23. Bill Hull, *Choose the Life* (Grand Rapids: Baker, 2004), 38.

24. A. W. Tozer, *A Treasury of Tozer*, ed. Warren W. Wiersbe (Grand Rapids: Baker, 1980), 98.

25. See Dallas Willard, *The Great Omission: Recovering Jesus' Essential Teachings on Discipleship* (San Francisco: HarperSanFrancisco, 2006), 120–21. The chasm between understanding what we ought to be in Christ and our actual experience is sometimes called the "sanctification gap." See John Coe, "Spiritual Theology: Bridging the Sanctification Gap for the Sake of the Church," *Journal of Spiritual Formation & Soul Care*, 2.1 (Spring 2009): 4–43.

the Spirit but as people who are still worldly—mere infants in Christ" (1 Corinthians 3:1).

Theologian J. I. Packer wrote:

> The experiential reality of perceiving God is unfamiliar territory today. The pace and preoccupation of urbanized, mechanized, collectivized, secularized modern life are such that any sort of inner life ... is very hard to maintain ... And if you attempt it, you will certainly seem eccentric to your peers, for nowadays involvement in a stream of activities is decidedly "in," and the older idea of a quiet, contemplative life is just as decidedly "out." The concept of a Christian life as sanctified rush and bustle still dominates, and as a result the experiential side of Christian holiness remains very much a closed book.[26]

The fact is that the church has not suffered from a lack of effort. But evidence suggests that typical regimens of sanctification commended to congregants are too programmatic, too superficial, and too fast to cultivate a vibrant spirituality. Professing Christians often find themselves notionally correct but spiritually undernourished.

Enter Christian Spirituality

During the past several decades, God graciously has wrought a revival of Christian spirituality and formation in the broader church. Although the word *spirituality* is not found in the English Bible, this proves not to be a show-stopping issue; other common terms such as Trinity, seeker-sensitive church, and seminary likewise do not occur in Scripture. The term *spirituality* corresponds to the Latin noun, *spiritualitas*, which is related to the Greek noun *pneuma* ("spirit") and the adjective *pneumatikos* ("spiritual")—the latter referring to qualities produced in persons empowered by God's Spirit (1 Corinthians 2:14–15; Galatians 6:1). Christian spirituality embraces devotion to the triune God, abiding in Christ, pursuit of holiness, and cultivation of virtues—in short, the whole of life lived under the direction and power of the Holy Spirit. Note that the New Testament, contrary to Greek philosophy, never sets spirit in opposition to physical matter. It does, however, distinguish qualities born of the Spirit (*pneumatikos*) from qualities that are worldly or carnal (*sarkikos*).

---

26. James I. Packer, *Keep in Step with the Spirit* (Old Tappan, N.J.: Revell, 1984), 74–75.

Until quite recently, the word *spirituality* was largely the province of Eastern Orthodox, Roman Catholic, and Anglican traditions. In the seventeenth and eighteenth centuries, Puritans, Pietists, Wesleyans, and others represented spirituality by terms such as piety, godliness, holiness of life, devotion, and Christian perfection. We may affirm, preliminarily, that Christian spirituality embraces the whole of godly life and practice, inclusive of vocation, politics, economics, sexuality, physical and emotional health, and creation care. The term *spirituality* also is used for the academic study of humans' holistic relation to God, to others, and to the surrounding environment. Several definitions of Christian spirituality will inform our study:

- the whole of human life viewed in terms of a conscious relationship with God, in Jesus Christ, through the indwelling of the Spirit and within the community of believers.[27] — Philip Sheldrake
- lived experience of God in Christ through the Spirit and reflection on this experience.[28] — Barry L. Callen
- the Christian life in the presence and power of the Holy Spirit; being conformed to the person of Christ and united in communion with God and others.[29] — Michael Downey
- the art of living with Jesus, or the "with-God" life.[30] — Richard J. Foster
- our continuing response to the reality of God's grace shaping us into the likeness of Jesus Christ, through the work of the Holy Spirit, in the community of faith, for the sake of the world.[31] — Jeffrey Greenman

The apophatic and the cataphatic traditions represent two ways of nurturing Christian spirituality. Apophatic ("without images") represents the path of knowing God by sheer negation. Advocates aver that the divine Reality, dwelling in a realm beyond human comprehension,

---

27. Philip Sheldrake, *Spirituality and Theology* (Maryknoll, N.Y.: Orbis, 1998), 35.
28. Barry L. Callen, *Authentic Spirituality* (Grand Rapids: Baker, 2001), 17.
29. Michael Downey, *Understanding Christian Spirituality* (New York: Paulist, 1997), 146.
30. Richard J. Foster, *Life with God* (New York: HarperOne, 2008), 7.
31. Jeffrey Greenman, "Spiritual Formation in Theological Perspective," in *Life in the Spirit*, ed. Jeffrey P. Greenman and George Kalantzis (Downers Grove, Ill.: InterVarsity, 2010), 24.

cannot be known by ideas, images, and language. Rather, God is known in the darkness by detachment, prayerful silence, and contemplation. Proponents appeal to Moses' approach to God in "thick darkness" (Exodus 20:21), as well as in a "cloud" (Exodus 24:15). Robust apophatic spirituality is found in Gregory of Nyssa (c. 335–c. 395), Meister Eckhart (c. 1260–c. 1328), *The Cloud of Unknowing* (fourteenth century), John of the Cross (1542–1591), and Eastern Orthodoxy.

Cataphatic ("with images") refers to the path of knowing God by affirmation, namely, through his self-revelation mediated by the intellect and senses. This path affirms that truths about the Almighty are disclosed via biblical teaching, the sacraments, and other symbols of the faith. Cataphatic spirituality is prevalent in Augustine, Luther, Calvin, the spiritual Exercises of Ignatius, and the teachings, liturgy, and art forms of the Catholic and Protestant traditions. Both apophatic and cataphatic ways direct sincere seekers to God and spiritual life.

A contemplative spirituality may be distinguished from an active or apostolic spirituality. The former emphasizes prayerful abiding in the divine Presence, whereas the latter stresses active service to God and others. The contemplative path is seen in biblical figures such as Mary and the apostle John and in historical persons such as Julian of Norwich, John of the Cross, and Thomas Merton. The activist path is evidenced in Mary's sister, Martha; the apostles Paul and Peter; together with Francis of Assisi, David Brainerd, and Mother Teresa. Many Christian authorities (e.g., Richard Rohr, Richard Foster) rightly commend the integration of contemplation and action.

The preceding suggests that Christian spirituality focuses, subjectively, on the "with-God" life in all its lived dimensions. It concerns the manner by which, individually and corporately, we understand our existence and live in communion with Christ in response to the Spirit in pursuit of holiness and service. Christian spirituality thus embraces thoughtful reflection on the faith, the existential process of spiritual growth in godliness, and compassionate care for others. It intentionally integrates head and heart—intellect, volition, affections, morality, relationships, and behaviors or actions.

Objectively, spirituality focuses on the scholarly study of the aforementioned realities. What is often described as spiritual theology includes the study of biblical documents (e.g., the Pauline letters), spiritual authorities (e.g., Francis de Sales), denominational perspectives (e.g., Pentecostal), ecclesial orders (e.g., Benedictine), and major Christian traditions, as in this volume's study of Eastern Orthodox, Roman Catholic, progressive Protestant, and evangelical spirituality.

The Four Christian Traditions

To understand how spirituality is understood in the church and how it nurtures the "with-God" life, we explore four leading Christian traditions: Orthodox, Roman Catholic, progressive Protestant, and evangelical. We recognize at the outset that North American Christianity is strong at change and innovation and relatively weak at welcoming faithful tradition. Although change simply for change's sake should be avoided, both continuity and change must be honored and embraced. Examination of the four major Christian traditions constitutes the task of this book in quest of an integrated and viable spirituality.

This study intentionally has been limited to the four Christian traditions cited above. Others might have been considered, such as Anglicanism and Pentecostalism, but in many respects these embody features common to one or more of the four chosen traditions. Anglican spirituality, for example, reflects many perspectives from Roman Catholic and evangelical spirituality.[32] Consistently conservative, Pentecostal or charismatic spirituality bears close affinities to the evangelical model. As we examine the spirituality of the four Christian traditions we are likely to discover that, in spite of differences, they offer constructive insights into spiritual protocols that facilitate life transformation and ministry effectiveness in our complex and threatening world.

What Is Eastern Orthodoxy?

The Orthodox Church is a communion of churches situated primarily in the eastern Mediterranean, eastern Europe, and the Middle East, governed by patriarchs or metropolitans who look to the ecumenical patriarch of Constantinople as the "first among equals." Separated from the church of the West following the so-called "Great Schism" in 1054,

---

32. See Frank C. Senn, ed., *Protestant Spiritual Traditions* (New York: Paulist, 1985). Similarities in the area of spiritual companionship and soul care are reflected in Gary W. Moon and David G. Benner, *Spiritual Direction and the Care of Souls* (Downers Grove, Ill.: Inter-Varsity, 2004), chapters 3–8.

Orthodoxy is defined by the teachings of the ancient fathers and the seven ecumenical councils from Nicea I (325) to Nicea II (787) that dealt with issues of the Trinity, the divine-human person of Christ, the virgin Mary, and the role of icons.

Orthodox distinctives include the incomprehensibility of the divine essence to the human mind, the infallibility of the seven ecumenical councils, the authoritative role of tradition, veneration of icons as portals to the divine, baptismal regeneration, elaborate sacramental and liturgical worship, the perpetual virginity of Mary the "God-bearer" (i.e., *theotokos*), and veneration of saints and relics. Orthodoxy generally rejects several Western theological tenets such as the *filioque* addition to the Nicene Creed, the Augustinian doctrine of original sin, and the supremacy and infallibility of the Roman pontiff.

Whereas Western theology stresses Christ's substitutionary atonement, Orthodoxy highlights the incarnation of the Word, whose life, death, and resurrection conquered the Devil and redeemed alienated humanity, thus enabling the faithful to "participate in the divine nature" (2 Peter 1:4) or become "deified" (i.e., made Christlike). Athanasius of Alexandria (c. 296–373) aptly summarized the fundamental *theosis* doctrine: "God became man that we might become God."[33] Jesus' radiant transfiguration on the mountain (Mark 9) is viewed as paradigmatic of humanity elevated into the mystery of the divine life. Some suggest that Orthodoxy represents "a profound Christ-centered mysticism of dynamic transformation."[34] Prominent Orthodox theologians and churchmen in recent times include Sergei Bulgakov (1871–44), Georges Florovsky (1893–1979), Vladimir Lossky (1903–58), John Meyendorff (1926–92), and Timothy (Kallistos) Ware (1934-).

What Is Roman Catholicism?

Catholicism, which traces its history back to the New Testament apostles, consists of the body of professing Christians under the authority of the bishop of Rome. At the Great Schism of AD 1054, Eastern and Western churches broke communion, and the sixteenth-century

---

33. Athanasius, *On the Incarnation of the Word of God*, ch. 8, par. 54.

34. John A. McGuckin, "The Eastern Christian Tradition," in *The Story of Christian Spirituality*, ed. Gordon Mursell (Minneapolis: Fortress, 2001), 129.

Reformation differentiated Roman Catholicism from Protestantism. The Roman church is a complex and diverse communion consisting of numerous philosophical traditions and theological schools. In common with Orthodoxy and Protestantism, Rome holds many central doctrines, including inspired Scripture (with the Apocrypha added); the Trinity; the divine-human person of Christ; salvation by grace (variously interpreted); gospel proclamation; commitment to social, economic, and political justice; and the return of Christ at the end of the age. Principal councils of the church—Trent (1545–63), Vatican I (1869–70), and Vatican II (1962–65)—propounded essential matters of doctrine and practice.

Leading Catholic emphases include the Roman pontiff as historical successor of Peter and infallible spokesman on matters of doctrine and morals, the more or less parity of tradition and Scripture, the merging of justification and sanctification, the role of meritorious works in salvation, and seven sacraments that convey saving grace *ex opera operato*. Other prominent emphases include the doctrine of transubstantiation wherein the bread and wine become the very body and blood of Christ, the sacrificial nature of the Mass, invocation of saints, prayers for the departed, and belief that all humanity is destined for salvation.

Various Marian dogmas central to Catholic faith and spirituality that evolved historically include Mary's immaculate conception, sinless life, perpetual virginity, heavenly assumption, and intercession for the faithful. The Second Vatican Council shifted the focus on Mary from soteriology to ecclesiology with renewed emphasis on our Lord's mother as model of the church and its most exemplary member. Mary nevertheless retains among others the title "mediatrix."

Additional Vatican II distinctives include emphasis on Scripture study, lay participation in certain forms of ministry, the church envisioned as a community rather than a hierarchical institution, the universal call to holiness, ecumenical cooperation with other Christian bodies, and optimism that non-Christian religions embody moral and spiritual truths that enlighten adherents and, by implication, lead to God. Prominent Roman Catholic theologians and spiritual writers include Karl Rahner (1904-84), Hans Urs von Balthasar (1905–88), Thomas Merton (1915–68), Henri Nouwen (1932–96), Sandra M. Schneiders (1938–), and Susan Muto (1943–).

What Is Progressive Protestantism?

Progressive Protestantism is comprised of historic denominations such as the Episcopal Church, United Methodist Church, American Baptist Church, Christian Church (Disciples of Christ), Evangelical Lutheran Church in America, and Presbyterian Church (U.S.A.), as well as numerous smaller bodies. Progressive Protestantism is a diverse movement that was stimulated by the Enlightenment, modern scientism, evolutionism, the social sciences (particularly psychology and sociology), comparative religions, feminism, the gay rights movement, and globalization.

The progressive Protestant tradition typically affirms God as love and Jesus as a moral teacher and prophet who differs from other humans in degree, not in kind. It upholds human goodness and moral progress, as well as the primacy of human reason and religious experience. It tends to highlight the exemplarist or moral influence theories of the atonement; structural evils such as poverty, racism, and militarism; the ethical implications of Christianity; and social and political change. Its teaching often centers on the kingdom of God as a social entity that will transform human culture. In its more radical forms, the tradition endorses liberation theology, process theology, feminist theology, and gay and lesbian theologies.

Progressive Protestantism ostensibly traces its origins to biblical times, further influenced by eighteenth- and nineteenth-century biblical criticism and authorities such as F. D. E. Schleiermacher (1768–1834), Albrecht Ritschl (1822–89), and Adolph von Harnack (1851–1930). Progressive Protestantism tends to favor current cultural values rather than classical creeds (reflecting H. Richard Niebuhr's "Christ of culture"). It also interprets the Bible more figuratively than literally and questions the validity of original sin, the historicity of Christ's resurrection, and the exclusivity of the Christian faith vis-à-vis other world religions. During the last century, the brutality of two world wars, numerous regional conflicts, as well as Karl Barth's critique of liberalism, have softened more radical perspectives. Prominent progressive Protestant thinkers and spiritual writers in recent times include Evelyn Underhill (1875–1944), Dietrich Bonhoeffer (1906–45), Marcus Borg (1942–), Kathleen Norris (1947–), and Rowan Williams (1950–).

What Is Evangelicalism?

The transdenominational movement that is evangelicalism traces its history and identity to New Testament apostolic teaching, the early Christian creeds, and orthodox faith through the centuries. It received clear definition with Luther, Calvin, and Zwingli during the sixteenth-century Protestant Reformation and is reflected in later movements such as Puritanism, continental Pietism, Methodism, Pentecostalism, and fundamentalism. It has been additionally shaped by the two Great Awakenings, revivalism, the African-American experience, and contemporary seeker-sensitive and emerging churches.

The term *evangelicalism* derives from the Greek *euangelion*, meaning "gospel," or "good news." Major theological tenets of the movement include the glory of the triune God, the divine-human person of Jesus Christ, primary revelation through inspired and authoritative Scripture, the guilt and depravity of the human race, and justification by grace through faith alone grounded in the sinless life, atoning death, and resurrection of Jesus Christ. Additional evangelical emphases include Bible-centered preaching, need for a personal relationship with the Savior, the church as the community of the redeemed, two ordinances or sacraments (baptism and the Lord's Supper), and worldwide evangelization of the unconverted.

Other prominent characteristics include God-centered worship, Bible study and prayer, the quest for holiness of life, incarnating the gospel in one's daily vocation, pursuit of justice and social improvement, and anticipation of Christ's return to dispense rewards and punishments. Prominent evangelical theologians and spiritual writers include Francis Schaeffer (1912–84), James M. Houston (1922–), Eugene Peterson (1932–), Dallas Willard (1935–), and Richard Foster (1942–). Evangelicalism, according to Ian Rennie, "is live orthodoxy" where "the whole of the evangelical theological enterprise is for the glory of God."[35] The term *born again* (John 3:3) refers to all those who have made a personal commitment to Jesus Christ as Lord and Savior.

---

35. Ian S. Rennie, "Evangelical Theology," in *New Dictionary of Theology*, ed. Sinclair B. Ferguson and David F. Wright (Downers Grove, Ill.: InterVarsity, 1988), 240.

Core Issues in Christian Spirituality

The present volume explores how the four major Christian traditions address humans' perennial quest for God and desire to live out a relationship with him. Diverse expressions of spirituality have arisen through the centuries and have been shaped by historical, cultural, and political factors. As expressed by Michael Downey, "Different responses to the presence and activity of the Holy Spirit throughout history have given rise to different paths of integration, wholeness, holiness. These may be recognized as diverse spiritualities."[36] In other words, our study is unlikely to uncover any uniform expression of Christian spirituality, since protocols for nurturing spiritual life and living out the gospel have been envisioned by the major Christian traditions in different ways throughout history. Critical engagement and evaluation of these several perspectives can serve to enrich our understanding of how to enter into and live out the transforming gospel of Jesus Christ.

In the chapters that follow, leading scholars from the four Christian traditions will expound prominent features of spirituality, addressing in the process the following issues:

- definition and key emphases of Christian spirituality
- the relation of spirituality to spiritual formation
- the means, disciplines, or regimens by which spirituality is achieved
- the role of Jesus Christ and the Holy Spirit in spirituality
- the function of the institutional church in spirituality
- the goals or endgame of Christian spirituality

Thereafter, the four contributors will respond to the perspectives of the other three contributors, highlighting commonalities and differences of belief and practice. Finally, the editor will undertake an integration of perspectives, noting perceived strengths and weaknesses of each tradition that hopefully will lead to a clearer sense of truth, mutual understanding, and the spiritual unity between Christians for which our Lord so passionately prayed (see John 17:11, 21–23).

---

36. Downey, *Understanding Christian Spirituality*, 46.

CHAPTER ONE

ORTHODOX SPIRITUALITY: A QUEST FOR TRANSFIGURED HUMANITY

BRADLEY NASSIF

A famous story is told in the *Russian Primary Chronicle* how, in the tenth century, Prince Vladimir of Kiev sent representatives to the various countries of the world in search of the true religion for his people. After going to the Muslims in the Volga, the envoys observed that there was no joy among them, and so they left. Next they traveled to Germany and Rome, where the worship was more pleasing. But the services were said to have lacked beauty. Finally the messengers journeyed to Constantinople, the capital of the Byzantine Empire. As they observed the Divine Liturgy in the great Church of the Holy Wisdom, they discovered what they had longed for. "We knew not whether we were in heaven or on earth," they reported to Prince Vladimir, "for surely there is no such splendor or beauty anywhere on earth. We cannot describe it to you. All that we know is that God dwells there and their service surpasses the worship of all other places. For we cannot forget that beauty."

In this story, Bishop Kallistos Ware finds three characteristics of Orthodox Christianity that are particularly relevant to our essay. There is first the emphasis on spiritual beauty: "We cannot forget that beauty," declared the envoys. The power of perceiving the beauty and mystery of the spiritual world, and expressing that beauty in worship, seems to be the particular gift of the Orthodox Church. Second, Orthodox worship embraces two worlds at once: "We knew not whether we were in heaven or on earth." The liturgy is the place where heaven and earth join in common worship of the triune God. The third principle this story illustrates is that "the rule of prayer is the rule of faith" (*lex orandi lex est credendi*). True prayer reveals the true God. The very word *orthodox* signifies correct belief as well as correct worship. Doctrine is doxological. Truth is understood in the context of worship. Prayer and theology are inseparable and interdependent. When the Russians wanted to discover the true faith, they did not ask about moral principles or a rational defense of doctrine, important though they are. Instead, they observed the different nations at prayer. They saw how the Orthodox approach to faith is fundamentally a liturgical approach.[1]

This story sets the tone for our essay. Our task is to describe Orthodox spirituality in terms of its key emphases, disciplines, and goals as they relate to the role of the church, Christ, and the Spirit in the life of the believer.[2] Posing the task in this way is understandably necessary for the overall unity of this book. However, it presents us with a challenge. First, the Orthodox tradition is so vast that in order to achieve this goal, we must necessarily limit ourselves only to a selection of the most essential and abiding features of its spiritual life. This essay can offer no more than an overture to the larger score of the church's spiritual life. Our approach must also avoid describing Orthodox spirituality in a strictly systematic or scholastic way that might lead readers to think it can be reduced to a set of emphases and practices each believer is to follow. The nature of communion with God cannot be reduced to a list of propositions or spiritual practices that will automatically bring about the desired closeness to God and others. On the contrary, Orthodox spirituality is caught more than it is taught. It is relational more than it is legal. It is experienced more than it is analyzed. So the best we can do is to describe what spiritual life is all about as it is experienced within the total life of the church. Finally, although our essay will not be a "history of spirituality," we will draw our answers largely, though not exclusively, from the early and Byzantine church of the first fifteen centuries of Christian history. That is because the

---

1. Timothy (Kallistos) Ware, *The Orthodox Church*, rev. ed. (New York: Penguin, 1993), 264–66. Though the story is possibly legendary, it represents well the character of Orthodoxy.

2. The term *spirituality* simply means "our life in Christ." It is an all-inclusive description of the Christian life, even if the term itself has not been customarily used in the church's tradition.

Orthodox Church today is thoroughly grounded in the classic expressions of Christian faith. The church sees herself as heir to a unified, consistent, and continuous tradition of faith that has been handed down from Jesus Christ to the apostles and church fathers through successive centuries.

The procedure will be as follows: We will start by defining "the gospel" as it has been understood in the Orthodox tradition. That definition is important because *Orthodox spirituality is above all else a gospel spirituality*. The gospel is like a mountain on which all the trees of the forest are planted. The individual trees of Orthodox spirituality—such as worship, sacraments, doctrine, and the like—must be rooted in the soil that gives them their life, namely, the gospel of Jesus Christ. Too often we see the trees but overlook the mountain on which they rest. After describing the centrality of the gospel, we will turn next to the trees. The trees are the emphases and practices that have manifested that gospel within the life of the church (its liturgy, sacraments, doctrine, monastic life, and missions). Each tree will be examined in relation to the gospel and its contribution to spiritual formation. Finally, we will conclude by describing the ultimate goal to which all of Orthodox spirituality leads, namely, the deification or glorification of the believer. Together, the mountain and trees are the means by which our humanity is renewed and transfigured into the likeness of Jesus Christ.

The Centrality of the Gospel in Orthodox Spirituality

My friend and colleague, Scot McKnight, is an evangelical Christian. He is widely recognized as one of the top gospel scholars in the world today on the life of Jesus. In his new book *The King Jesus Gospel*, Scot critiques contemporary evangelicals as being "soterians" for reducing the gospel to the "gospel plan of salvation." By "soterians," he means those evangelicals who limit the gospel to what God has done for us on the cross and how we are to respond if we want to get saved. He believes evangelicals have reduced the life of Jesus to Good Friday and therefore reduced the gospel to the crucifixion and transactions of a Savior. McKnight believes this is the wrong definition of the gospel. Rather, the gospel is the whole life of Jesus, not just a part of it. The gospel writers were themselves "gospeling" through the retelling of the whole story of Jesus. And the story of Jesus, the second Adam, is about Jesus' kingdom vision and how he fulfilled the stories of Israel and creation. Thus, in Peter's sermon in the book of Acts,

> Peter's gospeling ... involved telling the full Story of Jesus Christ, including his life, his death, his resurrection, his exaltation, the gift of the Holy Spirit, his second coming, and the wrapping up of history so that God would be all in all. The reason we have to say this is because too often we have ...
>
>> reduced the life of Jesus to Good Friday, and therefore reduced the gospel to the crucifixion, and then soterians have reduced Jesus to transactions of a Savior.
>
> Not so in the early gospeling, for in those early apostolic sermons we see the whole life of Jesus. In fact, if they gave an emphasis to one dimension of the life of Jesus, it was the resurrection ... The clearest example of Peter's whole-life-of-Jesus with an emphasis on cross-leading-to-resurrection gospel is seen at Acts 10:36–42, and I would urge you to read this entirely and slowly.[3]

McKnight's definition of the gospel comports well with the Orthodox vision. In Orthodoxy, the gospel is *the saving message of the Bible as a whole. It is the whole story of Jesus and not just a part of it.* The gospel includes Christ's connection with creation, with Adam, and with Israel. The good news of salvation comes from his eternal Trinitarian relations, his life, his death, his resurrection, his exaltation, the gift of the Holy Spirit to the church at Pentecost, his ascension, his intercession, and his second coming. As Messiah and Savior, he is preeminently the crucified and risen Lord and Son of God. These are the many streams of the gospel that flow into the spiritual lives of Orthodox Christians.

Put succinctly, Orthodox spirituality is defined by the center of its faith, and that center is the gospel of Jesus Christ. That is why a book called the Book of the Gospels rests on the center of the altars of every Orthodox Church in the world. Its contents and location in the sanctu-

---

3. Scot McKnight, *The King Jesus Gospel: The Original Good News Revisited* (Grand Rapids: Zondervan, 2011), 109. He believes gospel also includes the way it was preached with persuasion. A similar call to recover the fullness of the gospel in the Orthodox Church is developed at length by Fr. Theodore Stylianopoulos, *The Way of Christ: Gospel, Spiritual Life and Renewal in Orthodoxy* (Brookline, Mass: Holy Cross Orthodox, 2002).

ary bear witness to the church's priorities and focus. It is worth noticing that the Book of the Gospels does not contain the Old Testament or the epistles of the New Testament, but only the four gospels. On one side of the cover is an engraving of the crucifixion, and on the other side is the resurrection. The pages in between the two covers contain the story of Jesus as told by Matthew, Mark, Luke, and John. The Book of the Gospels proclaims the centrality of the gospel as the heart of the Orthodox faith while emphasizing the death and resurrection of Jesus as the climactic events of his saving work.

It is correct, therefore, to describe Orthodox spirituality as thoroughly evangelical. Why? Because the gospel of Christ is the soul of the church. Fr. Theodore Stylianopoulos, a senior professor of New Testament and Orthodox Spirituality at Holy Cross Greek Orthodox Seminary, is convinced that "at the core of the Orthodox tradition, whether we turn to the Eucharist or the lives of the great saints, the same truth has primacy, namely, Christ and the gospel ... The challenge of rediscovering the centrality of the gospel, as well as of energizing the evangelical ethos deeply enshrined in the Orthodox tradition, [is our highest task]."[4] This is reinforced by a well-known but anonymous author simply named "A Monk of the Eastern Church":

> There can be noticed all through Orthodox history the existence of a spirituality which we might call "evangelical." This spirituality takes care to identify Christian life neither with the rigorous asceticism of the desert nor with ritual worship; it lays stress on the spirit and virtues of the gospel, on the necessity of following Christ, on charity toward the poor and afflicted. St. John Chrysostom is the most eminent representative of this trend.[5]

St. Ignatius Brianchaninov, a nineteenth-century bishop of Russia, also makes an impassioned plea to monks, and to all Christians, to keep the gospel clear and central in all they do. It is the fundamental principle that is to guide their reading of the church fathers, saints, canons, and rules for worship. The gospel opposes legalism, rigidity,

---

4. Stylianopoulos, *Way of Christ*, 49.

5. A Monk of the Eastern Church, *Orthodox Spirituality: An Outline of the Orthodox Ascetical and Mystical Tradition*, 2nd ed. (Crestwood, N.Y.: St. Vladimir's Seminary Press, 1978). It is now known that the anonymous author was Lev Gillet.

narrowness, and barren ritualism. Failure to follow this basic rule was the cause of the bishop's own problems given to him by "spiritual directors suffering from blindness and self-delusion."[6]

Thus we see from the church's Book of the Gospels and the writings of its bishops, monks, and scholars that the gospel is the centerpiece of the Orthodox faith. If we lose sight of the gospel, we lose sight of everything the church has to offer.

Gospel Emphases and Spiritual Practices

Orthodox spirituality is above all else a gospel spirituality that is centered on Jesus Christ in his Trinitarian relations. By that I mean Orthodox spirituality can only be understood in the context of how Jesus Christ relates to the other members of the Trinity, namely, the Father and the Spirit. Christ, in his Trinitarian relations, is the focus of our life in God. As one of the Holy Trinity, Christ is the unifying medium through which the church interprets the whole range of Christian doctrine, worship, and spiritual life. This incarnational Trinitarian spirituality is expressed most fully in the church's liturgy, sacraments, dogmas, monastic life, and mission. Starting with the liturgy, we will now highlight some of the distinctive features within each of these areas to see how they work together in Orthodox spiritual formation.

Gospel Liturgies: A Paschal Spirituality that Celebrates the Victory of Christ over Sin, Death, and the Demonic

Liturgies are simply worship services of the church. They are the rituals that comprise preaching, prayer, and celebration of the sacraments. The centrality of the gospel in the worshiping life of the church is best summed up in the word *pascha* or Easter. *Pascha* is a Greek term that means "Passover." It emphasizes Jesus' completion of Israel's story by dying on the cross and rising victoriously from the grave in order to deliver humanity and all of creation from bondage to sin, death, and Satan. Fr. Theodore Stylianopoulos sees the gospel in numerous hym-

---

6. Ignatius Brianchaninov, *The Arena: An Offering to Contemporary Monasticism*, trans. Lazarus Moore (Jordanville, N.Y.: Holy Trinity Monastery, 1997), 3–10. For a theological exposition on this subject that complements our present essay, see Bradley Nassif, "The Evangelical Theology of the Eastern Orthodox Church," in *Three Views on Eastern Orthodoxy and Evangelicalism*, ed. James Stamoolis (Grand Rapids: Zondervan, 2004), 27–87.

nological passages of the New Testament, such as John 1:1–18; Philippians 2:6–11; and the doxologies of the book of Revelation. Liturgical confessions of faith pertaining to the good news of God's saving work through Christ are also seen in the sacramental passages of John 6:25–70; Romans 6:1–12; and 1 Corinthians 10 and 11.

In subsequent centuries after the apostolic age, the gospel continued to be presented through ancient hymns, some of which are still used in Orthodox worship today, such as the doxological song to the Holy Trinity known as the Trisagion Prayer: "Holy God, Holy Mighty, Holy Immortal One: have mercy on us." Another hymn titled "Only-Begotten Son" proclaims the incarnation, death, and resurrection of Christ and exalts him as "one of the Holy Trinity." Then there is the hymnographical cycle in church worship (the eight tones) that has developed over the centuries. The weekly hymns for Saturday vespers and Sunday matins are heavily resurrectional in emphasis as they set forth the gospel of the death and resurrection of Christ that goes back to the apostle Paul (for example, 1 Corinthians 15:1–8). An excerpt from the lyrics of the Matins hymn praises the death and resurrection of Christ:

> Though the tomb was sealed by a stone and soldiers guarded Your pure body, You arose, O Savior, on the third day, giving life to the world. Therefore, O Giver of life, the heavenly powers praise You: glory to Your resurrection, O Christ, glory to Your kingdom, glory to Your plan of redemption, O loving God.
>
> You were nailed upon the cross willingly, O Merciful One, and were placed in a grave as dead, O Giver of life. You trampled the power of death by Your death, O Mighty One. The gates of hell trembled before You and You raised with You those who were dead for ages, O loving God.[7]

Stylianopoulos goes on to note:

Sometimes one hears or reads about a false generalization that Eastern Orthodoxy features a "theology of the resurrection" as compared to the "theology of the cross" of the Western Christian tradition. In fact Orthodoxy has a profound vision of the cross both

---

7. Stylianopoulos, *Way of Christ*, 33–35.

in worship and spirituality. Orthodoxy knows no resurrection without the cross and no cross without the resurrection, viewing these redemptive events as inseparable.[8]

These liturgical proclamations of the gospel are not the only ones in the church's worship. The basic structure of the entire liturgical year is thoroughly biblical and evangelical in content and spirit. The weekly Sunday service, known as the Divine Liturgy, is like a mini-Easter service that takes its inspiration from the Feast of Pascha. The annual liturgical cycle takes a comprehensive view of Jesus' entire ministry as recorded in the Gospels. It centers around twelve major feasts whose source and goal are also rooted in Pascha—"the Feast of Feasts," the sacred Passover and resurrection of Christ. Most of the feasts focus on key events in the life of Jesus from his conception to his second return as judge. The themes include his annunciation, birth, baptism, transfiguration, death, resurrection, and ascension, and the gift of the Spirit and Christ's second coming.

Nowhere is the comprehensive victory of the gospel more strongly emphasized than in the liturgical symbolism of the resurrection service. Even though the cross and resurrection are held together, there is a clear emphasis on the resurrection of Christ that goes back to the apostle Paul (1 Corinthians 15). This deeply moving service proceeds in the following way:

A little before midnight on Saturday evening, an Easter procession begins. The priest and people circle the church building as they sing a triumphal hymn in anticipation of the victory of Christ. The connection between resurrection and overcoming the passions is sung aloud:

Thy Resurrection, O Christ our Savior, the angels in heaven sing.
Enable us on earth, to glorify Thee in purity of heart.

During the procession the church bells ring ceaselessly as they announce the approaching victory of Christ over the grave. It is the procession of the holy Passover from death to life, from earth to heaven, from this age to the age to come. The procession recalls the original baptismal passage from death to life in the kingdom of God (Romans

---

8. Ibid., 50, n.4.

6:1–12). It takes the faithful back to the beginning of their Christian life and announces God's creation and re-creation of human nature through his Son.

After circling the building three times, the people return to the closed doors at the front of the church. The priest faces the congregation with the doors behind his back as he intones a prayer to the "holy, consubstantial, life-creating, and undivided Trinity." He reads the gospel story of the empty tomb. Then a lively drama takes place in the form of a dialogue. The priest, holding a candle in one hand and the cross in the other, turns to speak to a man behind the closed doors of the church. The man symbolizes the Devil, who presently holds the keys of death and Hades. An animated dialogue ensues. The priest strikes the closed doors three times with the cross, commanding Satan in a loud voice with the verses of Psalm 24 (Psalm 23 LXX): "Lift up your heads, O you gates; be lifted up, you ancient doors, that the King of glory may come in!"

Satan: "Who is this King of glory?"

Priest: "The LORD strong and mighty, the LORD mighty in battle."

Priest (again striking the doors): "Lift up your heads, O you gates; be lifted up, you ancient doors, that the King of glory may come in!"

Satan: "Who is this King of glory?"

Priest: "The LORD strong and mighty, the LORD mighty in battle."

Priest (again striking the doors): "Lift up your heads, O you gates; be lifted up, you ancient doors, that the King of glory may come in!"

Satan: "Who is this King of glory?"

Priest (opening wide the doors of the church and declaring the last line): "The LORD of hosts—he is the King of glory!"

The people reenter the sanctuary, led by the priest, who is holding a lighted candle and the Book of the Gospels as they all sing the triumphal hymn:

Let God arise! Let his enemies be scattered! Let those who hate him flee from before his face!

Christ is risen from the dead, trampling down death by death, and upon those in the tombs bestowing life.

This is the day which the Lord has made, let us rejoice and be glad in it!

As the people enter, they pay reverence to an Easter icon in the center of the church that shows Christ destroying the gates of hell and freeing Adam and Eve from the captivity of death. There is continual singing and a vigorous censing of the icons and people. With antiphonal responses, priest and people proclaim aloud to one another, "Christ is risen!" "Indeed, he is risen!"

This paschal service sounds the keynote to all of life and liturgy in the Orthodox tradition. It reveals how Orthodox spirituality is above all else a paschal spirituality. It is where death to sin and newness of life has been won through the victory of the cross and Christ's triumphant resurrection from the dead. It is a victory that restores to humanity the possibility of the glorification that was originally lost in the garden of Eden (developed below; see Deification: The Quest for Trinitarian Love, pp. 52–55).

Gospel Sacraments: A Spirituality Centered on the Healing Mysteries of the Gospel

Closely connected to liturgical life is the Christian's lifelong participation in the sacraments. The Holy Spirit imparts grace (divine life) through the sacraments and makes present the healing gifts of the gospel. The church takes the material things of this world—water, oil, bread, wine, wheat, fruit—and offers them as healing gifts of the Holy Spirit. The sacraments are often called "mysteries," not because they conceal Christ, but because they reveal and make him present (Colossians 1:5, 26–27; 2:2–3). Fr. Alexander Schmemann saw the entire gospel story of Jesus contained in the word *mystery*:

> [The Greek Christians] called "mystery" the entire ministry of Christ, through whose life, death, resurrection, and glorification God saves man and the world. Christ thus both reveals and accomplishes the divine plan of salvation, kept secret ("mystery") until his coming. And since the church is to proclaim that mystery and communicate it to men, the essential acts by which she is accomplishing this are also called mysteries ... Through all these acts (mysteries or sacraments) we are made participants and beneficiaries of the great mystery of salvation accomplished by Jesus Christ.[9]

---

9. Quoted in Anthony M. Coniaris, *Introducing the Orthodox Church* (Minneapolis: Light and Life, 1982), 127. In 1 Corinthians 2:7 and 4:1, Paul uses "mystery" to denote things once hidden but now revealed by God to his people.

In Orthodoxy, the most profound presentation of the gospel is the Divine Liturgy of St. John Chrysostom. It is the weekly Sunday service that celebrates the Last Supper of Jesus. The Divine Liturgy makes present the gospel through the preaching of the Word of God and partaking of the Eucharist. The two are sacramentally connected. It is not possible to separate the proclamation of the crucified and risen Lord from the bread and wine of the Eucharist. The Word prepares the people's hearts for receiving the life-giving Eucharist and then calls them to embody that saving eucharistic presence of Christ in the world. The inspired Word of God expressed through the human words of the preacher becomes a divine vehicle of saving grace. The public reading of Scripture and the proclamation of it is a sacramental act. The pulpit is to agree with the altar by proclaiming the story of Jesus. That is why the Sunday reading is always taken from the Book of the Gospels. Preaching is tied to the Eucharist because the Eucharist makes present the gospel by "proclaim[ing] the Lord's death until he comes" (1 Corinthians 11:23; see John 6:52–58).[10]

How does divine initiative and human response to the gospel relate to Orthodox spiritual formation? Fr. Theodore Stylianopoulos explains:

> The Orthodox bear testimony to their own stream of tradition, which is largely unencumbered by the dichotomies of Scripture and tradition, word and sacrament, gospel and law, grace and will, faith and works, faith and reason. In the Orthodox tradition, all these elements have been held together as parts of the same truth in which unquestionably the revealed initiative and saving action belong to God, yet require the positive response of human beings. The sovereign efficacy of grace is confessed, while the active role of the receptive will is recognized. The primacy of faith is declared, while the necessity of works according to which believers will be judged is affirmed. The supreme authority of Scripture is unquestioned, but the obvious necessity of its discerning use and normative interpretation is acknowledged.[11]

---

10. See Alexander Schmemann, *For the Life of the World: Sacraments and Orthodoxy* (Crestwood, N.Y.: St. Vladimir's Seminary Press, 1977).

11. Stylianopoulos, *Way of Christ*, 39–40.

We may wonder how this holistic vision of God's relationship with humans relates to the church's sacraments. Since the seventeenth century, under the influence of Roman Catholic opposition to the Protestant Reformers, the Orthodox Church has numbered the sacraments as seven. But scholars now know this is not consistent with traditional Orthodox faith. The church never limited sacraments to seven. A sacrament happens whenever God's grace is communicated through the created order. In one way or another, everything in the church is a sacrament, including the whole of creation, everyday labor, homemaking, and a multitude of daily tasks. In the church, other sacramentals include icons, prayer, the blessing of water, homes, fields, relics, and even the funeral service, to name only a few. Indeed, the incarnation of Christ himself is the supreme sacrament of God's presence in the world.

Nevertheless, there are special moments when the Holy Trinity applies the mystery of salvation to particular sacraments that are expressly given for the nourishment and healing of body and soul (especially baptism and Eucharist). Notice their *life-giving* character in the brief descriptions below:

Baptism: Baptism is the "womb" of new birth in Christ and the "tomb" where one dies to the power of sin through the cross. Here the physical and spiritual unite as a vehicle of the Spirit to bring new life to the believer (John 3:5; Romans 6:1–12; Titus 3:5–6; and other passages).

Chrismation: Immediately after being baptized, the person is anointed with oil (chrism) to indicate the presence of the Holy Spirit given to empower the believer during his earthly pilgrimage as a continued Pentecost. Chrismation is also a sacrament of reconciliation for those Orthodox who may have left the church and wish to be reunited to it. It is also used when Catholic or Protestant Christians wish to join the church for the first time, thereby completing the spiritual life that was previously lacking in their backgrounds.

Eucharist: Orthodox spirituality is supremely a eucharistic spirituality. Directly after baptism and chrismation, the newborn life is nourished with the real presence of Christ in the bread and wine. The church does not view it as a metaphor, any more than it views baptism as figurative. It is essentially an eschatological meal that deifies the believer and anticipates the future banquet in the kingdom of God. The Eucharist constitutes the central act of worship in the Orthodox tradition.

Repentance or Confession: The sacrament of repentance heals the heart by restoring the believer to Christ and the church. When an Orthodox Christian confesses his sins, he confesses them to Christ in the presence of a priest, who stands as a witness to that confession.

Holy Orders: Through the sacrament of ordination, Orthodox clergy govern the church and manifest the saving action of Christ among his people. The pastor manifests the gospel through words and actions. As a liturgical leader, he not only preaches but also acts out the content of the gospel through a plethora of ritual proclamations and actions. Gospel themes from the Old and New Testaments are cited from the moment he begins to robe himself with clerical vestments at the start of each Sunday. Each part of his liturgical clothing is a symbolic communication of the gospel message. For example, the white robe worn underneath his vestments symbolizes the baptismal garment of salvation. A long stole that hangs from his neck represents the pastoral care of his flock that is patterned after Christ, "the good shepherd" (John 10).

Marriage: Marriage is a sacred state of life that reflects the mystical union between Christ and the church.

Anointing of the Sick: Holy unction is not reserved only for those who are dying, but it is offered in times of need for physical, mental, or spiritual healing.

This sacramental and synergistic approach to the Christian life has characterized Orthodox spirituality from the beginning and pervades it. It is important to state that the sacraments do not impose on our freedom or work automatically apart from faith. They do not work mechanistically. It is up to each Christian to make the sacraments bear fruit in their lives. The Orthodox Church has always upheld the doctrine of synergy, a collaboration between free will and God's grace. It is an unequal emphasis in which God takes the initiative in saving grace; yet it also is one that requires a response by human beings. The church recognizes that we are all saints by grace, but we must also become saints by our actions.

Alongside communal rites and sacramental practices, the church prescribes periods of personal prayer, fasting, and almsgiving. Congregants are to fast from meat, oil, and dairy products every Wednesday and Friday to commemorate special events in the life of Christ. They are to fast with especially great severity during the fifty days of Great Lent and Holy Week leading up to Easter. Orthodox Christians fast with an austerity that is alarming to Christians of the West, as well as to the Orthodox themselves. Under the guidance of their pastors, and as they are able, during the fifty days of fasting they are to refrain from all meat, certain types of fish, oil, cheese, eggs, milk, butter, and other dairy products. The purpose of fasting is to clear away the stony rubble in the heart so that the grace of God can take root and grow. Fasting is a refraining not just from food and drink but from all the passions that get in the way of our love for God (gluttony, greed, anger, lust, pride, and the like). The goal is not just to subdue the flesh but also to positively restore body and soul to their spiritual purpose, so that both, together, may serve God in a holistic and integrated manner.

Along with carrying out seasons of intense fasting and prayer, families are also encouraged to have devotional altars in their homes where they pray before the icons of Christ and the saints, read the Bible, and venerate the cross. The prayers come from manuals whose words are taken from the service books used in public worship. In that way, personal devotions are integrated with community life. Parishioners are, of course, encouraged to pray spontaneously in their own words as well.

These are just a few of the most important liturgies, sacraments, and seasons of prayer and fasting that Orthodox Christians do in their quest for a transfigured humanity.

Church Dogmas: A Spirituality Grounded in the Saving Ontologies of the Gospel

This section of our essay is the weightiest in theological content, so the reader should be alerted ahead of time to its character. Yet any account of Orthodox spirituality cannot afford to overlook its theological foundations as they relate to the Christian life. Christian spirituality and worship are the primary articulators of biblical faith in the Orthodox tradition. But we must also look back and ask, "What is the faith that Orthodox spirituality and worship seek to articulate? How does that faith shape the emphases and practices of the spiritual life?"

It is impossible to understand the spiritual life of the Orthodox Christian apart from the doctrinal underpinnings that define the way he is to pray, worship, and conduct everyday life. The church's dogmas shape the contours of his life in Christ. Dogmas are those authoritative teachings of the Orthodox Church that pertain to salvation through Christ and the Holy Trinity. Dogmas are derived supremely from Scripture and witnessed to through a chorus of voices in the church's tradition (the church fathers, councils, liturgy, iconography, hymnography, and disciplinary canons). Vladimir Lossky explains the inseparable connection between theology and spirituality:

> The term "mystical theology" denotes no more than a spirituality which expresses a doctrinal attitude ... The Eastern tradition has never made a sharp distinction between mysticism and theology; between personal experience of the divine mysteries and the dogmas affirmed by the church ... Far from being mutually opposed, theology and mysticism support and complete each other. One is impossible without the other ... Mysticism is the perfecting and crown of all theology: as theology *par excellence*.[12]

This experiential approach to the knowledge of God is based on a distinction the church fathers made between *cataphatic* (*via positiva*) and *apophatic* (*via negativa*) ways of knowing.[13] Cataphatic statements are positive affirmations about God (e.g., "God is merciful"), while apophatic ones negate those assertions without abolishing them (e.g., "God is not merciful in exactly the same way as we know mercy; he is far beyond our definitions."). Both ways of knowing God are interdependent. In noncontradictory ways, negative theology denies

---

12. Vladimir Lossky, *The Mystical Theology of the Eastern Church* (Crestwood, N.Y.: St. Vladimir's Seminary Press, 1976), 8–9.

13. For a fuller account, see Aristotle Papanikolaou, *Being With God: Trinity, Apophaticism, and Divine-Human Communion* (Notre Dame: Notre Dame University Press, 2006).

assertions about God while leading one to a positive encounter with him. Christians know God through this unknowing. They can grasp him but can never completely put their arms around him. One example among the many that demonstrate how apophaticism shapes our communion with God comes from the Divine Liturgy. During the prayer of consecration (the *Anaphora*), the priest prays apophatically:

> It is meet and right to ... worship Thee in every place of thy dominion: for Thou art God ineffable, inconceivable, invisible, incomprehensible, ever existing, and eternally the same.

This and other apophatic prayers foster a deep sense of mystery in our relationship with God and underscore the limitations of our knowledge and speech about him. Spiritual writers and church councils of the early and Byzantine church, from whom much of our mystical theology derives, make frequent use of the apophatic approach (literally a "turning away from speech"). Apophatic spirituality creates a posture of profound reverence in the heart of an Orthodox believer who understands that God is God and they are not. He or she realizes that the primary path to communion with God is through a direct relationship with the risen Christ, who is accessible to each and all of us in the community of the church, even though certain truths transcend human reasoning. The apophatic way, however, does not negate the use of the mind. On the contrary, the church fathers recognized that rationality is perhaps the noblest feature of the image of God in humans. Christ died so that we may lose our sins, not that we may lose our minds. Thus in Orthodoxy, there is an essential link between the mystical language of the church's dogmas and the spiritual fruit that those dogmas bear. Right faith (*orthodoxia*) is not only correct doctrine; it is also sound spirituality and worship. It is a true way of thinking, a mentality or mind-set (*phronema*) reflecting the mind of Christ. It is also, and above all, a right way of living according to the gospel.

The dynamic relation between doctrine and experience can further be discerned in how the very title of "theologian" is used in the Eastern Orthodox tradition. The term does not ordinarily convey the same meaning it has had in the Christian West. A theologian is not someone who primarily engages in the academic study of concepts about God as a professional discipline in a seminary or university. Rather, a genuinely Orthodox theologian is someone who pursues Christ himself, in his Trinitarian relations. He or she experiences and reveals the living Lord as he is known and confessed in the church's liturgical, sacramental, and dogmatic tradition. Evagrius Ponticus (345–399), a desert father in Egypt, gives a classic description of a theologian: "If you are a theologian, you truly pray. If you truly pray, you are a theologian."[14] Vladimir Lossky adds,

> There is, therefore, no Christian mysticism without theology; but, above all, there is no theology without mysticism. It is not by chance that the tradition of the Eastern Church has reserved the name of "theologian" peculiarly for three sacred writers of whom the first is St. John, most "mystical" of the four Evangelists; the second St. Gregory Nazianzen, writer of contemplative poetry; and the third St. Symeon, called "the New Theologian," the singer of union with God.[15]

If mystical theology is lived doctrine (spirituality) in the Eastern Orthodox tradition, what then are those doctrines that we live? The starting point may appear to be the story of creation in Genesis 1–2. Surprisingly, this is not where the church fathers begin. Rather, the interpretive key that unlocks the original purpose and goal of creation is found in the historical appearance of Jesus of Nazareth, "the Word made flesh" (John 1:14). For the early church fathers, Christ is the key that unlocks the meaning of everything, everyone, and everywhere— the Old and New Testaments as well as all of creation. That is why the dogmas of the seven ecumenical councils (325–787) are so central to Orthodox spirituality. Next to the Bible, the ecumenical councils occupy the highest place of authority in the church.[16] All the ecumenical councils ground the source of spiritual life in the Trinity (the common divinity and eternal relations between the Father, Son, and Holy Spirit)

---

14. Evagrius Ponticus, *Chapters on Prayer*, trans. John Eudes Bamberger (Kalamazoo, Mich.: Cistercian, 1981), 65.

15. Lossky, *Mystical Theology of the Eastern Church*, 8.

16. See Bradley Nassif, "'Authority' in the Eastern Orthodox Tradition," in *By What Authority? The Vital Questions of Religious Authority*, ed. Robert Millett (Macon, Ga.: Mercer University Press, 2010), 36–54.

and the incarnation (the Son of God becoming human). The dogmas of the incarnation and Trinity constitute the very heart of Orthodox spirituality. They shape the way Orthodox people worship and pray. They inform their understanding of God, their concept of the human person, and how we are saved and sanctified. The dogmas affirm that the basis of communion with God is not psychological but ontological.[17] Communion with God is rooted not in mental and subjective states of the soul but in the objective person of Christ, who offers salvation to all who embrace him in faith. Christ, in his Trinitarian relations, constitutes the ontological grounds of all Orthodox spirituality.

It is crucial to understand that the ecumenical councils were deeply concerned with human salvation. They were not concerned simply with abstract formulas of "Christological chemistry." Rather, the various heresies that were condemned by the ecumenical councils were anathema precisely because they undermined the possibility of salvation through the incarnate Lord. Incarnation and deification went hand in hand in Christian living. The person of Christ, his fully divine and fully human natures, the cooperation between his divine and human wills, and his eternal relationships with the Father and Spirit are the ontological realities that make deification possible through prayer, works of love, and especially through the sacramental life of the church.

We cannot give a full account of all that transpired in the councils, nor will we explain their positive contributions. Some of the positive contributions are already well-known, such as those of the Nicene Creed and the Chalcedonian Definition, which affirmed the co-equality and co-eternity of the triune God and the personal union of the fully human and fully divine natures of Christ. Instead, we will look at the heretical teachings that were condemned and briefly highlight the ontological dangers they imposed on the gospel and thus on the spiritual life of the Christian. In one way or another, all the heresies undermined the mediation of Christ in human salvation.[18] I have identified the perils of each heresy below to show how their teachings adversely impact

---

17. *Ontology* is a term that is concerned with the nature of being. Here it refers to the being of the Trinity and the being of Christ in his incarnate state.

18. For more, see Thomas F. Torrance, *Incarnation: The Person and Life of Christ* (Downers Grove, Ill.: InterVarsity, 2008); *Atonement: The Person and Work of Christ* (Downers Grove, Ill.: InterVarsity, 2009), both edited by Robert Walker.

salvation and Christian spirituality. Many of them lie at the center of our differences with liberal Protestant theology and their concepts of spirituality today. They highlight the dangers of a faulty understanding of Christ and the Trinity. A faulty Christology, for example, leads to a faulty life of prayer, worship, and the sacramental life.

Councils of Nicea (325) and Constantinople (381): Both councils rejected Arianism. St. Athanasius declared, "God became humanized so that humans might become divinized."[19] If Christ was not fully God, as the Arians asserted, then salvation is not possible, because only God can be the Savior.[20]

Councils of Ephesus (431), Chalcedon (451), and Constantinople II (553): These rejected Nestorianism, Monophysitism, and Apollinarianism. If Christ, the Logos, did not unite God and humanity in one person, as implied by Nestorius, then Christ could not have destroyed the middle wall of partition that existed between God and humanity. If the Son is not truly united with our humanity, then we are still in our sins, for he who died on the cross would not be able to mediate between God and humans.

Nestorius's chief adversary, Cyril of Alexandria (378–444), provided much of the Christology of these councils based on Holy Scripture. Closely associated with the "two natures in one person" doctrine of the Council of Chalcedon was the inseparable connection Cyril made between Christology and the Eucharist. For Cyril, and for the Orthodox Church today, God communicates his divine life to believers in the church through the Eucharist. Real communion with God is possible through the bread and wine because of the mystery that God ontologically united himself to humanity through the incarnation of the Word. A biblical Christology supports the real presence of Christ in the Eucharist; conversely, a faulty Nestorian Christology, which separates the two natures into two distinct persons, leads to a faulty conception of Christ and the Eucharist because no real union between God and

---

19. Athanasius, *On the Incarnation of the Word of God*, ch. 8, par. 54 (my translation; though a bit colloquial, it captures the nuances of the Greek in modern idiom).

20. The Cappadocian Fathers emphasize God's self-revelation as a trinity of persons. For a theology of the *filioque* and its implications for Christian spirituality, see A. Edward Siecienski, *The* Filioque: *History of a Doctrinal Controversy* (New York: Oxford University Press, 2010); G. L. Prestige, *God in Patristic Thought* (London: SPCK Press, 1952), 242.

humans would be possible in Christ or the bread and wine (cf. John 6:53–56; 1 Corinthians 10:16–17). We are never more human than at the Eucharist, where Christ communicates his life to us while drawing us into his life of communion with the Father and with one another. This is a major reason that the Eucharist is the supreme expression of Orthodox unity and spirituality then and now.[21]

Likewise, the condemned Apollinarians and Monophysites denied the fullness of Christ's human nature. If Christ had not assumed the fullness of human nature, then only a portion of our humanity could be saved and enter into union with God. By rejecting these heresies, the church wanted to affirm that Christ assumed and saved our humanity in its totality.

Council of Constantinople III (680/1): Condemned the Monothelites, who believed Christ had only one divine will after uniting with human nature. A free and perfect cooperation between the human and divine wills of Christ must have occurred within Christ in order for salvation to be achieved. Christ lived a sinless, obedient life and offered himself willingly on the cross for our sins. The council declared that Christlikeness or deification is possible for believers because Christ united in himself both wills, not just one, thereby achieving the perfect cooperation of the human and divine in salvation.

Nicea II (787): Condemned the iconoclasts, whose rejection of artistic representations of Christ amounted to a rejection of the incarnation, since the "Word became flesh" (e.g. John 1:14). Basing their conclusions on Scripture, the Fathers, and the Chalcedonian Definition (451), the council concluded that icons affirm the incarnation and the divine realities they represent. The council supported the making and reverencing (Greek *proskynesis*) of icons while strictly forbidding their worship (Greek *latreia*).

Icons continue to occupy a central place in the liturgy and personal piety of Orthodox Christians. The grace of God in the saints is made

---

21. Henry Chadwick, "Eucharist and Christology in the Nestorian Controversy," *Journal of Theological Studies* 2 (1951): 145–64; John McGuckin, *Saint Cyril of Alexandria and the Christological Controversy* (Crestwood, N.Y.: St. Vladimir's Seminary Press, 2004); John McGuckin, "The Concept of Orthodoxy in Ancient Christianity," *Patristic and Byzantine Review* 8.1 (1989): 5–23. The liturgical veneration of Mary as the *theotokos* ("God-bearer") is more of a Christological than a Mariological affirmation. The subject of her birth was the eternal Son of God.

accessible to believers through their icons. This creates a sacramental bond of communication with those who venerate their images. The major function of icons is to bear witness to the incarnation while furthering Christlikeness (deification) in the believer. They also teach the faith, inspire holiness, and bear witness to the coming eschatological transformation of the cosmos into "a new heaven and a new earth" (Revelation 21:1). As such, icons are the visual gospel of the church in lines and color.[22]

To these councils, add **Council of Constantinople (1354) and successive councils:** These local assemblies of bishops acquired universal authority in the Orthodox world. They are anti-Barlaamite councils that condemned Barlaam the Calabrian for opposing the possibility of humans having a genuine, saving knowledge of God. In response, Gregory Palamas, his opponent and defender of the Orthodox faith, drew a distinction between the impossibility of humans to know God in his essence (Greek *ousia*) and the possibility of their knowing God in his energies or actions (Greek *energeia*). Palamas identified "grace" with God himself and affirmed, on the basis of Chalcedonian Christology, that humans can know God in his energies but can never know God in his essence. This Palamite distinction plays a crucial role in the church's ascetical and mystical theology with its stress on the relation between grace and free will in spiritual progress.

The heresies described above constitute what the church has opposed in its theological foundations for the spiritual life. Any form of spiritual life (then or now) that rests on the premises of any of these doctrinal errors ends up with a spirituality that is dangerously devoid of the saving gospel of Jesus Christ.

Monasticism: A Baptismal Spirituality and the Quest for Scriptural Holiness

Monasticism has profoundly shaped the Orthodox Church in its worship structure, austere fasting practices, spiritual disciplines, and ideals. Even though monastic life is a calling that is not meant for all

---

22. For an interpretation of the more widely used icons, see Solrunn Nes, *The Mystical Language of Icons* (Grand Rapids: Eerdmans, 2004). For a short history and theology of the iconoclastic controversy, see Bradley Nassif, "Kissers and Smashers: Why the Orthodox Killed Each Other Over Icons," in *Christian History* (Spring 1997).

Christians, its path is one and the same for monks and laypeople alike. The simplest way to explain its ideals is through the life of St. Anthony of Egypt (251–356), the most renowned father of monastic life.

St. Athanasius, Anthony's biographer, tells the story of his calling. Shortly after his parents died, when he was about twenty years old, Anthony went to church and heard the gospel reading about detachment from worldly possessions: "Sell everything you have, and come, follow me," said Jesus to the rich young ruler (Mark 10:21). Anthony took these words literally as a personal command from God. In obedience, he sold all his property and gave it to the poor. He soon moved to the outskirts of his village, where he apprenticed himself to an old hermit. His devotion to Scripture was legendary: "For he paid such close attention to what was read that nothing from Scripture did he fail to take in—rather he grasped everything, and in him the memory took the place of books."[23] Soon thereafter, he took up residence in the Egyptian desert, where he would remain for most of his life. There he prayed, fasted, engaged in spiritual warfare, reconciled enemies, encouraged the weak, and healed the sick and suffering. Such great numbers were helped that Athanasius declared, "It was as if he were a physician given to Egypt by God."[24]

This story illustrates several characteristics that we still find in Orthodox spirituality. First, Christ's call to radical discipleship occurred within the liturgical life of the church. Once more, we see that personal spirituality is rooted in worship. Anthony was already a Christian when he heard Christ's call through the public reading of Scripture. Not every person is called to such radical detachment from this world's possessions, but all are called to live out the meaning of their baptism by dying daily to their own will and rising with Christ to walk in newness of life (Romans 6:1–12). Today, when a monk is tonsured, baptismal texts such as Galatians 3:27 (KJV) are still read to announce their calling: "As many of you as have been baptized into Christ have put on Christ."

Second, Anthony demonstrates that the Christian's primary vocation is prayer. Some refer to this as "union" with God or deification. Closely connected is the need to live under the guidance of a spiritual

---

23. *Athanasius: The Life of Antony and Letter to Marcellinus*, trans. Robert Gregg (New York: Paulist, 1980), 32.

24. Ibid., 94.

father or elder as he did with the old hermit.[25] Self-guidance is a grave danger to be avoided for fear that it can lead to delusion. Orthodox laypeople are not required to live in obedience to an elder, as monks are asked to do. Most often, it is their local pastor who shepherds them through counseling and confession. At special times, however, some consult the guidance of a spiritual father or mother, whom they often find in a monastery or within their own communities.

Third, Orthodox spirituality is less taught than caught. It is a whole way of life, not a list of regimens for developing the spiritual life. It is certainly true that there are appointed seasons of fasting and prayer in the liturgical calendar that all Orthodox are invited to follow as they are able. Daily prayers and Bible readings are appointed throughout the year. It is also wise to identify specific areas of need and to purposefully work on them (such as Evagrius Pontincus's "eight deadly thoughts," which later became known as the "seven deadly sins"). Yet Anthony did not facilitate spiritual growth by using a predetermined plan of special techniques complete with ascetical practices. There is no systematic way of talking about *the* way of prayer or *the* way of obtaining guidance.[26] Prayer, guidance, and other practices are simply part of the hard work of holiness learned over a lifetime of striving to love God and neighbor. Anthony fasted because he was hungry to love God more; he prayed because he wanted closer communion with God; he contemplated so he could better fix his gaze on his divine spouse; he practiced silence because he yearned to hear God. There is no notion of "merit" in these works, as developed in later medieval theology in western Europe.[27] Following the relational

---

25. For the role of spiritual fathers and mothers, see Kallistos Ware, "The Spiritual Guide in Orthodox Christianity," and "The Fool in Christ as Prophet and Apostle," in *The Inner Kingdom* (Crestwood, N.Y.: St. Vladimir's Seminary Press, 2001), 1:127–80.

26. Such as used in the Ignatian exercises of the Roman Catholic tradition, although some Orthodox have used them with great profit (e.g., St. Nicodemus, an eighteenth-century compiler of *The Philokalia*). Gregory of Nyssa (c. 335–394) articulated the classic three-path journey into communion with God — the ways of purgation, illumination, and union with God. This approach was taken up later by Byzantine spiritual writers, but we must not make absolute what is merely relative. Outside of monastic circles, this path is not widely practiced among the faithful.

27. The best of all monastic literature on this in the Christian East is by Mark the Ascetic, "Concerning Those Who Imagine That They Are Justified by Works," in *Counsels on the Spiritual Life: Mark the Monk*, vol. 1, trans. Tim Vivian and Augustine Casiday (Crestwood, N.Y.: St. Vladimir's Seminary Press, 2009), 113–40. Mark argues that prayer, fasting, vigils, and all other monastic disciplines are dangerously misguided without a prior grounding in the "unmerited, free gift" of grace as the prime motivation for all Christian living. For

qualities within the Trinity, the source and goal of every spiritual activity is love for God.[28] Love is more relational than legal.

A fourth observation on the life of Anthony for discerning the principles of Orthodox spirituality is his emphasis on Scripture in the quest for holiness. Any attempt to understand Orthodox spirituality must give full weight to the centrality of Scripture in Christian formation. In a classic collection of monastic wisdom called *The Sayings of the Desert Fathers*, two elders are discussing what is most profitable for their souls. Abba Amoun of Nitria says to Abba Poemen, "When I am obliged to speak to my neighbor, do you prefer me to speak of the Scriptures or of the sayings of the Fathers?" The old man answered him, "If you can't be silent, you had better talk about the sayings of the Fathers than about the Scriptures; it is not so dangerous."[29]

This is just one story among many that illustrates the supremacy of Scripture in the spiritual life. Scripture is far more authoritative than the voice of the Fathers, though they are inseparably united in the church's tradition. In order to internalize the Scriptures, the monks memorized large portions of the Bible, recited them out loud throughout the day, meditated on them, and applied them to their daily lives.[30] They were convinced that one cannot really know the Scriptures until he or she has lived them. The Scriptures were also essential for discerning and defeating the demonic. Spiritual warfare against the powers of darkness still constitutes a major emphasis in Orthodox spirituality and prayer—a topic that, unfortunately, we cannot develop here.

As we think about the role of spiritual practices in our communion with God, we turn to the late Fr. John Meyendorff, who has cautioned,

---

an interpretation of this text, see our essay "*Concerning Those Who Imagine That They Are Justified by Works*: The Gospel According to St. Mark—the Monk," in *The Philokalia: Exploring a Classic Text of Orthodox Spirituality*, ed. Brock Bingaman and Bradley Nassif (New York: Oxford University Press, 2012).

28. Bradley Nassif, "The Poverty of Love," *Christianity Today* (May 2008), 34–37.

29. *The Sayings of the Desert Fathers*, rev. ed., trans. Benedicta Ward (Kalamazoo, Mich.: Cistercian, 1984), 31–32.

30. The *lectio divina* method used by later monks in the Latin West is consistent with this tradition, but the technique was not widely used by the Eastern Church. For inspirational reading of the desert fathers and mothers, see Bradley Nassif, *Bringing Jesus to the Desert* (Grand Rapids: Zondervan, 2012). For advanced studies, see Douglas Burton-Christie, *The Word in the Desert* (New York: Oxford University Press, 1993); William Harmless, *Desert Christians: An Introduction to the Literature of Early Monasticism* (New York: Oxford University Press, 2004).

"The Church does not canonize any particular form or method of devotion, but merely sanctions the holiness of those who have been able to express the reality of the Kingdom of God in their lives and in their words."[31] This is important to keep in mind since we previously noted that Orthodox spiritual life does not normally utilize a set of special techniques. The exception, however, is a monastic practice known as hesychasm ("holy silence"). For centuries, Orthodox monks, known as hesychasts ("those who practice silence"), have practiced this form of contemplation. It is a hallmark of Orthodox spirituality. At its core lies an apophatic experience of stillness and silence. St. Gregory Palamas (1296–1359) rooted it in the church's dogmas of the Trinity, Christology, and the sacraments of baptism and Eucharist.

Hesychasm is a form of mental prayer, or prayer of the heart, that combines breathing techniques with a short petition known as "the Jesus Prayer": "Lord Jesus Christ, Son of God, have mercy on me" (the words "a sinner" are sometimes added).[32] By gazing at the region of the heart or navel while regulating one's breathing and reciting the Jesus Prayer, one may see and partake of the divine glory in this life. We may experience a vision of the visible uncreated light of God's energies that shone forth from the body of the transfigured Christ on Mount Tabor (Matthew 17:2). In so doing, we too may become more deified in our body and soul. But Christians who pray the Jesus Prayer are to seek the Giver, not the gift, of the uncreated light.

The simplicity of the Jesus Prayer became the most traditional way in which communion with God has been expressed. It is still widespread, not only among the monks, but also the laity. Yet it is not the only way to communion with God, nor is it required of all Orthodox Christians. It is one significant room among many in the larger castle of the church's spirituality. Bible reading, listening to sermons, almsgiving,

---

31. John Meyendorff, *The Orthodox Church*, 4th rev. ed. (Crestwood, N.Y.: St. Vladimir's Seminary Press, 1996), 187.

32. Next to the Bible, the most widely read book in the Orthodox Church today is a collection of ascetical writings known as *The Philokalia* (trans. G. E. H. Palmer, Philip Sherrard, and Kallistos Ware, vols. 1–4, vol. 5 forthcoming [London: Faber and Faber, 1979–1999]). This anthology of monastic texts from the fourth to fifteenth centuries covers a range of topics, but especially the Jesus Prayer. Its emphasis on ceaseless prayer (2 Thessalonians 5:17) became the subject of the nineteenth-century Russian classic *The Way of a Pilgrim*. A companion collection of interpretive essays is in *The Philokalia: Exploring a Classic Text of Orthodox Spirituality*.

evangelism, and the frequent saying of the "Our Father" (Lord's Prayer) are other rooms in the church's castle.

Gospel Missions: A Social Spirituality of an Incarnational Trinitarian Faith

In what little space remains, it is imperative that we highlight the missionary implications of the Orthodox Church's Trinitarian spirituality. The nature of Trinitarian dogma requires love in action. The church's mission is rooted in the triune being of God himself. In the language of the Greek Fathers, the inner life of the Trinity is *perichoretic*, which simply means that the Father, Son, and Holy Spirit mutually indwell each other in an eternal bond of love and intimacy. That internal bond, however, expresses itself in the Father's sending of the Son in the incarnation. After his death and resurrection, the Son says, "'As the Father has sent me, I am sending you'" (John 20:21–22). At Pentecost, the people of God receive the Spirit (Acts 1:4–5; 2:4) and reach out to the uttermost part of the world with the message of the gospel. The mission of the church is to preach the good news of new life through Christ, given by the Holy Spirit in baptism in the name of the Trinity and nourished by the Eucharist in the church.[33]

The Trinitarian and incarnational models of love for the neighbor have also inspired the social outreach of the church. Sts. Basil the Great and John Chrysostom, its two greatest exponents, stressed the urgency of Christian philanthropy for the poor and needy. Orphanages, hospitals, schools, hospices, and other forms of social work are practical expressions of a spirituality centered on Christ's incarnate love.[34]

Deification: The Quest for Trinitarian Love

Up to now, we have seen the central role that the gospel plays in the outworking of Orthodox spirituality. We have also identified some of

---

33. For the conversion theology of the church, see my essay, "The Evangelical Theology of the Eastern Orthodox Church," in *Three Views on Eastern Orthodoxy and Evangelicalism*, 68–81; see also James Stamoolis, *Eastern Orthodox Mission Theology Today* (Maryknoll, N.Y.: Orbis, 1986).

34. For Orthodoxy's characteristic approaches to issues of social theology, see M. J. Pereira, ed., *Philanthropy and Social Compassion in Eastern Orthodox Tradition* (New York: St. Sophia Institute, 2010).

the major liturgical and sacramental emphases and practices that draw Orthodox Christians closer to the triune God and to each other. We have also discussed the dogmatic foundations and missionary imperatives of the spiritual life. But what is the ultimate goal toward which all these lead? Two texts summarize everything Orthodoxy teaches about the spiritual life. Both are tied to the common purpose of creation and the incarnation:

> "Then God said, 'Let us make human beings in our image, to be like ourselves." (Genesis 1:26 NLT)

> "God became humanized so that humans might become divinized." (St. Athanasius)[35]

In these texts, the definition and destiny of the human person is to become divine. Communion with God is the goal of creation and salvation. The church calls this goal *christification* or, more commonly, *deification* (from the Greek *theosis*).[36] Deification is the goal that integrates all Eastern Orthodox theology and spirituality. While acknowledging that the term has Greek philosophical origins, it is nevertheless thoroughly biblical. The gospel of John and the epistles of Paul clearly speak of a mystical union between Christ and the believer and a personal indwelling of the Holy Spirit. The church fathers and ecumenical councils, discussed above, base their understanding of deification on the reality of the incarnation. By participating in Christ, who united our humanity with his divinity, believers "participate" in the very life of God himself. It is by such intimate union that we "are being transformed into the same image [of the Lord] from one degree of glory to another" (2 Corinthians 3:18 ESV). The best biblical term that is equivalent to the Greek word *theosis* or deification is probably *glorification*.

The goal of glorification is seen in the creation account in Genesis 1–2. Orthodox Christians believe that at creation Adam and Eve were fashioned after a Trinitarian likeness. This is of great importance because, as we saw in the dogmas of Christ and the Trinity, it is *out of* that Trinitarian love and *for* that Trinitarian love that humans were first

---

35. Athanasius, *On the Incarnation of the Word*, ch. 8, par. 54 (my translation).
36. Norman Russell, *Fellow Workers with God: Orthodox Thinking on* Theosis (Crestwood, N.Y.: St. Vladimir's Seminary Press, 2009).

created. Humanity's ultimate goal is to live as God lives, namely, in love. But our first parents were not fully developed in their relationship with God. Unlike an Augustinian interpretation of Adam and Eve, our first parents were not created in a full-grown state of physical and spiritual perfection in complete communion with God. Rather, humanity was more like a developing young child who was charged with growing ever more deeply into the divine likeness through the process of deification. *Theosis* includes growth in the characteristics of God, such as love, compassion, and mercy. But it also includes the idea of growing in communion with God, resulting in a continued state of immortality. Accordingly, the fall into sin was not a drastic withdrawal from a perfected state. Instead, it was a failure to achieve the original purpose God had set for humanity. It was a departure from the path of deification.

This understanding of humanity's original purpose and the nature of the fall directly impacts Orthodox concepts of the incarnation and salvation as deification. Through the incarnation and atonement, humans can become by grace what Christ was by nature. The purpose of the incarnation was to give us a new humanity. As we saw in our earlier discussion of the gospel in the liturgy, this incarnational view sees the person and work of Christ as a victory over sin, death, and the demonic. Since the immortal Son of the Father became human and died, he overcame the powers of death and corruption and thus enabled people to acquire immortality. It is a victory that restores to people the possibility of a new humanity through becoming like Christ.

In the words of the apostle John, the Father sent the Son so that we may participate in the Son's love for the Father (see John 13–17).[37] *That is what Orthodox spirituality is finally all about: love for God and love for neighbor through union with Christ in the life of the church (Mark 12:29–31).* The experiential coherence of the gospel through the church's liturgy, sacraments, dogmas, ascetical life, and mission have one object as their ultimate goal—the deification of the human person into the image of Jesus Christ (Romans 8:29; 2 Peter 1:4). This Christ-likeness is not such that can make one a fourth person of the Trinity.

---

37. See Donald Fairbairn, *Life in the Trinity* (Downers Grove, Ill.: InterVarsity, 2009); John A. McGuckin, *Standing in God's Holy Fire: The Byzantine Tradition* (Maryknoll, N.Y.: Orbis, 2001).

That, of course, would be blasphemous. It is also not pantheistic because in this union with God we do not lose our personal identity. Rather, we are deified by becoming truly ourselves, and we cannot become truly ourselves unless we are in communion with Christ in his Trinitarian relations.

This ideal portrait of glorified humanity in the Orthodox tradition is emphasized in the transfiguration of Christ (Matthew 17:1–13). Yet the eschatological glory of the transfigured Christ can only be known partially in this life. And so, as we end this essay, we return to the story of St. Anthony of Egypt to see what a fallen portrait of a deified Christian can look like here and now. After living an ascetic life for nearly twenty years in the desert, several of Anthony's friends tore down the fortress door where he had lived in relative seclusion. The following describes what they saw:

> Antony came forth as though from a shrine, having been led into divine mysteries and inspired by God. This was the first time he appeared from the fortress for those who came out to him. And when they beheld him, they were amazed to see that his body had maintained its former condition, neither fat from lack of exercise, nor emaciated from fasting and combat with demons, but was just as they had known him prior to his withdrawal. The state of his soul was one of purity, for it was not constricted by grief, nor relaxed by pleasure, nor affected by either laughter or dejection ... He maintained utter equilibrium, like one guided by reason ... Through him the Lord healed many of those present who suffered bodily ailments; others he purged of demons, and to Antony he gave grace in speech.[38]

This portrait of Anthony as a Spirit-filled man shows what a human being renewed in the image and likeness of God can become in this world. Athanasius could explain the transformation of Anthony only in light of the conviction that the deification of a mortal creature depends entirely on the power of the Son of God, who became human so that humans might become like God. One can only explain Anthony's holiness—and ours—in the light of that mystery.

---

38. *Athanasius: The Life of Antony*, 42.

SCOTT HAHN

Bradley Nassif gives a beautiful account of a beautiful life. For me, it brought back the memory of the first time I attended a Catholic liturgical event — a vespers service at a Byzantine seminary. My Calvinist background had not prepared me for the experience — the incense and icons, the prostrations and bows, the chants and bells. All my senses were engaged. Afterward a seminarian asked me, "What do you think?" All I could say was, "Now I know why God gave me a body — to worship the Lord with his people in liturgy." It was a life-changing moment for me.

For the Orthodox believer, the church's worship is not merely good and true; it is beautiful. The Christian makes worship beautiful because it is for God.

For the Orthodox believer, as for the Catholic believer, the church's spiritual life is not reducible to practices and phenomena. It is helpful to focus instead on the common ground and goal that unifies the external signs and efforts, and Nassif does this very well as he focuses our attention on deification and on Trinitarian life. The Catechism of the Catholic Church tells us, "The mystery of the Most Holy Trinity is the central mystery of the Christian faith and of Christian life," and "from the beginning ... the very root of the Church's living faith."[39] The Orthodox believer, again like the Catholic, understands salvation in terms that are not merely negative (saved from sin), but positive (saved for a share in Christ's sonship). Orthodox Christians have spoken this way, as the Catechism says, "from the beginning," and so the Scriptures describe a graced exchange (2 Corinthians 8:9), a share of divine sonship (Galatians 4:4–6; 1 John 3:1–2), our transformation into God's

---

39. *Catechism of the Catholic Church* (New York: Doubleday, 1995), par. 234, p. 69; par. 249, p. 74.

image (1 Corinthians 15:49–52), and our participation in the divine nature (2 Peter 1:4). The early church fathers richly developed this doctrine in terms of deification and divinization, and their language pervades the liturgies of the Orthodox churches. To live Christian life to the fullest is to live divine life, heavenly life, even here on earth.

Western Catholics may not be familiar with all of the vocabulary and cultural expressions of Eastern Christianity, but they are part of the church's patrimony. They appear throughout the Catechism and other documents of the church. The West can only be enriched by greater exposure to the traditions of the East. Pope John Paul II dreamed of a day when the church would "breathe with both lungs" once again, and Christians East and West would enjoy a relationship of profound mutual influence and respect—a relationship of true communion.

What a Catholic usually misses in any account of Orthodoxy is the note of catholicity—the affirmation, empirically verifiable, that the church is one and is universal. As the Catechism puts it, "The Church was ... catholic on the day of Pentecost, and will always be so until the day of the Parousia" (see Acts 2:1–14).[40] This is a distinctive mark of the new covenant: that it cannot be identified with an ethnic group, nation, empire, language, or culture. Catholicity was supremely important for the earliest of the church fathers, and it is evident in Clement of Rome, Ignatius of Antioch, Polycarp of Smyrna, Irenaeus of Lyons, and Eusebius of Caesarea, among others. These bishops looked for apostolic succession, but also communion—and in many cases, quite specifically, communion with the Church of Rome.

Orthodoxy creedally affirms such unity, but for a millennium it has increasingly had to identify its locus exclusively in the invisible heavens rather than on the visible earth. For the first millennium, even the enemies of Christianity knew that the church was one and universal. Yet, in recent years, world Orthodoxy has suffered from the autocephaly, factionalism, and rivalry among patriarchs and among local bishops. We have seen the scandal of new imperial capitals seeking to supplant Constantinople. We have seen the inability of the Orthodox in America—or even simply the *Russian* Orthodox in America—to gather in practical, administrative unity. I have heard more than one Orthodox

---

40. Ibid., par. 830, p. 239.

theologian lament the fact that to count the number of Orthodox bishops of New York requires the use of all ten fingers and all ten toes. In light of these problems, great theologians such as John Meyendorff and Thomas Hopko have concluded that the idea of a pan-Orthodox council can only be seen as an eschatological hope.

In speaking of the sacraments, Nassif helpfully explains that these signs are not mechanistic or automatic, but rather synergistic. The word comes from St. Paul, who referred to us as God's co-workers (*synergoi*, 1 Corinthians 3:9). It is important, however, to add that our partnership is not fifty-fifty. Whatever we have, we have received as a gift, a grace. Augustine of Hippo is helpful in clarifying this matter. He explains that when God rewards our merits, he is simply crowning his own gifts.

As a theologian I am especially grateful for Nassif's high standard for my profession. He is right to complain about the degradation of the field, as it has become just another academic career path. He writes, "A genuinely Orthodox theologian is someone who pursues Christ himself, in his Trinitarian relations." I would say the same applies to a truly Catholic theologian, and I would add that this is indeed what the term has meant in the Christian West. We see it in the lives and works of Bernard of Clairvaux, Albert the Great, Thomas Aquinas, Bonaventure, Teresa of Avila, and Therese of Lisieux, all of whom are recognized in Catholicism as doctors of the church. Seminaries (whether Catholic or Orthodox) that have sought secular accreditation in the West have sometimes also compromised with the spirit of academic careerism, but our office remains our office, whether or not we live up to it, and the saints remain the standard by which we will be judged.

As a theologian I am grateful also for Nassif's recognition of the Fathers' high regard for human reason, a quality often disparaged by the Protestant Reformers and those who followed after them. I would suggest only a slight adjustment. Nassif states that "rationality is perhaps the noblest feature of the image of God in humans." The Catholic tradition, however, has always subordinated rationality to love.

The Catechism states this in a way, I believe, that Catholics and Orthodox can agree on: "The whole concern of doctrine and its teaching must be directed to the love that never ends. Whether something is proposed for belief, for hope or for action, the love of our Lord must always be made accessible, so that anyone can see that all the works of perfect

Christian virtue spring from love and have no other objective than to arrive at love" (quoting verbatim from the old Roman Catechism).[41]

Christ prayed that we should be united in that love, which is the life of the Trinity manifest in the church on earth. I wait in joyful hope for his prayer to be answered and for all of us to "arrive at love" in sacramental communion. This need not be an eschatological hope.

---

41. Ibid., par. 25, p. 15.

JOSEPH DRISKILL

The opportunity to respond to the presentations of three Christian faith communities using the lens of Christian spirituality is an opportunity to affirm what is sacred and life-giving in each while pointing out differences that distinguish progressive mainline faith from those who share much of its heritage. Approaches to varying faith expressions that begin with doctrine or history seem naturally to turn rather quickly to those aspects of faith that divide members of the Christian community.

Frequently, such divisions are prematurely lauded as lines in the sand, with truth on one side and error on the other. My aim is to promote a deeper understanding of differences — one that grows out of mutual respect, with an eye to deepening one's own faith through the encounter with those whose lived experiences of faith differ. Once a hermeneutic of appreciation or generosity has been exercised, it is then possible to affirm differences without disrespecting the integrity of those whose faith communities and practices offer alternative patterns of Christian living.

Key Emphases

The key emphases of Orthodox and progressive Protestant spiritualities are shaped by the worldviews that provide the differing contexts of their formative periods. Orthodox spirituality is clearly shaped by the worldviews of the early and Byzantine church. Nassif identifies three theologians whose works are formative for Orthodox spirituality: John the Evangelist, Gregory Nazianzen, and Symeon the New Theologian. He also points out that the dogmas of the first seven ecumenical councils, meeting between AD 325 and 787, are essential to Orthodox spirituality. Nassif points out that these councils understood that the spiritual life is grounded in the Trinity and in the incarnation. Christ, in his Trinitarian relations with God the Father and the Holy Spirit, "constitutes the ontological grounds of all Orthodox spirituality." The worldview of Orthodox liturgy is the meeting of heaven and earth. In the wonderful story Nassif shares from Bishop Kallistos Ware, visitors sent by Prince Vladimir to an Orthodox liturgy do not know whether they are "in heaven or on earth."

Progressive Protestant spirituality since the Enlightenment has been shaped by and is in dialogue with the foundational categories of the modern and, of late, the postmodern world as ancient notions of a three-story universe (heaven, earth, and underworld) were challenged by the rise of science. For progressive Protestants, the category of heaven not only became increasingly problematic, but the understanding of the world itself was transformed. This transformation problematized many traditional faith categories, such as resurrection and miracles, and raised profound questions about Jesus' nature. Questions that the answers of early church councils had settled for Orthodox spirituality were now on the table for progressive Protestants, albeit in forms shaped by the modern and now postmodern worldviews. The distance between the assumptions and questions raised by the disparate social locations of these faith communities might make a dialogue seem fruitless if the goals were to seek institutional change. However, speaking as a progressive Protestant, I believe a number of our shared commitments and values make such an exchange meaningful.

Means for Implementing Spirituality

A dialogue between Orthodox spirituality and progressive mainline Protestant spirituality has the potential to enrich the way progressive Protestants implement or engage their spiritual practices. For example, Orthodox spirituality emphasizes the importance of holding together such binaries as prayer and action, mysticism and rationality, faith and works, faith and reason, mysticism and theology, apophatic and cataphatic prayer, and doctrine and experience. Progressive Protestants, on the other hand, have frequently privileged one side of the binary while to a greater or lesser degree devaluing or even dismissing the other. The recovery of these aspects of faith deemed less significant offers the possibility for a more meaningful lived religious experience.

In this brief response, I lift up two binaries bifurcated by progressive Protestants where each side needs to be valued and embraced—social action and prayer, mysticism and rationality. A dialogue with Orthodox spirituality can assist progressive Protestants along this path. In progressive Protestant communities of faith, social action clearly receives more attention than prayer, especially personal prayer or contemplative prayer. Not only have prayer traditions been largely ignored in mainline theological curricula, but in many congregations the prayers of public worship have been the primary forms of prayer engaged in by congregants. While it was customary for members to pray before meals and at bedtime and for religious leaders to pray at the bedsides of the ill, prayer itself was generally de-emphasized. Many progressive mainline Protestants believed that personal prayer was largely a matter of individual preference and that formal public prayer sufficiently addressed the needs of the community.

Orthodox spirituality understands that prayer is at the heart of faith. Nassif points out that members of the faith community are encouraged to have devotional altars in their homes and to pray in front of icons of Christ and the saints using words from manuals derived from the service books. This establishes a link between the prayers used in private devotions and public worship that Protestant Reformers, including Luther and Calvin, also valued highly. As the influence of the modern worldview deepened, many progressive Protestant communities lost sight of the link between personal and corporate prayer. Orthodox spirituality has kept these connections alive and vital. Progressive Protestants seeking to transform the world through engagement and action would benefit from a commitment to spiritual practices that nourish an experiential relationship with God. Such commitments nourish visions of justice and keep leaders spiritually nourished. Such prayer also has the power to foster actions that are truly altruistic rather than ego driven.

The bifurcation of mysticism and rationality was even more marked for Protestants. Progressive Protestants wanted little to do with mysticism and much to do with rationality, a spirituality profoundly influenced by the Enlightenment. The reliance of a worldview shaped by Enlightenment rationality resulted in lived experiences of faith that were largely dismissive of mysticism. When I was in seminary in the late 1960s, while we were reading Paul Tillich's *Systematic Theology* our professor said, "You will no doubt find much of Tillich's work enlightening. But when you get to his comments on mysticism, you can skip over them. I don't have a clue what he is trying to say." This view of mysticism was commonplace for progressive Protestants and reveals the extent to which binaries held together and celebrated by Orthodox spirituality were parsed and evaluated as worthy or unworthy by progressive Protestants. Recovering the importance of various life-giving forms of prayer, along with integrating the insights of the mystics into progressive Protestant spirituality, has the potential to ground the commitments to justice and compassion on firmer soil.

The Role of Christ in Spirituality

The Orthodox emphasis on the incarnation of Christ and its implications for salvation rather than on the fall—the redemption theology central in the thought of Augustine—provides a much-needed corrective to what progressive Protestants see as the fall, that is, an overemphasis on sin. While many progressive Protestants have seriously questioned or abandoned substitutionary atonement theology, alternative theological positions have not sought to draw on the Orthodox focus on incarnation and deification. Through the incarnation Christ was both fully human and fully divine. This union of the human and the divine allows for cooperation between the human and divine. Nassif explains that in Orthodox spirituality the fall is not understood as a drastic departure from a perfected state. Rather, it is a failure to live up to God's purpose for humankind, namely, following the path of deification. The belief that God became human (incarnation) so that humans could become more like God (deification) offers a foundation for ethical reflection in which one's lifestyle is guided not only by values taught by Jesus but also by one's relationship to the divine. Deification requires growing in the characteristics associated with God—love, compassion, mercy, and justice. Protestants, nevertheless, remain skeptical of anything that seems like an abandoning of "justification by faith" in favor of using spiritual practices to earn God's favor. However, the Orthodox emphasis on deification grounds spiritual practices and ethical living in an understanding of sanctification based not on earning God's favor but on being in an authentic relationship with the Holy One. Because progressive Protestants have since the waning years of modernity sought a long-missed experiential relationship with God, the Orthodox understanding of deification offers fruitful possibilities for continued reflection.

Turning to another difference, the Orthodox emphasis on heresy differs markedly from progressive Protestants' approach to doctrine. When Nassif turns to the early church councils, he highlights their findings by identifying the heresy that each addressed. He notes that the heresies "undermined the mediation of Christ in human salvation" and as such "lead to a faulty life of prayer, worship, and the sacramental life." He notes that many of these heresies "lie at the center of our differences with liberal Protestant theology ..." As a liberal Protestant I agree with Nassif's observation not only as it identifies differences between the spiritualities of our communities but also as it echoes through my own life experience. In the late 1960s when I was gaining my first academic exposure to church history and the events of the early church councils, I remember numerous times identifying with those who were declared heretics. As I reflect back on that experience, I see myself bringing my modern worldview, with its implicit anthropological and cosmological assumptions, to texts whose assumptive world was very different. I remember someone saying, "In the patristic period, people could not imagine how Jesus could be human. Now we find it difficult to believe that Jesus could be divine." The theological understanding of Christ and the Trinity provide Orthodox spirituality with a theological center that undergirds the worship, sacraments, and spiritual practices of the community. Thus, the Orthodox concern with early church heresies regarding the nature of Christ and the Holy Spirit highlights an area where progressive Protestant spirituality differs from its Orthodox counterpart.

In progressive Protestant faith communities there is much less focus in general on doctrinal conformity than in the other spiritualities described in this book. The history of biblical interpretation has deeply influenced mainline Protestant denominations and has contributed to more latitude for individual interpretation of texts. As a result, there is not a major emphasis on errant belief or on personal acts of sin. However, there is considerable concern with social sin, that is, with the injustices resulting from systemic and institutional ills. For example, racism, sexism, and homophobia are frequently embedded in social and legal systems. Working to rectify systems in which injustice is perpetrated is, from the vantage point of progressive Protestant spirituality, holy labor and is deemed of more importance than conformity to church doctrines.

The Function of the Institutional Church

Orthodox spirituality has the potential to enrich progressive Protestants' lived experience of faith by the way it understands and values beauty in its liturgical life. Orthodox worship engages and activates all five senses in worship and thereby implicitly acknowledges the way in which human beings have been created. We are more than our capacity for reason, as important as the role of reason and critical thinking are for a faith that seeks understanding. As progressive Protestants in America focused increasingly on issues of justice and compassion, notions of sacred space, where material objects might beckon a worshiper to bow down, were exchanged for that which is "useful" or benevolent. The history of Protestant protests, fighting these battles in one arena or another since the sixteenth century, resulted in an ambivalent attitude toward beauty. Utilitarian notions of beauty which view that which is beautiful as a luxury rather than a window to the divine have resulted in many Protestant houses of worship that are neither beautifully ornate nor beautifully simple. Consciously investing resources to create spaces that invite believers to see worship as more than fellowship with one another was in many progressive churches viewed as either a luxury or a misuse of scarce resources. Reclaiming the importance of beauty has the potential to enliven public worship.

If I suspend my postmodern worldview and enter the Orthodox framework, I can appreciate the many gifts Orthodox spirituality brings to its followers as well as to a dialogue with progressive Protestant spirituality. However, I notice that although the Orthodox Church engages in outreach to the world, it does not emphasize such outreach in its spirituality. While there is considerable discussion of the role of love, mercy, and compassion in the life of Jesus and in the interior relations of the Trinity, reaching out to care for the world is seen primarily as a fruit of the Spirit rather than as an integral aspect or central tenet of being faithful. This, of course, identifies a major difference between progressive Protestant spirituality and Orthodox spirituality.

RESPONSE TO BRADLEY NASSIF

I consider it an honor to respond to Bradley Nassif's essay. I have known of Dr. Nassif (thanks to Grant Osborne of Trinity Evangelical Divinity School) since he first founded the Society for the Study of Eastern Orthodoxy and Evangelicalism in 1990 and have appreciated his efforts at Orthodox-evangelical dialogue ever since. His expertise in navigating Orthodox and evangelical theologies is well-known. In the present essay, however, we move from theology to the exploration of spirituality. Nassif has openly declared that, with regard to evangelical-Orthodox relations, the area of spirituality is "very likely the most dynamic manifestation of their common ground."[42] I look forward to our exploration of that sentiment in the essays and responses published in this volume. My own responses to Nassif's essay will loosely take the form of comments on some of the core issues in Christian spirituality listed in Bruce Demarest's introduction to this book.

Definitions of Spirituality and Orthodoxy

Nassif does not provide a definition of spirituality. "Orthodox spirituality is caught more than it is taught," he states. Orthodox spirituality and *theology as well*, I would say. I remember years ago walking into the library at the Patriarch Athenagoras Orthodox Institute in Berkeley, California, and asking for manuals of systematic theology. I was instructed that this genre of literature was not the norm in Orthodoxy. With a few exceptions, liturgical studies, patristic research, and explorations of particular issues are the common forms of Orthodox theological exploration. This is the material Nassif uses in his essay. He makes almost no reference to the many biographies, spiritual writings, and

---

42. Bradley Nassif, "The Evangelical Theology of the Eastern Orthodox Church," in *Three Views on Eastern Orthodoxy and Evangelicalism*, ed. James Stamoolis (Grand Rapids: Zondervan, 2004), 74.

devotional manuals respected in Orthodox circles. What we have before us, then, is a presentation of an Orthodox *theology of spirituality*—how relationship with God is ideally lived in light of the structure of Orthodox theology, liturgy, and polity.

Nassif also does not provide a definition of Orthodoxy. He simply describes Orthodoxy as a "vast" tradition. The impression given is that Orthodoxy is also a *single* tradition. And yet I was struck as I read the essay—this is not any of the Orthodoxies I had known or experienced elsewhere. This is not the social-formalist Orthodoxy many have known, particularly overseas but also in ethnic churches in America. This is not the progressive Orthodoxy of Russians such as Nikolai Berdyaev, Fyodor Dostoyevsky, Pavel Florensky, or Alexander Men. This also is not the postexile Orthodoxy of Vladimir Lossky, John Meyendorff, or Kallistos Ware—an Orthdoxy that speaks much more of such matters as *penthos*, the manifestation of thoughts, watchfulness, and spiritual conflict.

Indeed, Nassif speaks with a new voice. He drinks from the wells of contemporary biblical studies. He also actively receives from the evangelical traditions both personally and theologically. He has stated that he considers himself deeply indebted to evangelical Christians who helped bring him into a personal relationship with Jesus Christ. He teaches in evangelical institutions and reads evangelical books. Indeed, if I understand his life project correctly, Nassif is passionate about offering the riches of Orthodox Christianity to evangelicals *and* seeking to infuse American Orthodoxy with a spiritual renewal fueled through a recovery of the Orthodox tradition and sparked by the fires of evangelical Christianity. Nassif's emphasis on the gospel, for example, is nearly unique in my reading of Orthodoxy. What we have before us then, is a presentation of a vision of Orthodox spiritual theology written in the context of a desire for mutual influence between Orthodox and evangelical traditions. We must keep this in mind in order to fairly evaluate both Nassif's essay and Orthodox spirituality more generally.

Key Emphases and Practices of Spirituality

Nassif does not appear to separate his treatment of the key emphases of the Orthodox tradition from his treatment of the "means, disciplines, or regimens by which spirituality is achieved." Furthermore, as he places his treatment of "dogma" within his presentation of the key emphases and spiritual practices of the Orthodox tradition, it would seem inappropriate to divorce Nassif's treatment of the "role of Jesus Christ and the Holy Spirit" from his treatment of the key emphases and spiritual practices of Orthodox spirituality. What I understand from this way of ordering the material is that for Nassif, Orthodox spirituality, rooted in the gospel of Christ, is lived out characteristically through liturgy, sacrament, attention to dogma, and a life informed by monastic history and culture.

This brings us to the question, in light of Nassif's earlier claim: Are these emphases "the most dynamic manifestation" of the common ground between Orthodoxy and evangelicalism?

I begin with *gospel, dogma*, and the *role of Jesus Christ and the Holy Spirit*. Nassif, building on his reference to evangelical Scot McKnight, identifies the Christian gospel as "the saving message of the Bible as a whole." "Orthodox spirituality is defined by the center of its faith, and that center is the gospel of Jesus Christ," he proclaims. Consequently, "it is correct, therefore, to describe Orthodox spirituality as thoroughly evangelical." The centrality and fullness of the person, life, and work of Jesus Christ are at the center of Orthodox spirituality.

Evangelicals would for the most part be in complete agreement with Nassif regarding the importance and basic framework of gospel belief and life. Indeed, evangelical Protestants may have more in common doctrinally with Orthodox Christians than with either Roman Catholics or progressive Protestants. The importance of the saving message of the Bible for evangelicals hardly needs to be mentioned. And, as Nassif's reference to Scot McKnight demonstrates, evangelicals are developing an ever richer understanding of the fullness of salvation, due not only to what we have learned from Orthodox Christians but also to dialogues with progressives and Roman Catholics.

With regard to the role of the Holy Spirit, I suspect that evangelicals would be somewhat uncomfortable with Nassif's presentation. Nassif mentions the gift of the Holy Spirit as an integral part of the Christian message of salvation, but after this, refers to the Holy Spirit rarely and only in sacramental contexts. For evangelicals, spirituality is an ongoing relationship with Christ through the Holy Spirit. The work of the Spirit is not simply a matter of grace communicated by and recognized through sacraments, but rather a moment-by-moment interaction with the living God.

This brings us to Nassif's discussion of *liturgy* and the *sacraments*. He is clear on these points. Spirituality (grace) is mediated to believers through the sacraments and through the liturgy. He leads us on a thorough tour of the sacraments and sacramentals of the Orthodox faith. Grace is communicated not only through baptism, Eucharist, and repentance but also through icons, homemaking, and many other ordinary activities. These do not work automatically apart from our faith, but they combine with faith to foster growth in the spiritual life. In one sense, some evangelicals could not agree more with this approach. Evangelical Anglicans distinguish between "dominical" and "minor" sacraments. John Wesley and the Methodists outlined both "instituted" and "prudential" means of grace. There are vehicles that seem especially important to the Christian faith and to our growth. These are "instituted," "dominical," *special* means of grace. But then again, all kinds of spiritual activities are sacramental, used by the Spirit to draw us closer to Christ. Other evangelicals, however, are cautious about elevating any particular means of grace above the freedom of the Spirit to "blow wherever it pleases" (John 3:8).

Perhaps it is a matter of emphasis. Aside from theological disputes (and the heated disputes among Protestants only demonstrate how important sacrament is to us), what we are looking at with regard to a *spirituality* of sacrament is the role it plays in our lives as Christians. What is the relationship between true religion and the means of grace? When worded in this manner, the evangelical concerns become clearer. The means of grace *are* means of grace. Many evangelical Anglicans, for example, are very serious about their use of the sacraments. Yet, for the evangelical, one must be cautious, for sacraments can also easily become hindrances to true religion. For true religion is a lived union with God. Formalism, nominalism, and ceremonialism can be enemies of true religion, just as heresy and licentiousness can destroy authentic relationship with the living God. Thus evangelical spiritual writer Thomas Wilcox, for example, declares, "Thou mayest be high in duty, and yet a perfect enemy and adversary to Christ, in every prayer, in every ordinance."[43] Nassif is not ignorant of this danger. Indeed, when, in his

---

43. T. W. (Thomas Wilcox), *A Choice Drop of Honey from the Rock Christ: Or a Short Word of Advice to All Saints and Sinners* (London, 1757), www.kirjasilta.net/wilcox/choice/choice.html (accessed December 7, 2011).

works, he writes of the weaknesses of Orthodoxy, he is eager to warn of the dangers of nominalism.

A final central emphasis or practice identified in Nassif's essay is *monasticism*. He is quick to communicate that monasticism is a path that is "the same for monks and laypeople alike." He presents four features of this every-person monasticism: (1) the call arises from within liturgical life; (2) its primary vocation is prayer; (3) it is more caught than taught; and (4) it is an embodiment of Scripture. If there is one expression of Christianity that has *not* influenced evangelicalism greatly, it would probably be monasticism. If Nassif is saying that a characteristic of Orthodox spirituality is its connection to historic monasticism (which many other writers on Orthodox spirituality mention), then there is little manifestation of common ground here. If, however, Nassif is merely saying that attention to prayer, Scripture, and a mysterious life with God are important in Christian life, then certainly any evangelical will concur.

The Goal or Endgame

The goal or endgame of spirituality for Nassif, and for virtually all other Orthodox writers on spirituality as well, is deification or *theosis*—a full realization of our humanness through the assimilation of the energies of the Godhead. While hairsplitting details about the nature of the image of God in human beings, the nature of the "fall" and original sin, and the consequent character of restoration might be thrown back and forth at this point, there is really no need to do so. Protestants have debated the precise details of this issue among themselves for centuries. The point of the matter is that both for evangelicals and for Orthodox believers (and indeed for Roman Catholics and for progressive Protestants), growth in likeness to God and harmony with God is what it is all about in the end. I say, *Amen*.

Institutional Church

I close with a few comments on Nassif's views of the function of the institutional church in spirituality. I suspect that the reason Nassif never explicitly addresses this core issue of spirituality is because he implicitly makes the case that in Orthodox spirituality, virtually every aspect of our relationship with God is mediated through the institutional church.

We are converted through baptism, as he fleshes out more fully in other essays. We become recipients of grace through the liturgy and sacraments administered by the institutional church. The dogma is established, confirmed, and maintained by the institutional church. The days of fasting, prayer, and almsgiving are prescribed by the institutional church. The call to the every-person monastic life arises in the context of the liturgical life of the institutional church. When looked at from one perspective, Nassif's presentation of Orthodox spirituality is an attractive spirituality of "receiving": we receive the fullness of God's salvation — in the context of the comprehensive doctrinal orthodoxy received by the church — as we receive through the church the sacraments, the liturgy, and the life ordered by the church calendar and prescriptions. This is certainly not a salvation of "works." Everything is received. And to that extent many evangelicals would applaud Nassif's presentation of Orthodoxy.

And yet, as mentioned in my essay, evangelicalism is characteristically a *lay* movement. Part of this is a reflection on the modern individualism in which evangelicalism emerged (and out of which postmodern, nonindividualistic evangelicalisms are developing). But part of this is a simple belief in the ordinary Christian. We permit a lot to happen from the ground up. True, it gets messy at times. That's what happens when you allow influence from people other than trained, approved clergy. You get Methodist circuit riders, camp meetings, gospel churches, and church splits. While many evangelicals might be comfortable with a spirituality of receiving, few would feel satisfied with only receiving from the same sources in the same ways. The body of Christ is too diverse and too Spirit-led for this.

Conclusion

Is the field of spirituality the most dynamic manifestation of evangelical-Orthodox common ground? We have explored the foundations of the Christ-centered gospel, the place of liturgy and sacrament, the every-person monastic life, and the goal of that spirituality — a shared life with God. We have also seen the context of this spirituality in the institutional Orthodox Church. In the end, I suspect that a great deal has to do with true religion. Individually and corporately, evangelicals believe that true religion is about union with Christ. As evangelicals, we welcome into communion any corporate body or any particular individual who appears (or perhaps professes) to exhibit the signs of that union. Our efforts at fostering spiritual growth will make use of any means (or any rejection of means) that serve this purpose best. As evangelical and Orthodox Christians make authentic union with Christ our deepest common ground, differences between liturgical and institutional forms (though real) will take second place.

"COME TO THE FATHER": THE FACT AT THE FOUNDATION OF CATHOLIC SPIRITUALITY

SCOTT HAHN

My friends who aren't Catholic often think of the Catholic faith as monolithic. I used to imagine it that way myself. I was raised a Presbyterian and even served in the Presbyterian ministry until shortly before I became a Catholic in 1986.

Our impressions of Catholic spirituality come, perhaps, from the images we see most often on television, in novels, in the movies, or in the lives of our neighbors. We know the final scene of *The Godfather*, with its depiction of the rite of infant baptism. Maybe we've seen Catholics praying the prayers of the Rosary while fingering a string of beads at a vigil. Maybe we've seen Hispanic Catholics in procession with a banner that shows the image of the Virgin of Guadalupe. Maybe we've attended a wedding or funeral Mass.

We take this handful of phenomena and try to connect them somehow, and we come up with our idea of Catholic spirituality. This approach may work for defining the spirituality of some religious groups, but it breaks down when we apply it to the church that calls itself "Catholic."

The name itself hints at the problem we immediately encounter. *Catholic* means "universal," and if we're deriving spirituality from external phenomena, we have to process a world of religious phenomena and somehow find its common ground, common sense, or common thread.

Think about what must fall within the range of Catholic spirituality: the silence of the Trappists and the Pentecostal praise of the

Charismatic Renewal; the rarefied intellectual life of the Dominicans and the profound feeling of the Franciscans; the wealth of the Knights of Malta and the elected poverty of the Missionaries of Charity; the strict enclosure of the Carthusians and the world-loving secularity of Opus Dei; the bright colors of Central American devotional art and the austere blocks of the German cathedrals; the warrior spirit of the Templars and the serene *pax* of the Benedictines; Ignatian detachment and Marian warmth.

Catholic spirituality must encompass movements, schools, orders, and disciplines in every period of historical development: the desert fathers of the first millennium; the consecrated virgins and widows; the cenobites, anchorites, solitaries, brotherhoods, and the various syntheses in the rules of Basil, Augustine, and Benedict. Yet it must also include the rise of the friars of the Middle Ages; the mendicants, itinerant preachers, crusaders, reformers, founders, artists, and guilds of artisans; and the lay confraternities. Catholic spirituality must somehow also contain the rise of kaleidoscopically diverse lay movements in the twentieth century: Catholic Worker, Communion and Liberation, Cursillo, Focolare, L'Arche, Legion of Mary, Madonna House, Neocatechumenal Way, Sant'Egidio, Schoenstatt—a list alone could weigh down our discussion!

There are two main avenues of approach to spirituality. One considers the external phenomena of religions—prayer forms, disciplines, methods, devotions, and so on. The other approach focuses on interior phenomena—states of consciousness, emotion, mysticism (variously defined). The problem with these approaches is that they tend to boil spirituality down to a style of worship or a temperament.

Either way, Catholic spirituality presents a forest indiscernible because of the variety and number—and even the age—of its trees. In fact, if you look in older textbooks, you'll find that until recently (the last half century or so) "spirituality" didn't exist as a discipline within Catholic theology. The word *spirituality*, when it appeared at all, was defined simply as "the opposite of materiality."

I believe it is futile, then, to try to circumscribe Catholic spirituality by reducing it to a lifestyle or psychological profile. It is just too large. By necessity, it must contain multitudes.

What we can do, however—and what I hope to do in the course of this essay—is discern some basic points common to Catholics. Call them facts, truths, or a basic orientation. They are doctrines, yes, but they are more than doctrines. They are certainly more elemental and primal than style or temperament; they must accommodate every Christian style and temperament. Moreover, they must be catholic not only in spatial terms, uniting believers of India's Malabar Rite with Latin Rite Americans; they must be catholic also in temporal terms, uniting the great saints of the apostolic and patristic generations with their coreligionists in the Middle Ages, the Counter-Reformation, and the wake of the Second Vatican Council.

Saving Grace and Sonship

At the foundation of Catholic spirituality is an idea we find poetically expressed in the first postapostolic generation by Ignatius of Antioch: "My love has been crucified, and there is no fire in me desiring to be fed; but there is within me a water that lives and speaks, saying to me inwardly, 'Come to the Father.'"[1]

As Ignatius wrote those lines, he was en route from Syria, where he had served as bishop, to Rome, where he would be executed for his Christian faith. Deprived of everything he could love in the world — his home, his congregation, his title — he found that he still had all he needed. He rested upon the divine sonship he had received in baptism. This he depicts as a current of living water that speaks to him as it bears him home. His statement is a compact poetic image, compressing so many New Testament motifs: living water (John 4:10; Revelation 7:17), a voice that calls *Abba* (Romans 8:16; Galatians 4:6), participation in the cross (Romans 6:6; Galatians 2:20), but most importantly divine sonship (Romans 8:14–17; Galatians 3:26–27).

This "divine filiation" is the foundation of Catholic spirituality. In the Western church it is often called the *life of grace*. In the East it is called *deification*, *divinization*, or *theosis*. It is, quite simply, the fact of salvation — encompassing everything that goes with that fact: justification, sanctification, the remission of sin, the infusion of grace, and spiritual regeneration.

It describes the life that begins when a believer is baptized and receives the redeeming grace of Jesus' cross and resurrection. In the Catholic view,

1. Ignatius of Antioch, *The Letter to the Romans* 7.

we are not merely saved *from* something, but *for* something. We are saved *from* our sin, but *for* sonship. Freed from bondage to sin, we may at last enjoy "the freedom and glory of the children of God" (Romans 8:21).

This life of grace is a life of growth that will be complete only when its earthly phase is complete. "See what great love the Father has lavished on us, that we should be called children of God! And that is what we are!... Dear friends, now we are children of God, and what we will be has not yet been made known. But we know that when Christ appears, we shall be like him, for we shall see him as he is" (1 John 3:1–2). If we can describe Catholic spirituality at all, we must begin by examining this life and this process of growth.

Sharing God's Life

Come to the Father! At the heart of the gospel is the revelation of God's fatherhood. Christians accept this today as part of the standard vocabulary of received religion, of revelation. In the first century, however, it represented a revolution. That message was reason enough to get a person killed. In John's gospel we learn: "For this reason [the Jewish leaders] tried all the more to kill [Jesus]; not only was he breaking the Sabbath, but he was even calling God his own Father, making himself equal with God" (John 5:18).

It was customary for Jews to call on God as Father of their nation (see John 8:41), but not as Father to an individual. To make such a claim, they rightly assumed, was in some way to make oneself "equal with God," for earthly children always share a common (human) nature with their earthly fathers.

Jesus spoke of his own sonship in unique terms. He alone was the eternal Son of God. Yet he also encouraged everyone to consider God a Father. Consider the words that he held up as the model prayer: "Our Father in heaven, hallowed be your name" (Matthew 6:9). God's fatherhood extended to each and to all; that motif recurs throughout the Sermon on the Mount (Matthew 5–7), which we can call a compact summary of Jesus' teaching. The Sermon is thick with father-child language, and most of it refers to God's relationship with each individual in the crowd of Jesus' listeners.

How could human beings — persons possessing *human* nature — come to be children of a *divine* person who possesses *divine* nature? It's impossible. A father must share a common nature with the child he calls his "son" or "daughter." I may feel strong affection for my dogs or cats, but I cannot legally adopt them.

The shocking truth is that Jesus wants human beings to share God's life: "he has given us his very great and precious promises, so that through them you may participate in the divine nature, having escaped the corruption in the world caused by evil desires" (2 Peter 1:4). Jesus empowers us to *escape corruption* so that we may *participate in the divine nature*. As we noted earlier, salvation is not merely *from* sin, but *for* sonship—for the sake of divine adoption.

Through baptism, we have come to share in Christ's eternal relation with the Father. Paul speaks of us repeatedly as living "in Christ" (see Romans 8:1). He also speaks of Christ as living in us (Galatians 2:20 and elsewhere).

In love, God "predestined us for adoption to sonship through Jesus Christ, in accordance with his pleasure and will" (Ephesians 1:5). "So in Christ Jesus you are all children of God through faith" (Galatians 3:26). Though Christ had the "very nature of God" (Philippians 2:6), he poured himself out to take on "human likeness" (2:7). He took on our poverty so that we might assume his riches (see 2 Corinthians 8:9).

We are sons and daughters *in* the eternal Son of God. To use the formula favored by the early church fathers, we have become "sons in the Son"—"children in the Son." We possess by grace—the grace of adoption—the life that the divine Word has by nature. We have by gift what is his by right.

All Catholic spirituality proceeds from this fact. In the words of the twentieth-century abbot and spiritual writer Columba Marmion, "Just as the whole of Christ Jesus can be summed up by his Divine Sonship, so the whole of a Christian can be summed up by participation in this Sonship, through Jesus Christ, in Jesus Christ."[2]

Or better yet, in the words of St. Paul, "Those who are led by the Spirit of God are the children of God. The Spirit you received does not make you slaves, so that you live in fear again; rather, the Spirit you received brought about your adoption to sonship. And by him we cry, '*Abba*, Father'" (Romans 8:14–16).

---

2. Blessed Columba Marmion, *Christ, the Life of the Soul* (Bethesda, Md.: Zaccheus, 2005), 28.

Life in the Trinity

Salvation creates a family bond—which in biblical terms is a covenant bond—a new relation between two formerly unrelated parties. That is the key to understanding Catholic spirituality. Christ has given his Father to be our Father. Thus, in Christ all Christians are truly brothers and sisters, inhabiting "[God's] household" (Ephesians 2:19).

Salvation for a Catholic is "a translation from that state in which a man is born a child of the first Adam to the state of grace and of the 'adoption of the sons' [Romans 8:15] of God through the second Adam, Jesus Christ, our Savior."[3]

If we understand the gift of divine adoption, we can begin to see the sense of many Catholic customs and practices: for example, addressing Mary as "Mother," calling nuns "Sister," speaking of baptism as a "rebirth," and gathering together on Sundays for a solemn ritual meal. Moreover, if Christ is our brother, then *his* Father is *our* Father; *his* home is *our* home; *his* table is *our* table; *his* mother is *our* mother.

It all comes down (or goes up) to living the family life of God himself. For Christianity is the only religion whose one God is a family. Pope John Paul II put it memorably: "God in his deepest mystery is not a solitude, but a family, since he has in himself fatherhood, sonship, and the essence of the family, which is love."[4]

God is not *like* a family; he *is* a family. From eternity, God alone possesses the essential attributes of a family, and the Trinity alone possesses them in their perfection. Earthly households have these attributes, but only imperfectly.

Of course, Father, Son, and Holy Spirit are not "gender" terms, but relational terms. The language of the divine family is theological, not biological. The terms describe the eternal relations of the divine persons who dwell in communion.

---

3. Council of Trent, Decree on Justification, quoted in Heinrich Denzinger, *The Sources of Catholic Dogma* (Fitzwilliam, N.H.: Loreto, 2002), 811.

4. Pope John Paul II, *Puebla: A Pilgrimage of Faith* (Boston: Daughters of St. Paul, 1979), 86; see also Bertrand de Margerie, S.J., *The Christian Trinity in History* (Still River, Mass.: St. Bede's, 1982), xix: "The directive idea, underlying our Trinitarian analysis and synthesis is this: in the created world the total, though not adequate nor still less exhaustive, image of the Trinitarian mystery is man, personal and familial." And see my book-length study, *First Comes Love: Finding Your Family in the Church and the Trinity* (New York: Doubleday, 2002).

The Trinity is who God eternally is. It is his personal identity, which does not depend on creation. Other titles—such as Lord, Lawgiver, Creator, Architect, and Physician—are metaphorical terms, describing his relationship to creatures. Only the Trinity—Father, Son, and Holy Spirit—describes God in metaphysical terms.

Yet because the Trinity reveals the deepest mystery of who God is, it also reveals the deepest meaning of what God does. "The mystery of the Most Holy Trinity is the central mystery of Christian faith and life," states the Catechism of the Catholic Church.[5] "It is the mystery of God in himself. It is therefore the source of all the other mysteries of faith, the light that enlightens them." Thus, our understanding of God as family should also profoundly affect our understanding of all his works—of creation, redemption, and sanctification.

In short, in everything that exists, we may discern with the eyes of faith a familial purpose, what Catholic tradition calls "the footprints of the Trinity" (*vestigia Trinitatis*).

Reflection on the mystery of God and the mysteries of creation, then, becomes mutually enhancing. Declares the Catechism, "God's works reveal who he is in himself; the mystery of his inmost being enlightens our understanding of all his works. So it is, analogously, among human persons. A person discloses himself in his actions, and the better we know a person, the better we understand his actions."[6]

And furthermore, "God has left traces of his Trinitarian being in his work of creation and in his revelation throughout the Old Testament."[7] The whole of the Scriptures, in fact, can be viewed as the story of how God repeatedly strove, as Father, to invite people into his household, to keep his family together, and to draw his wayward children home.

God's relationship with Israel was defined by a *covenant*, the ritual, legal means by which ancient peoples created family bonds. God made covenants with Adam, Noah, Abraham, Moses, and David. With each succeeding covenant, God opened membership in his covenant family to ever more people: first to a married couple, then to a household,

---

5. *Catechism of the Catholic Church* (New York: Doubleday, 1995), par. 234, p. 69.

6. Ibid., par. 236, p. 70.

7. Ibid., par. 237, p. 70.

then to a tribe, then to a nation, then to a kingdom—until finally the invitation was made universal with Jesus. Christ's "true family" consists of those who receive new birth as children of God through baptism (John 3:3–8) and who do the will of the Father in heaven (see Matthew 12:49). They become his younger brothers (see Romans 8:14–15, 29).

Baptism and Eucharist are now the means by which men and women are incorporated into God's covenant family. They mark the Christian's covenant oath, common meal, and sacrifice. The word *sacrament* itself witnesses to this truth. *Sacrament* comes from the Latin *sacramentum*, which means "oath," and the word was applied to baptism and the Eucharist from the earliest days of the church. The pagan Roman historian Pliny the Younger recorded that, in his time (the end of the first century), Christians would gather before sunrise to sing hymns to Christ, after which they would "bind themselves by oath."[8] This is the *sacramentum*, the "oath," that seals the covenant: the Holy Eucharist. Jesus himself described his relationship with the church in explicitly covenantal terms. At the Last Supper, he blessed the cup of the "new covenant" in his blood (see Luke 22:20; 1 Corinthians 11:25).

This makes a profound difference in a Christian's life, for now he can call God "*Abba*, Father" (Galatians 4:6). Christians are truly children of God (John 1:12; 1 John 3:1–2), brothers and sisters and mothers of Christ (Mark 3:35), who is the "firstborn among many brothers and sisters" (Romans 8:29). Christians are "members of [God's] household" (Ephesians 2:19), which is the church (1 Timothy 3:15; 1 Peter 4:17).

The book of Revelation (19:9) makes clear that this new covenant is the closest, most ecstatic, and most intimate of family bonds. John's vision concludes with the marriage supper of the Lamb (Jesus) and the Lamb's bride (the church). With this event—which tradition has understood as the Eucharist—Christians seal and renew their family relationship with God. With this sacrament—which is at once an oath, a sacrifice, and a covenant meal—they call God himself their true Brother, Father, and Spouse.

---

8. Pliny the Younger, *Letters* 10.96–97, www.fordham.edu/halsall/source/pliny1.html (accessed July 29, 2011).

Church: Hierarchy and Home

The family theme that dominates Scripture continues through the earliest centuries of the church. St. Polycarp of Smyrna, in the generation immediately after the apostles, wrote, "For if we continue to love one another and to join in praising the Most Holy Trinity—all of us who are sons of God and form one family in Christ—we will be faithful to the deepest vocation of the Church."[9]

Even before St. Polycarp, St. Ignatius of Antioch had set forth the divine family, the Trinity, as the model of concord in the church: "Be obedient to your bishop and to one another, as Jesus Christ in his human nature was subject to the Father and as the apostles were to Christ and the Father. In this way there will be union of body and spirit."[10] And again, "As the Lord was united to the Father and did nothing without him ... so neither should you do anything without the bishop and priests."[11]

St. Irenaeus emphasized the fatherly role of the hierarchy and of teachers. Tertullian developed the notion of ecclesial motherhood, calling the church "Lady Mother Church."[12] For Tertullian, the church on earth reflects the family model that is implicit in the Trinity: "Not even the mother, the Church, is passed by—that is, if in the Son and Father is recognized the mother, by whom the names of both father and son exist."[13] Elsewhere he exhorted candidates for baptism to pray to the Father "in the house of your Mother ... with your brethren." St. Cyprian of Carthage summarized this line of thinking with his famous aphorism: "He can no longer have God for his Father, who has not the Church for his mother."[14]

Thus the teaching continues throughout the patristic era. It is no exaggeration to say that family imagery saturates the teachings of the fathers of the church. Indeed, the very title "fathers" flows from a

---

9. *Catechism*, par. 959, p. 272.

10. Ignatius of Antioch, *Letter to the Magnesians*, 13.2.

11. Ibid. 7.

12. Tertullian, *Ad Martyras*, 1. See J. C. Plumpe, *Mater Ecclesia: An Inquiry into the Concept of the Church as Mother in Early Christianity* (Washington, D.C.: Catholic University of America Press, 1943).

13. Tertullian, *On Prayer*, 2.

14. Cyprian of Carthage, *On the Unity of the Church*, 5.

familial understanding of the church! In the fifth century, St. Augustine wrote, "The apostles were sent as fathers [see 1 Corinthians 4:15]; to replace those apostles, sons were born to you who were constituted bishops ... The Church calls them Fathers, she who gave birth to them, who placed them in the sees of their Fathers ... Such is the Catholic Church. She has given birth to sons who, through all the earth, continue the work of her first Fathers."[15]

God is a family, and Christians are his. By establishing the new covenant, Christ founded one church — his body — as an extension of his incarnation. By taking on flesh, Christ divinized flesh, and he extended the Trinity's life to all humanity through the church, his body (1 Corinthians 12:27; Ephesians 4:12). Incorporated into the body of Christ, Christians become "sons in the Son." They become children in the eternal household of God. They share in the very life of the Trinity.

The earthly household of the Trinity is the church. This is a dominant motif in recent documents of the Catholic Church, especially the Catechism of the Catholic Church, whose opening paragraph states that God "calls together all men, scattered and divided by sin, into the unity of his family, the Church." Elsewhere, the Catechism states, "The Church is nothing other than 'the family of God.'"[16]

The Catholic Church is the universal family of God. Non-Catholic Christians are, however, considered "separated brethren," united to the family by the sacrament of baptism. The Catechism declares this truth in moving terms: "All who have been justified by faith in baptism ... are accepted as brothers in the Lord by the children of the Catholic Church."[17]

Within the church, as within the family, there are clearly defined roles. From the time of the apostles, the Christian faithful have viewed the clergy as spiritual fathers. Indeed, even in the Old Testament, priests were identified this way. In the book of Judges, when the Levite appears at Micah's door, Micah pleads, "Live with me and be my father

---

15. Quoted in Henri Cardinal de Lubac, S.J., *The Motherhood of the Church* (San Francisco: Ignatius, 1982), 90. De Lubac (ibid., 105) also shows how, in the early church fathers, "the authority of the bishop has an essentially paternal character. If he is the head, it is because he is father."

16. *Catechism*, par. 1655, p. 461.

17. Ibid., par. 818, p. 235.

and priest" (Judges 17:10). In the New Testament, St. Paul clearly sees his role as paternal: "For in Christ Jesus I became your father through the gospel" (1 Corinthians 4:15). And this attitude would continue in the early church. St. Jerome wrote: "Be obedient to your bishop and welcome him as the father of your soul." The great earthly father of the church is, of course, the "Holy Father," the Pope.

Yet the family is not only global. It is also supremely local. Pope John Paul II wrote, "The great family which is the Church ... finds concrete expression in the diocesan and the parish family ... No one is without a family in this world: the Church is a home and family for everyone."[18]

From Heaven to Hearth

The "family of God" model offers a more intimate experience of the communion of saints—as the church's covenant family extends through time as well as space. "Becoming a disciple of Jesus means accepting the invitation to belong to *God's family*."[19] In this context we can understand the solicitude of the saints in heaven for the church on earth, and we can understand the care of the church on earth for the souls in purgatory. For the members of the church—militant, triumphant, and suffering—are siblings in a close-knit family. Even in Christianity's first generation, St. Paul expressed his kinship with the saints on earth—for example, in the church at Colossae (Colossians 1:2, 4)—as well as with the saints in heaven, "in the kingdom of light," as he put it in the same chapter (Colossians 1:12).

In the supernatural family of the saints, Mary, the Mother of God, holds an eminent place. Of all creatures, Mary is directly related to God by a natural bond of covenant kinship. She is the mother of Jesus, to whom she gave her own flesh and blood. This bond enabled mankind to share in the grace of Christ by adoption. Thus, as brothers and sisters of Christ, Christians are also children of Mary, and so are bound to honor her as their mother. Indeed, Jesus himself is legally bound by his Father's law ("Honor your father and mother") to share his honor with

---

18. Pope John Paul II, Apostolic Exhortation *"Familiaris Consortio:* On the Role of the Christian Family in the Modern World," November 22, 1981, n. 85.

19. *Catechism*, par. 2233, p. 597 (original emphasis).

Mary. And he fulfilled this law more perfectly than any son has ever done, by bestowing the gift of his glory on Mary. Christians, then, are called to imitate him in this way, as in all other ways.

The church and the family are more than "communities"; each is, like the Trinity, a *communion* of persons. And so they also bear a family resemblance to one another. As the church is a universal family, the family constitutes an *"ecclesia domestica"* (domestic church).[20]

Through marriage, which is a sacrament of the new covenant, a household receives a new family resemblance to God. St. Paul wrote, "For this reason I kneel before the Father, from whom every family in heaven and on earth derives its name" (Ephesians 3:14–15). Earthly families, then, receive their "name," their identity, from God himself.

In his "Letter to Families," Pope John Paul II wrote, "The primordial model of the family is to be sought in God himself, in the Trinitarian mystery of his life. The divine 'We' is the eternal pattern of the human 'we,' especially of that 'we' formed by the man and the woman created in the divine image and likeness."[21]

The Catechism further reflects this understanding: "The Christian family is a communion of persons, a sign and image of the communion of the Father and the Son in the Holy Spirit. In the procreation and education of children it reflects the Father's work of creation. It is called to partake of the prayer and sacrifice of Christ."[22]

Thus, as an image of God who is faithful and who is One, the family bond between husband and wife must be permanent and indissoluble. Thus, too, as God is fecund and generous, a married couple must be open to life, willing to cooperate with the Father in the conception of children. In this context, it should be clear why the Catholic Church forbids acts of contraception, abortion, homosexuality, and adultery—all acts that distort the sanctity of marriage and the divine image in the family.

Within the domestic church, all members, but especially fathers, exercise the "priesthood of the baptized" and evangelize "by word and example."[23] Further, the family is holy because Christ himself lived in a

---

20. *Catechism*, par. 1656, p. 461.
21. Pope John Paul II, "Letter to Families," February 2, 1994, n. 6.
22. *Catechism*, par. 2205, p. 589.
23. Ibid., pars. 1656–57, p. 461–62.

family. The Catechism teaches that "Christ chose to be born and grow up in the bosom of the holy family of Joseph and Mary. *The Church is nothing other than 'the family of God.'* From the beginning, the core of the Church was often constituted by those who had become believers 'together with all [their] household' ... These families who became believers were islands of Christian life in an unbelieving world."[24]

This understanding of God, church, and family has profound implications for the inner life of the Christian. Grace, which by definition is "a *participation in the life of God*," is suddenly revealed as family life because grace "introduces us into the intimacy of Trinitarian life: by baptism the Christian participates in the grace of Christ ... As an 'adopted son' he can henceforth call God 'Father,' in union with the only Son. He receives the life of the Spirit who breathes charity into him and who forms the Church."[25]

By baptism, we are "co-heirs" with Christ and so, in the words of St. Augustine, "Grace has gone before us; now we are given what is due ... Our merits are God's gifts."[26]

Among these gifts of grace is prayer, and this, too — with all its varieties, methods, and phenomena — we may understand in a familial way. No less an authority than the Catechism presents prayer in the context of covenant, communion, and family resemblance: "Christian prayer is a covenant relationship between God and man in Christ ... In the New Covenant, prayer is the living relationship of the children of God with their Father who is good beyond measure, with his Son Jesus Christ and with the Holy Spirit. The grace of the kingdom is 'the union of the entire holy and royal Trinity ... with the whole human spirit.' Thus, the life of prayer is the habit of being in the presence of the thrice-holy God and in communion with him."[27]

Even in its highest expressions, prayer remains, essentially, a family matter: "Contemplative prayer is the simplest expression of the mystery of prayer. It is a gift, a grace; it can be accepted only in humility and poverty. Contemplative prayer is a covenant relationship established by

---

24. Ibid., par. 1655, p. 461, emphasis added.
25. Ibid., par. 1997, p. 538.
26. Ibid., par. 2009, p. 541.
27. Ibid., par. 2565, p. 675.

God within our hearts. Contemplative prayer is a communion in which the Holy Trinity conforms man, the image of God, 'to His likeness.'"[28]

Doctrinal Applications

The notion of the family of God can be applied to doctrine as well. Consider three very broad categories.

Creator and Creation

"Then God said, 'Let us make mankind in our image, in our likeness'" (Genesis 1:26). Christian commentators have always drawn out the Trinitarian implications of the divine "us" in the book of Genesis. Seeing creation as the work of the Trinity enables us to see the world differently. God is more than our Creator; he is our Father by grace. We are more than mere creatures; we have a "family resemblance." We are made in his image and likeness to live as his sons and daughters. Instead of inhabiting a vast impersonal cosmos, we live in a world that the Father has fashioned to be our inheritance—a royal palace and a holy temple.

The church does not despise the world. In fact, traditional Catholic blessings and prayers often end, in Latin, with the phrase *per omnia saecula saeculorum*, meaning simultaneously "throughout the entire world" and "through all the ages of ages." Thus, an ordinary blessing consecrates the world and all that is in it. This is the extension in history of that most famous of gospel passages: "God so loved the world … For God did not send his Son into the world to condemn the world, but to save the world through him" (John 3:16–17).

Lay Catholics are called to sanctify the world from within. They need not leave the things of time in order to find the things of eternity. The temporal order is God's domain, and so it is the domain of his children as well. The Catechism cites the Second Vatican Council in this regard: "By reason of their special vocation it belongs to the laity to seek the kingdom of God by engaging in temporal affairs and directing them according to God's will."[29] The church's Code of Canon Law lays

---

28. Ibid., par. 2713, p. 715.
29. Ibid., par. 898, p. 258.

down that the laity's mission is "to permeate and perfect the temporal order of things with the spirit of the Gospel" (canon 225).

Monks and nuns, for their part, are called to renounce the world, but they do so precisely because the world is so good! They prefer God the giver to the exclusion of all his gifts—even the greatest, such as marriage and family. Their sacrifice makes no sense if they are offering up something valueless or evil.

Law and Morals

More than a legal contract, a covenant is a sacred family bond. So God's covenants in salvation history (with Adam, Noah, Abraham, Moses, David, and Jesus) reveal how he fathers his ever-expanding family and maintains its unity and solidarity.[30] Accordingly, the laws of the covenant are not arbitrary stipulations forcefully imposed by a superior power, but rather expressions of God's fatherly wisdom, goodness, and love. We obey them in order to mature, so that we can love as God loves. When God makes and keeps covenants with his people, he is just being true to himself, for the Trinity is a covenantal being—three persons living in eternal communion. Covenant is what God does because covenant is who God is.

Sin and Judgment

More than broken laws, sin means broken lives and broken homes. At root, sin comes from our refusal to keep to the covenant that binds our family. Thus, through sin we lose the grace of divine sonship. We sin because we do not want to love as much as God loves us. Yet sin is absurd and deadly, for in sinning, we stupidly prefer something other than the life and love to which our Father calls us. God punishes sin with death because sin is what kills his life in us. Judgment is not an impersonal legal process; nor are the covenant curses enactments of God's vindictive wrath. Like God's covenant law, the curses are expressions not of hatred but of fatherly love and discipline. They impose suffering that is intended to be remedial, restorative, and redemptive. God's wrath is not opposed to his love; it is an expression of his love. God is love (1 John

---

30. See *Catechism*, par. 759, p. 217.

4:8), but his love is a consuming fire (Hebrews 12:29). This fiery love reflects the inner life of the Trinity. Sinners do not escape God's love; they get burned by it, unless and until they reopen themselves to it. This is what repentance achieves, and this is what God's wrath is for. Seeing God as Father does not lessen the severity of his wrath, nor is a lower standard of justice implied. On the contrary, a good father requires more from his sons and daughters than judges require from defendants. And a good father also shows greater mercy.

Suffering and Death

These are particularly challenging and profound mysteries. We know they entered the world because of sin (Romans 5:12). We also believe that Christ has set us free from the power of sin and death (Romans 8:2). Yet if this is so, why must we still suffer and die? Catholics believe that Jesus Christ suffered, not merely as a substitute for sinful humanity, but as our representative. Thus, Christ's saving passion did not exempt us from suffering, but rather endowed our suffering with divine power and redemptive value.

St. Paul could even "rejoice" in his troubles, "knowing that suffering produces perseverance; perseverance, character, and character, hope. And hope does not put us to shame, because God's love has been poured out into our hearts through the Holy Spirit" (Romans 5:3–5). He concluded, "I consider that our present sufferings are not worth comparing with the glory that will be revealed in us" (Roman 8:18).

God gives his children everything he has, sharing even his divine nature. Nevertheless, he did not spare his eternal Son from suffering. Suffering was central to Jesus' mission as redeemer. And so it is part of our share in his life and mission. Thus, suffering is not an optional component of Christian life. St. Paul tells us, "We are God's children ... co-heirs with Christ, *if indeed we share in his sufferings* in order that we may also share in his glory" (Romans 8:16–17, emphasis added). So — no suffering, no glory.

Catholics, moreover, do not merely endure suffering; they "offer it up." For Christlike suffering has redemptive power. Christ offered his sufferings as a priestly sacrifice for the sake of others, and so should Christians. That is true love. Here is Paul again: "Now I rejoice in what I am suffering *for you*, and I fill up in my flesh what is still lacking in regard to Christ's afflictions for the sake of his body, which is the church" (Colossians 1:24, emphasis added).

A Sacramental Worldview

Sacramentality and sacraments are such important aspects of Catholic life that we should spend a moment examining them more closely. Sacraments are outward signs instituted by Christ and entrusted to the church. The church observes seven of them: baptism, Eucharist, confirmation, penance, anointing of the sick, matrimony, and holy orders (the ordination of deacons, priests, and bishops).

Apart from sacraments, church custom has hallowed many *sacramentals*: the wearing of devotional medals and scapulars, the use of holy water, the veneration of sacred images and books, and so on. Sacramentals dispose believers to receive grace from God and provide an occasion for such graces.

But the sacramental principle really applies to all of creation. It is evident from the biblical testimony that God's way of dealing with his people is profoundly sacramental. Even in the Old Testament, the chosen people spoke of creation in sacramental terms:

> The heavens declare the glory of God;
>> the skies proclaim the work of his hands ...
> They have no speech, they use no words;
>> no sound is heard from them.
> Yet their voice goes out into all the earth,
>> their words to the end of the world.
>
> Psalm 19:1, 3–4

God tends not to work in abstractions. His Word is not mere words; it is creative, living, and active. The Catechism of the Catholic Church puts it well: "God speaks to man through the visible creation. The material cosmos is so presented to man's intelligence that he can read there traces of its Creator. Light and darkness, wind and fire, water and earth, the tree and its fruit speak of God and symbolize both his greatness and his nearness."[31]

---

31. *Catechism*, par. 1147, p. 324.

God created the physical universe. He made it good, and he did not hesitate to use its most commonplace items to manifest his glory. Sometimes, too, he would even elevate those commonplace items for uncommon purposes, as channels of divine power.

The early Christians saw this clearly. In AD 383, St. Gregory of Nyssa preached a sermon in which he cited many sacramental uses of nature in the Old Testament:

> Moses' rod was a hazel switch — common wood that any hands might cut and carry and use as they please before tossing it into the fire. But God purposed to work miracles through that rod — great miracles beyond the power of words to express [see Exodus 4–14] ... Likewise, the mantle of one of the prophets, a simple goatskin, made Elisha famous throughout the whole world [see 2 Kings 2:8] ... A bramble bush showed the presence of God to Moses [see Exodus 3:2]. The remains of Elisha raised a dead man to life [see 2 Kings 13:21].[32]

St. John of Damascus added, "I do not worship matter; I worship the creator of matter who became matter for my sake, who willed to take his abode in matter; who worked out my salvation through matter. Never will I cease honoring the matter which wrought my salvation! ... God has filled it with his grace and power. Through it my salvation has come to me."[33]

Creation, then — even in the old covenant — could serve as a natural sacrament. Nature itself was a sign, but God showed it capable of conveying supernatural power as well. It was not in nature, however, that St. Paul found the preeminent sacraments of the Old Testament. He looked instead to the ritual worship of ancient Israel. Abraham and all of his male descendants had "cut" their covenant with God by the rite of circumcision. The New Testament even identifies the old covenant with its sacramental sign when Stephen refers to "the covenant of circumcision" (Acts 7:8).

We learn from St. Paul that the old covenant and the old sacrament — great as they were — foreshadowed something still greater:

---

32. Gregory of Nyssa, *On the Baptism of Christ.*
33. John of Damascus, *On Holy Images*, 1.16.

"You were also circumcised with a circumcision not performed by human hands. Your whole self ruled by the flesh was put off when you were circumcised by Christ, having been buried with him in baptism" (Colossians 2:11 – 12). The circumcision of infants prefigured the baptism of those who would be "newborn" in Christ. The old rite marked a child's "birth" as a son of Abraham; the new rite marks the still greater birth of a child of God.

We saw, with St. Paul, that the ancient Passover meal served as the renewal of the old covenant. Israelites sacrificed the Paschal lamb so that their firstborn children would be spared the plague of death. In the New Testament, it was at a Passover meal that Jesus established the new covenant in his blood (1 Corinthians 11:25). With the traditional unleavened bread and cups of wine, Jesus offered the first Mass at the Passover Seder on the night he was betrayed.[34]

In baptism and Eucharist, Christ's action was "new" in the sense of a renewal, but it was not a novelty. It did not abolish the Old Testament but fulfilled it and renewed it in a transformative way. The same could be said of all the sacraments.[35] They had been implicit in all God's dealings with his beloved Israel and with all of mankind. They would be explicit with the revelation of the church.

In the old covenant (as St. Augustine explained), the sacraments — the rituals of the law of Moses — had been many, weak, and difficult. In the new covenant, they are few, powerful, and simple. In the pages of the New Testament, we see the apostles practicing these rites frequently — baptizing, forgiving sins, breaking the bread, laying on hands to ordain the clergy, and anointing the sick.

Thus, the sacraments do not somehow demote the New Testament but rather bring it into sharper focus. Indeed, the New Testament was, in the generation of the apostles, not a book but a rite. It was the Eucharist, which Jesus himself had called the "new testament" (or "new covenant") in his blood (see Luke 22:20). He established the New Testament when he instituted the Eucharist and said, "Do this in remembrance of me" — not "read this" or "write this," but "*do this*." And the apostles went forth and celebrated the New Testament everywhere

---

34. See Luke 22:15; *Catechism*, par. 1340, p. 373.
35. See *Catechism*, par. 1150, p. 325.

they went. Very few of them wrote books; but all of them went forth and celebrated the Eucharist.

The Eucharist was the defining action of the primitive church: "They devoted themselves to the apostles' teaching and to fellowship [Greek, *koinonia*], to the breaking of bread and to prayer" (Acts 2:42). It is in the Mass that those actions come together, as they did in the generation before the New Testament documents were complete and the centuries before they were definitively compiled.

The documents weren't complete until the end of the first century, and even then they were not called the "New Testament" until the end of the second century. The documents only gradually took that name, again because of their liturgical proximity to the Eucharist, the original "New Testament" in Christ's blood. They were the *only* books approved for proclamation in the Mass, and they were "canonized" for that very reason. The New Testament was a sacrament at least a generation before it was a document.

The Bible as the Measure

One of the great modern scholars of Catholic spirituality was Father Jordan Aumann, O.P. In one of his greatest works, he wrote, "If Christian spirituality signifies a participation in the mystery of Christ, our first task is to contemplate that mystery with the help of the New Testament and then to discover how we share in it."[36]

The Bible does not stand apart from the church's life, but at the heart of it. Scripture is the content and the context of all the church's ritual and devotion. At every Mass, at least three extensive readings are proclaimed and preached on, drawn from the Old and New Testaments. The readings change every day, so that over the course of the three-year cycle worshipers will hear most of the Bible.

This is the way most Christians have received God's word throughout most of history, from the days before there was a canon of Scripture and the days before the printing press and widespread distribution of books and the days before literacy was widespread. It is the way we see congregations receiving the word in the Bible's own narratives—in the assembly gathered

---

36. Jordan Aumann, O.P., *Christian Spirituality in the Catholic Tradition* (San Francisco: Ignatius, 1985), 10.

for ritual public worship. Worship is the natural and supernatural habitat of Scripture. Liturgy is both the content and the proper context of Scripture.

Catholic life and practice are steeped in Scripture and answerable to it. Father Aumann writes the following:

> Everything must be understood and evaluated in the light of Scripture, and the closer any spirituality is to the Bible, the more authentic it is. This does not mean that the application of biblical teaching to the spiritual life does not admit of any variety whatever, but it does mean that Sacred Scripture ever remains the unifying factor and the ultimate standard. It transcends all diversity ...
>
> What we should seek in the New Testament is a spirituality that is valid for all persons everywhere and in every age, whether it be the twentieth century, the Middle Ages or the primitive church. But Christ lived within a particular historical context; the New Testament represents a variety of viewpoints, such as that of St. Matthew or St. Luke as compared with that of St. John or St. Paul; in primitive Christianity there was a Jewish-Palestinian and a Jewish-Hellenistic trend. Consequently, it is not always easy to abstract the essential and perennial elements of gospel spirituality from the New Testament writings or from the life of Christians in apostolic times. Further, gospel spirituality must be lived by particular persons at a particular time and in a particular place. In other words, the gospel must be constantly inserted into the historical situation; that is why there is a history of spirituality and schools of spirituality.[37]

Within Catholicism, then, there are schools of spirituality that are all imbued with a Catholic spirit, which is the spirit of adoption — which is the Spirit crying out, *Abba*, Father!

Home to the Father

So we return to Ignatius of Antioch and the summons he heard from the echoes of his baptismal waters: *Come to the Father*. So much about who we are as Catholics is packed into those words. Not just, "Come to God," but "Come to the Father." We're more than God's creatures; we're God's children.

---

37. Ibid., 3, 10.

It is Ignatius, too, who provides us the earliest surviving reference to the "catholic church," though he treats the phrase as an already established term: "Wherever the bishop appears, there let the people be; as wherever Jesus Christ is, there is the Catholic Church. It is not lawful to baptize or give communion without the consent of the bishop. On the other hand, whatever has his approval is pleasing to God. Thus, whatever is done will be safe and valid."[38]

Ignatius wrote in AD 107. He resounded with a voice that is the first echo of the apostles. Yet he described a catholic church recognizable to any Catholic in the twenty-first century—whether Byzantine, Chaldean, or Coptic; monastic or charismatic; Thomist, Scotist, or personalist; Carmelite, Carthusian, or Augustinian.

Ignatius proclaimed a church reborn through baptism and a church that feeds on the Eucharist, which he calls "the sacrifice" of "the blood of God" and "the flesh of Christ." He proclaims a church that is hierarchical, a church that shuns doctrinal aberration, a church that finds its earthly center of gravity in Rome.

In that Catholic Church, Christians still hear the call that welled up within Ignatius, and they answer. That is Catholic spirituality.

---

38. Ignatius of Antioch, *Letter to the Smyrnaeans*, 8.

RESPONSE TO SCOTT HAHN

BRADLEY NASSIF

It was enriching to read Scott Hahn's essay. It reflects integrity to the Church of Rome and an ecumenical openness that extends the spirit of Vatican II. In his section titled "Church: Hierarchy and Home," he roots Catholic spirituality in patristic ecclesiology and affirms that "the great earthly father of the church is, of course, the 'Holy Father,' the Pope." Since Vatican II, there has been a series of important Catholic encounters with Orthodoxy that shape Orthodox perspectives. For example, in 1964, the churches of Rome and Constantinople officially lifted the "anathemas of 1054" (the date of the "Great Schism" between Orthodoxy and Rome). This act did not put an end to the schism because the mutual excommunications of 1054 were canonically doubtful and were followed by many other excommunications that were never "lifted." Nevertheless, it was symbolically significant and followed by many meetings between representatives of Rome and Constantinople, as well as among other Orthodox leaders, including the patriarchates of Moscow and Antioch. In more recent times, the Orthodox and Roman Catholic churches have formed official theological dialogues at both the national and international levels, culminating in position papers and consensus documents.

Both sides recognize that Orthodoxy and Rome are the two major branches of historic Christianity and, in that sense, can be seen as "sister churches."[39] However, theological differences still separate us. Our known and continuing differences center on the particular issues of papal infallibility, universal jurisdiction, and the use of the *filioque* clause in the Nicene Creed, to which other Orthodox would add purgatory and the immaculate conception of Mary. Because our subject is

---

39. See Avery Dulles, S.J., "The Church as Communion," in *New Perspectives on Historical Theology: Essays in Memory of John Meyendorff*, ed. Bradley Nassif (Grand Rapids: Eerdmans, 1996), 125–39.

Christian spirituality, I cannot expound on these complex issues here but instead will focus on the overarching vision of Catholic spirituality as Hahn has presented it: the centrality of Trinitarian theology, sacramental theology, Marian piety, and the role of Scripture.

Key Emphases and Goals of Catholic Spirituality

Regarding the role of the Trinity in Christian spirituality, Hahn quotes the Catechism of the Catholic Church, which states, "The mystery of the Most Holy Trinity is the central mystery of Christian faith and life. It is the mystery of God in himself. It is therefore the source of all the other mysteries of faith, the light that enlightens them."[40] His exposition of this central mystery for Christian spirituality is masterful. It illustrates just how united Orthodox and Catholic theology are in this central dogma of the Christian faith (the *filioque* notwithstanding). We fully agree on the dogmas of the Trinity and Christology as expounded by the ecumenical councils of Nicea (325), Constantinople (381), Ephesus (431), and Chalcedon (451). As I explained in my essay, these councils bear witness to the ontological foundations for what the Greek Fathers called "deification" (*theosis*). Hahn concurs: "This 'divine filiation' [in the Trinity] is the foundation of Catholic spirituality. In the Western church it is often called the *life of grace*. In the East it is called *deification, divinization*, or *theosis*."

How, then, does the process of Catholic spiritual growth occur within this Trinitarian framework? Hahn answers:

> Come to the Father! At the heart of the gospel is the revelation of God's fatherhood ...
>
> The shocking truth is that Jesus wants human beings to share God's life: "he has given us his very great and precious promises, so that through them you may participate in the divine nature, having escaped the corruption in the world caused by evil desires" (2 Peter 1:4). Jesus empowers us to *escape corruption* so that we may *participate in the divine nature*. As we noted earlier, salvation is not merely *from* sin, but *for* sonship — for the sake of divine adoption.
>
> All Catholic spirituality proceeds from this fact.

---

40. *Catechism of the Catholic Church* (New York: Doubleday, 1995), par. 234, p. 69.

We agree, once again. This comports well with the teaching of Orthodox spirituality as expressed by St. Athanasius: "God became humanized so that humans might become divinized." Orthodox and Catholic teaching concurs that by virtue of the incarnation and "communication of idioms" (*communicatio idiomatum*) between Christ's divine and human natures, believers may participate in the deified humanity of Christ. We are called not merely to imitate Jesus' moral example, but to partake of Christ himself through the sacramental life of the church.

Disciplines for Implementing Spirituality

This leads to Hahn's following comments about Catholic sacramental theology:

> Baptism and Eucharist are now the means by which men and women are incorporated into God's covenant family ... The word *sacrament* itself witnesses to this truth. Sacrament comes from the Latin *sacramentum*, which means "oath," and the word was applied to baptism and the Eucharist from the earliest days of the church ... This is the *sacramentum*, the "oath," that seals the covenant: the Holy Eucharist.

We, of course, want to avoid magnifying minor disagreements. But it is worth observing that there is a different spiritual "ethos" that pervades the liturgical atmosphere in our two traditions. Catholic liturgical life describes the sacraments mainly in terms of Latin legal categories, such as "oaths," compared with the Greek Fathers, who viewed the sacraments as "mysteries." The numbering of "seven sacraments" in Catholicism also reflects a difference in theological methodology and mind-set that seems to rely more heavily on scholastic reasoning. Without wishing to overstate the case, in Orthodoxy the sacraments are seen more as relational gifts than rational realities. As the late Orthodox liturgical scholar Fr. Alexander Schmemann observed, Eastern Christians used the terminology of "mystery" because it communicates the *gospel story* of Jesus. Hahn recognizes these problems (numbering and scholasticizing the sacraments) by adding, "But the sacramental principle really applies to all of creation."

Yet there remains a certain rigidity in Catholic ecclesiology that seems to carry over to Catholic spirituality. This rigidity seems endemic not only to the vocabulary and structure of the "seven" sacraments, but also to the church's posture toward the papacy and hierarchical orders (matters beyond the scope of this response). Church order and sacramental life give the impression that the church has been overly defined and military-like in the way its life is lived out. It has become an institution with sacraments. But again, as Schmemann once said, the church is a sacrament with institutions, not an institution with sacraments. At one time, I believed this perspective to be a false characterization of Catholicism. But that viewpoint was actually reinforced recently when I heard a prominent Catholic bishop tell the story of how he was once asked by an evangelical Christian if was "saved." He replied, "Yes, but only within a sacramental *system* (his emphasis)." As an Orthodox, I can't help but quietly wonder if the "relational" life of the Father, Son, and Holy Spirit still needs to be more fully integrated into the Catholic sacramental vision. Surely the sacraments are understood better as "healing mysteries of the gospel" than they are as "systems" or "institutions" of salvation. God's Trinitarian love is more relational than legal. Herein lies an experiential difference between Catholic and Orthodox sacramental theology.

A similar sort of "agreement but with different emphases" arises over Catholic devotion to the Virgin Mary. Hahn asserts that Jesus "shared his honor with Mary." The Orthodox would largely agree with this, but only with extensive Christological qualifications. It is certainly true that the Orthodox and Catholic traditions share a common devotion to Mary as the God-bearer or Mother of God (*theotokos*), as she is called. The ecumenical councils of Ephesus (431) and Chalcedon (451) recognize Mary as the *theotokos* and solemnly declare the title to be a church dogma. But Marian devotion is noticeably different in Orthodox and Catholic piety. On the devotional level, there seems in Catholicism to be an excessive and sentimental veneration of Mary in and of herself, which causes an observer to think of Mary apart from her Son (contrary to official Catholic dogma). This de facto elevation of Mary apart from Christ is no doubt partly due to the legacy of geographical location, in which the theological teachings about the *theotokos* were originally hammered out in the eastern part of the Roman Empire, where the Greek Orthodox Churches flourished, rather than in the Christian West. It was among the Greek-speaking churches of the East where the Christological debates in the fourth and fifth centuries formed the context for understanding Mary's relation to Christ in the incarnation. The Latin West took part in these debates, but not to the same extent as the Eastern churches.[41] The tendency to honor Mary apart from Christ may also be a consequence of the Catholic emphasis on the "immaculate conception," promulgated by Pope Pius IX in 1854, according to which Mary, from the moment she was conceived by her mother, was delivered from all the stain of original sin—a dogma not shared by the Orthodox.

Regarding our approach to the role of Scripture, Hahn expresses a similarity in the Orthodox and Catholic traditions: "Liturgy is both the content and proper context of Scripture. Catholic [and Orthodox, I might add] life and practice are steeped in Scripture and answerable to it." Our common convictions confess that the church is answerable to Scripture, yet the Bible is still a liturgical book. The Word of God and the people of God are inseparably united.

But what have we to say about average laypeople in our parishes? Can we honestly say they know the Bible well? Or even as proficiently as evangelical Protestants do today? I don't think so. Fortunately, this is beginning to change. Orthodox Christians in America probably know the Bible better than their counterparts outside the continent due to the positive influence of evangelicalism on Orthodox parishioners. Likewise, Catholic laypeople in North America probably know the Bible better than their counterparts outside America for the same reason. The growth of Catholic biblical scholarship over the past thirty years has provided Catholic Christians with more books on the Bible than at any other time in history. We must admit that Catholic scholarship has directly impacted Catholic spirituality in a way that Orthodox biblical scholarship has yet to do.

In closing, I congratulate Scott Hahn for writing this beautiful and winsome essay on Catholic spirituality. I hope this brief analysis above will serve to further our dialogue and engender greater appreciation

---

41. See Jaroslav Pelikan, *Mary Through the Centuries* (New Haven, Conn.: Yale University Press, 1996).

for each other's tradition. Of all the essays in this volume, Hahn's is the closest to the Orthodox because it is the most "catholic" (small *c*, meaning "full, complete"). Metropolitan Kallistos Ware summarizes it best: "Among Western Christians, it is the Anglicans with whom Orthodoxy has enjoyed the most cordial relationship during the last hundred years, *but it is the Roman Catholics with whom we have by far the more in common.*"[42]

---

42. Timothy (Kallistos) Ware, *The Orthodox Church* (New York: Penguin, 1993), 314, emphasis mine.

JOSEPH DRISKILL

Scott Hahn has provided a description of Roman Catholic spirituality that sets out clearly the theological consistency of its doctrines of the Trinity, Christ, God, and the church, as well as the theological foundation for its stance on such issues as contraception, abortion, and gay marriage. By using the Catechism as the touchstone for that which shapes the "lived experience of faith" for Roman Catholics, Hahn focuses on key elements of Roman Catholic spirituality and demonstrates the way in which the church nurtures this spirituality.

The Role of Christ and the Holy Spirit

Hahn notes that "divine filiation," the sonship of Jesus Christ, is the foundation of Roman Catholic spirituality, and he establishes the metaphor of the family as the lens through which the many and diverse expressions of Catholic spirituality find their unity. The language of "sonship" in the Trinity makes Jesus "equal" with God in something of the way an earthly child shares a common human nature with his or her earthly father. Hahn notes, however, that the relationships within the Trinity are metaphysical and theological realities rather than biological or metaphorical realities. God is not like a family; God is a family— Father, Son, and Holy Spirit. Christ has given his Father to be our Father. Thus, with Christ as our brother, we become adopted sons of God. Through baptism we are united with the family. Mary becomes our mother; nuns are sisters; priests are fathers; the church is the household of God; the Eucharist is the holy meal through which commitment to Christ is affirmed. God's covenant is a family bond.

We see here that as with Orthodox spirituality, Roman Catholic spirituality posits a worldview in which a supernatural realm claims a metaphysical reality reserved for Father, Son, and Holy Spirit that is qualitatively different from earthly realities. Hahn points out that metaphorical terms that describe God's relationship with creatures—for example, Creator and Architect—do not have the status of the metaphysical terms of the Trinity. As a Protestant, I sense that this reliance on the theological notion of the Trinity to ground so much of one's spirituality is misplaced. Protestants have often been quick to point out that the word *Trinity* does not appear in the Bible. And while much is said about God, Jesus Christ, and the Holy Spirit, the early church's faith emerged without an articulated, consistent understanding of the internal relations of the Trinity. Therefore, to use patristic understandings of the internal relations of Trinity as the foundation for pastoral offices, such as marriage, which were deeply influenced by the cultural customs of their respective social locations, strikes mainline Protestants as anomalous.

The Function of the Institutional Church

Participation in the Christian family through baptism and membership in the church requires viewing earthly institutions as models of the divine relations. Marriage between a man and a woman is patterned on the marriage between Christ and his church. Thus, earthly marriage is perforce indissoluble. The purpose of marriage includes the act of procreating, mirroring the creative actions of God. Thus, contraception and abortion are wrong because they thwart the creative process. From my vantage point as a mainline Protestant, I find it difficult to accept what seems to be an idealized sense of the human condition. For example, the notion that the marriage vow between a man and a woman cannot be broken because it mirrors the internal relations of the Trinity seems implausible in the contemporary world. Marriage tribunals that decide if a "true marriage" ever existed when legal marriages blessed in the church break down after a number of years of shared companionship and the birth of children seems especially problematic. I understand that if one believes that the marriage covenant is not dissoluble, then a humane way to negotiate the brokenness of the human condition may be to determine that a true marriage never existed. Alternatively, the reality of the human finitude and humane requirements of the pastoral situation could result in other just and compassionate theological solutions. Both mainline and more theologically conservative Protestant churches have found more compassionate and humane theological ways to understand human brokenness. To use patristic understandings of these internal relations, whether they are Eastern or Western, as a justification for a belief that marriages cannot be dissolved is problematic for many mainline Protestants.

The church is understood as the household of God. God not only invites people into the church but through the discipline of the church brings the "wayward" home. Hahn's discussion of the role of sin and judgment in Roman Catholic spirituality also draws on the metaphor of the family. Here God's wrath is seen as not opposed to God's love, but as an expression of it. Hebrews 12:29 speaks of a fiery love that Hahn notes not only reflects the inner life of the Trinity but also burns those who sin. Thus, fatherly love and discipline impose a suffering that is "remedial, restorative, and redemptive." From this theological departure, God's wrath is understood as bringing about repentance in the life of the sinner. This focus on the judgment and wrath of God stands in contrast to the emphasis on God's love common in mainline Protestant traditions. Those who do pastoral or family counseling are well aware of the frequency with which child abuse is justified by the offending parent on religious grounds. Many mainline congregations have become havens for or gained members from those who have been judged and condemned by their religious community. Focusing on personal sins is not the agenda of mainline Protestant faith communities in which the emphasis is on the power of God's transforming love.

Some years ago, I attended an ecumenical gathering in which the panel included a Roman Catholic bishop. The bishop was speaking about the nature of judgment and mercy as applied in pastoral situations. In the course of the discussion, he noted that a priest who was his personal friend believed that God's mercy always exceeds or extends beyond his judgment. The bishop, a deeply caring and compassionate person, took exception to this and said that while it might be true of God, the church at times had to exercise judgment and that carrying out the judgment was a sign of mercy because only through this process could the sinner become reconciled to God. Personally, I agree with the priest, not the bishop, and I think most progressive Protestants when dealing with personal sin believe that ultimately God's love exceeds God's judgment and that the church should mirror this grace.

Not only does the metaphor of the family illuminate the Roman Catholic understanding of the church; it also addresses the nature of episcopal authority. Hahn quotes St. Cyprian of Carthage—"He can no longer have God for his Father, who has not the Church for his mother"—and Ignatius of Antioch's admonition to be obedient to the bishop. Apostolic succession is affirmed by noting in 1 Corinthians 4:15 that apostles were sent as fathers. Sons were then born who became bishops, and bishops continue the work of the first fathers. As a result, a male hierarchy is established during the early centuries of the church that is eventually centralized in the authority of the office of the bishop of Rome. Mainline Protestants' views of authority and the role of women are at variance with the Roman Catholic position. Clearly, the patriarchal authority of Roman Catholic spirituality reflects an institutionalization of gender roles dating to the early centuries of the church. One of the cultural shifts of the late modern world has been an increasing appreciation of the gifts and talents of women and an awareness of the injustices done to women not only by patriarchal attitudes but also by patriarchal institutions. These injustices are perpetuated by custom and tradition rather than on theological grounds. As Hahn notes, "Father, Son, and Holy Spirit are not 'gender' terms, but relationship terms." Mainline Protestants in the United States began to ordain women in the nineteenth century and gradually recognized over the last half century that the opposition to women's ordination reflected outdated social mores rather than sound theological arguments.

Mainline Protestant approaches to ecclesiastical authority differ sharply from Roman Catholic views. Hahn quotes Ignatius of Antioch to provide theological justification for obedience to a bishop. Members of the church, the family of God, are to be obedient to their bishop as Jesus in his human nature was to God and as the apostles were to Christ and God. In this ecclesiastical context, obedience to the bishop—and more generally to religious authority—results in an ethos and spirituality in which congregants are more deferential to clerical policies and power than in mainline Protestant contexts. Even in Protestant denominations where the office of bishop was retained following the Reformation, the nature of authority and obedience has a less hierarchical ethos than in the Roman Catholic Church.

The rise of Protestantism in the sixteenth century resulted from major challenges to clerical abuses of the time and to the authority of Rome. By concentrating power in the male hierarchical authority—

with few avenues for review and oversight by the wider church—there was little recognition that power itself easily corrupts those who are entrusted with authority. Sinfulness afflicts clerics and laity alike. While the correction of abuses by the Counter-Reformation restored the integrity of the Roman Catholic Church, it did not result in the profound structural change evidenced by the ecclesiastical structures of the emerging Protestant faith communities. Increasingly the laity was given a role in the decision-making processes of the Protestant Church. The rise of the Enlightenment and its accompanying modern worldview fostered an attitude toward critical thinking that abandoned unquestioned obedience and doubted ecclesiastical authority. The voice, influence, and vote that laypersons exercise in most mainline Protestant denominational structures reflects a post-Enlightenment approach to authority in which clerical power and influence are either subject to review or integrated into the decision-making process. This affords mainline Protestant laity a major role in the shaping of their religious institutions.

I have seen these contrasting approaches to authority exhibited in the ecumenical conferences and committees in which I have participated over the years, including my role as a faculty member at the Graduate Theological Union. My Roman Catholic colleagues have a respect for an ecclesiastical "office," even when they disagree with or hold strong opinions contrary to those providing leadership. Protestants, on the other hand, tend to have only modest respect for an ecclesiastical office per se and are most willing to be led when they respect the person holding the office. The Protestant views that any authority can be corrupted and that laity as members of the community of faith are called to provide leadership at all levels of church life place limits on clerical authority and affirm the vitality of lay leadership.

When Protestants at the time of the Reformation sought to escape what they viewed as the chains of church tradition, they turned to the Bible. Here especially in the New Testament they encountered the Word made flesh, Jesus Christ, as the source of revelation. This dependence on the Bible as the source of revelation was made possible, at least in part, because of the invention of the printing press in the fifteenth century. People now had access to the Bible in a way not previously possible. The seven sacraments of the Roman Catholic Church were reduced to two—baptism and Eucharist. These two sacraments were accepted because of their centrality in the biblical witness and not primarily because of their role in the traditions of the church. The tendency to see all of life as having a sacramental nature, that is, as having the potential to reveal in an outward way the working of God's grace, was de-emphasized by Protestants. With the focus on the Word, the role of God in the realm of nature was largely ignored. Hearing and reading the Word were emphasized as a means to guide ethical actions in the world. Discerning God's activity in the realm of nature or in the mundane activities of daily life was not an interest of mainline Disciples until their more recent liberation from modernity. Discovering spiritual practices kept alive in the Roman Catholic tradition after the Protestant Reformation has been a gift to many Protestants.

As a mainline Protestant clergyperson, I have over the years found Roman Catholic social teachings on economic justice and world peace— as delineated in pastoral letters from the U. S. Conference of Catholic Bishops and from liberation theologians in South America—a place of common ground between Roman Catholic and mainline Protestant spiritualities. As the Roman Catholic Church has in many quarters become more conservative during the last two pontificates, this voice seems to have been muted. As a result, a strong voice for economic justice and world peace has been diminished, and we are all the poorer for it.

Conclusion

Hahn demonstrates that Roman Catholic spirituality is grounded by an orderly view of the world whose foundation is the sonship of Jesus Christ. The picture created has such internal coherence that I found it quite compelling. However, the stumbling block preventing my acceptance comes both from my own life experience and from the brokenness I have encountered in the pastoral situations of those with whom I have ministered over the years. On the one hand, I wish my own faith were as systematic, logical, and all-encompassing as Roman Catholic spirituality; on the other, I am thankful that my church has allowed me to wrestle with profound theological questions—for example, ecclesiastical authority—without the fear that critiquing the church's position could have deleterious consequences.

RESPONSE TO SCOTT HAHN

EVAN HOWARD

Though Scott Hahn has written many books and articles, this essay was my first exposure to his work. I found him to be the quintessential catechist. Hahn's teaching is both accessible and winsome. He presents the biblical and theological foundations of the Roman Catholic faith and life in a way that not only educates but inspires. He shies from detailed analysis and draws his readers to the Scriptures. No wonder he has been such a gift to the church. I felt, as I read his essay, a bit of his passion for the new evangelization in the Roman Catholic Church, a passion that he suggests "is going to take place in conversation with evangelicals."[43] My hope is that his conversation with *this* evangelical facilitates not only the new evangelization encouraged by Pope John Paul II in 1992 but also the fulfilling of the Great Commission encouraged by Jesus Christ in AD 33.

My comments on Hahn's essay will take the form of brief reflections on a couple of the core issues listed by Bruce Demarest in his introduction. I will respond to Hahn's comments regarding the term *spirituality* and then address a few of the doctrinal points he mentions insofar as they relate to our approach to Christian spirituality. After this, I will comment on a couple of core issues less addressed in his essay.

The Definition of Spirituality and Catholicism

Hahn rejects in his essay some common approaches to spirituality because "they tend to boil spirituality down to a style of worship or a temperament." He finds it futile to "reduce spirituality to a lifestyle or a psychological profile." Indeed, Hahn argues that "until recently (the last half-century ago) 'spirituality' didn't exist as a discipline within

---

43. "A Conversation with Scott Hahn," recorded in Vancouver, B.C., www.youtube.com/watch?v=ifDRq0I1kEw&noredirect=1 (accessed October 14, 2011).

Catholic theology. The word *spirituality*, when it appeared at all, was defined simply as 'the opposite of materiality.'" For these reasons, Hahn chooses to approach the topic by discerning a few basic points that he identifies as doctrines. Nevertheless, before I respond to his doctrinal points, it might be valuable to comment on what he rejects.

The history of the term *spirituality* is well-known, and its relationship to particular Roman Catholic disciplines of theology is significant. The term *spirituality* in European languages has been used in a variety of ways—in the modern period, to emphasize interiority and devotion. It was this modern use that facilitated the connection of the term *spirituality* with a particular branch of Catholic theology. By the end of the medieval period, separate branches of dogmatic and moral theology had developed in the Roman Catholic community. Most of the matters regarding Christian life were understood to be a part of moral theology. Furthermore, some aspects of moral theology (namely, how we mature and experience growth in relationship with God) were eventually identified as *ascetical* and *mystical* theology, which in turn led to the development of "spiritual theology." Dogmatic theology established the first principles of the faith. Moral theology explored the nature of the obligations of this faith. Spiritual theology discussed "additional" material regarding spiritual maturity, religious experience, and the like. Particularly after the Second Vatican Council—in light of new biblical concerns, new liturgical developments, and new interests in recovering the original charisms of religious life—an emphasis was given to a more descriptive approach to spiritual development. Thus the theological discipline of Christian "spirituality" was born. Here the term was used not to distinguish immaterial from material but precisely to give room for the exploration of relationship with God insofar as it is embodied in the *whole* of life. Bruce Demarest has given us excellent representative definitions of this kind of approach to the term in his introduction (p. 18).

Thus, systematic reflection on the maturing experience of the Christian life has been a formal part of Roman Catholic theology in one form or another throughout its history. There are dictionaries of Catholic spirituality that summarize the state of research in this field. There are many volumes of classics that speak of Roman Catholic spiritual life, experience, and growth. There are manuals of Catholic spiritual direction, histories of the mystical experience of the Western church up to the Reformation, and societies and journals specifically specializing in reflection on the matters of the "scientific investigation of the spiritual life." None of these materials or approaches are represented in Hahn's essay on the Roman Catholic view(s) of Christian spirituality. Indeed, Hahn cites no source between John of Damascus (676–749) and J. C. Plumpe (1943).

Next, as a non-Catholic responding to Hahn's essay, it may be appropriate to share something of the "handful of phenomena" from which I gain my own perspectives on Roman Catholicism. After coming to personal faith in Christ through the ministry of the Jesus Movement in 1971, I found myself regularly seeking a place of private prayer after school. The nearby Catholic church building was open, and I enjoyed having devotional time there regularly. While attending an evangelical seminary, I went through what I call my "contemplative conversion." During this period, my wife and I monthly visited a monastery for a day of silent retreat and spiritual direction (offered by one of the nuns). This was a life-changing season for me. I went on to pursue graduate studies in Christian spirituality at a Roman Catholic university. I received a PhD in this field, studying under a wide range of Roman Catholic scholars. I have attended many Catholic services of various sorts and have—for years at a time—enjoyed spiritual direction from Roman Catholics. This past year, I traveled to Rome, where my wife and I attended more than one service each day in a different magnificent location, and to Assisi, where I taught on the history and significance of the Franciscan tradition. Although I have not joined a Roman Catholic church (we did flirt with the possibility of becoming Protestant Third Order Franciscans back in the early 1980s), I have received bountifully from the riches of the Roman Catholic community. It is out of this context that I write my response.

Key Emphases

What Scott Hahn has chosen to do in his essay is to discern a few points for reflection. He states, "They are doctrines, yes." So what we have in his essay is a reflection on the doctrinal prolegomena to spiritual theology, something generally covered in the first chapters of a manual of ascetical and mystical theology. In these chapters, a spiritual theologian generally lays out the principles of dogmatic theology insofar as they are relevant to a clear understanding of the nature of Christian growth toward perfection. Hahn presents in his essay reflections on the theological foundations of spirituality rooted particularly in the 1992 Catechism of the Catholic Church. As such, his reflections do not represent the opening chapters of the classic manuals of Catholic spiritual theology published in the past century, nor do they represent the theological interests of, for example, Catholic biblical theologians (such as Raymond Brown, SS, or Edward Schillebeeckx), Latin American theologians (such as Gustavo Gutiérrez, OP, or Leonardo Boff, OFM), or transcendental Thomists (such as Karl Rahner, SJ, or Bernard Lonergan, SJ).

Given what Hahn *has* presented, I am compelled to celebrate his primary points of theological foundation. For Hahn, spirituality is rooted in God's saving grace and in our adoption into the family of God. It is rooted in a sharing of the Trinitarian life of God. It is lived out in the context of the family of God. It has as its measure the Scriptures themselves. The Catholic faith affirms creation, interprets law and sin in terms of interpersonal (rather than merely legal) dynamics, and aims toward deification. The fact that Hahn identifies these points and describes them in this language is testimony to the riches that the contemporary Roman Catholic Church has received from the larger body of Christ. His treatment of the social Trinity is a Cappadocian/ Eastern rather than an Augustinian/Western portrait of the Trinity and its implications for spirituality. Similarly, his treatment of deification as a sharing of the divine life more resembles an Eastern theology than, for example, what we might find in John of the Cross or Teresa of Avila. He has learned from the Fathers of the East.

Hahn's description of law, sin, saving grace, and adoption reveals a sensitivity to the concerns voiced in the Protestant Reformation. He describes the theological dynamics that lead to spiritual life and growth as rooted in interpersonal — even familial — dynamics between the human being and God. A "button" I still have from my Jesus People days declares, "Not a Religion: A Relationship with Jesus." Hahn emphasizes this very point. And how could I possibly disagree with his claim that the Bible is the measure of it all? Since 1962, the Mass and the Scriptures have increasingly been proclaimed in the languages of the people. These are the very kinds of emphases that were central to the

Protestant Reformers, and in recent decades they have become valuable to the Roman Catholic community as well.

Furthermore Hahn's treatments of creation, sin, and even Mary are testimony to what Roman Catholicism—or at least his presentation of Roman Catholicism—has received from progressive mainline Protestants. It has been the mainline Protestants who have pressed us to reexamine our own faith with regard to the value of creation. True, we are discovering the affirmation of creation within our own traditions, but it has been the progressives that have led the pack. Similarly, our approach to sin and the work of Christ (both Roman Catholics and evangelicals) has sometimes been limited to narrow impressions of theological categories rather than reflecting the rich and interpersonal metaphors found in Scripture and the history of our own traditions. Why are we examining Duns Scotus or von Zinzendorf? Why are we all, as Hahn does in his book *First Comes Love*, exploring the connections between Mary and the feminine character of the Holy Spirit? True, we are finding resources on these matters within our own traditions. Yet we have been led to do so by the voices of progressive Protestants.

While I'm sure we could argue about various theological nuances— for example, what is the meaning of "merit" and its relationship with Christian spirituality? How does a believer approach the *interpretation* of Scripture (a topic I discuss in my response to Joseph Driskill)?—with regard to the basic thrust of Hahn's main points, I must simply offer praise. May we all continue to receive from one another, as Hahn demonstrates that Roman Catholics have received.

Institutions and Means

Nonetheless, while the Roman Catholic and the evangelical traditions appear to share doctrinal elements essential to developing an understanding and practice of growth in relationship with God, each is still a distinct tradition. Consequently, it is appropriate in a volume of this kind to articulate something of the differences between the two. In my own essay, I mentioned that evangelical spirituality has historically understood itself as *Protestant*. As such, evangelicals have tended to distance themselves from—among other things—the scholasticism of Catholic theology, the hierarchy of Catholic ecclesiology, the mechanics of late medieval spirituality, and the basic structure of late medieval Catholic ascetical and mystical consciousness. Interestingly, Hahn appears to distance himself from three of these aspects. Only the issue of hierarchy appears to divide evangelical from Roman Catholic. And somewhat attached to this issue is the question of the sacramental character of our respective spiritualities. For my discussion of hierarchy and the institutional church, see my response to Bradley Nassif.

While Hahn appears to distance himself, as do evangelicals, from the mechanics of late medieval devotion, I would be remiss in giving the impression that only institutional and sacramental issues divide Roman Catholic spirituality from evangelicalism. Roman Catholic devotions are alive and well. I would go so far as to say that while they are not prescriptively *normative* for the believer, they are descriptively *characteristic* of Roman Catholicism both historically and globally. Adoration of the Blessed Sacrament or Devotion to the Sacred Heart, devotions to saints, Masses on behalf of the dead, and other similar practices are quite common across the globe. Just as evangelicalism reflects today something of the popular emphases of its origins (preaching, hymn singing, private reading of Scripture), so Roman Catholic spirituality today reflects something of its medieval development.

Conclusion

Scott Hahn is eager to promote a new evangelization, one that he suggests will be advanced in dialogue with evangelicals. This dialogue, with regard to spirituality, has just begun. We have taken a small step forward, I hope, with regard to the theological foundations of spirituality. Nevertheless, we have much work ahead of us. I look forward to the evangelization—no, the *revival*—that may come as our dialogue matures.

CHAPTER THREE

THE PROGRESSIVE FACE OF MAINLINE PROTESTANT SPIRITUALITY

JOSEPH DRISKILL

Stephen Sondheim's lyrics to "I'm Still Here" tell the story of an aging actress who celebrates her survival of the difficulties experienced over many years. "Good times and bum times, I've seen them all and, my dear, I'm still here ... Seen all my dreams disappear, but I'm here ... I got through all of last year, and I'm here."[1] Sociologists of religion have for forty-five years been tracking the decline of mainline Protestant denominations with a variety of measures: loss of members, reduced attendance, relocation to less expensive offices, and smaller congregations.[2] Denominations structures, once the organizational and symbolic centers of North American Christianity, are a shadow of an earlier existence.[3] However, in the last five years, these losses, which signaled shrinkage, accelerated beyond a pace that allowed for business as usual. Shrinking numbers brought shrinking budgets to the breaking point. Dan Aleshire's provocative title for his 2010 address to the Association of Theological Schools, "The Future Has Arrived," reflects the urgency of transitions occurring in many mainline theological schools.[4] Given

---

1. Stephen Sondheim, *Finishing the Hat: Collected Lyrics (1954–1981) with Attendant Comments, Principles, Heresies, Grudges, Whines and Anecdotes* (New York: Knopf, 2010), 221.

2. William McKinney, "Mainline Protestantism 2000," *The Annals of the American Academy of Political and Social Science* 558 (July 1998): 57–66.

3. For example, on October 12, 2010, the Evangelical Lutheran Church of America announced it would lay off 60 of its 358 employees, effective February, 2011.

4. Daniel Aleshire, "The Future Has Arrived: Changing Theological Education in a Changed World," lecture at ATS/COA biennial meeting, June 2010.

the state of mainline Protestant spirituality, one might well celebrate that our spiritual traditions are, in the words of the lyric, "still here."

The current situation necessitates examining mainline Protestant spirituality as the denominations themselves are in flux, navigating, among other things, the transition from the modern to the postmodern worldview. While all of us writing for this volume face these changing tides, mainline Protestant spirituality seems more vulnerable and more in need of changing course than the other interlocutors because of its enmeshment with the modern worldview.[5] As a result, in this chapter I will identify salient features of progressive mainline Protestant spirituality with an eye on both its ties to the modern worldview of twentieth-century inheritances and the emerging characteristics in its twenty-first-century future that "has arrived." First, however, I will locate myself within the progressive sector of my religious social location, define my use of the term *spirituality*, delineate the denominations subsumed by the term *mainline Protestant*, and then turn to the issues that shape the contrasting spiritualities of this volume.

In our postmodern world, each of us speaks from the influences and assumptions of the various social locations we inhabit. Therefore, the reader will be assisted by knowing that I am a white, heterosexual, middle-class male in my mid-sixties, ordained in the Christian Church (Disciples of Christ) as a third-generation clergyperson. Although I was reared in the "Land of Lincoln" in and near Springfield, Illinois, my worldview was shaped significantly by a progressive theological education and by additional study in the history of religions. After pastoring a Disciples congregation in Regina, Saskatchewan, I served as a campus minister for twelve years with the United Church of Canada, a progressive denominational voice. In midlife I completed a PhD at the Graduate Theological Union and for the past eighteen years have served as professor of spirituality and dean of the Disciples Seminary Foundation at Pacific School of Religion, Berkeley, California. While all of these formative religious influences are easily encompassed by the "mainline Protestant" moniker, they represent in a number of identifiable ways the more progressive points of view associated with the mainline Protestant

---

5. See Graham Ward, "The Future of Protestantism: Postmodernity," in *The Blackwell Companion to Protestantism*, ed. Alister E. McGrath and Darren C. Marks (Malden, Mass.: Blackwell, 2007), 453–67.

religious spectrum. Representing this perspective will contribute to the counterpoints that this volume seeks to highlight as it investigates the spiritualities of four major Christian traditions.

Spirituality and *mainline Protestant spirituality* are both conceptual terms fraught with ambiguity that require further definition and elaboration. The definition of spirituality which informs my work is influenced by Sandra Schneiders' focus on "the lived experience of faith" as it manifests itself through a variety of expressions.[6] This perspective concerns itself with "the experience of the concrete believing subject(s)."[7] My definition maintains that spirituality is concerned with the lived experience of faith, the communities that shape the experience, the practices that sustain it, and the moral life that embodies it. This definition acknowledges the socially situated nature of meaning making and the way in which the community of faith contributes to the shaping of a life of faith. It highlights the practices that undergird faith development and sustain religious commitments. In addition, the embodied moral life is viewed as a fruit of the spirit. Here one sees concrete evidence of the believers' commitments, as well as the particular manner in which they are expressed. Using the prism of "lived experience" to investigate selected beliefs and significant characteristics of the progressive side of mainline Protestant Christianity keeps the focus grounded in the experience of its various communities of faith.

Throughout the chapter I will attempt to describe salient features of progressive mainline Protestant communities of faith by drawing on resources to which large numbers of their members and leaders have been exposed. This chapter will not focus on the spirituality of key denominational leaders in these faith communities or emerging cutting-edge theologies. For the most part, my sources will draw on theologians who have and are being read not only by clergy and seminarians but also by congregational leaders and members. Exposure to those who shape mainline Protestant spirituality comes in congregational study groups, and public lectures, as well as in lay schools of theology and through continuing education. Most of my references will be to writings from authors who are members of mainline faith communities.

---

6. Sandra Schneiders, "Approaches to the Study of Christian Spirituality," in *The Blackwell Companion to Christian Spirituality*, ed. Arthur Holder (Malden, Mass.: Blackwell, 2005), 15–33.

7. Ibid.

The term *mainline Protestant* is widely used today, even though its meaning is, to a considerable extent, fluid. The Protestant faith traditions of colonial America, including Congregational, Episcopal, and Presbyterian, were first identified as "mainline." While there was no uniform relationship between religious groups and the governing structures of the various colonies, two groups wanted little separation between the church and the governing structures of the colonies. The Puritans in the northern colonies and the Anglicans in the southern colonies both advocated for the support of their particular religious institutions through civil collection processes.

Although the adoption of the First Amendment to the Constitution ultimately provided for the separation of church and state, the participation of civic leaders in religious institutions ensured that these familiar denominations would continue to enjoy their preeminent position as "mainline." Later, the immigrants of the eighteenth and nineteenth century brought with them the Reformed and Lutheran traditions. These immigrants settled in geographic areas (the Upper Midwest, for example) where their very numbers ensured a "mainline" status to their faith traditions. In addition, the faith traditions producing large numbers of followers on the America frontier—Methodist, Christian Church (Disciples of Christ), and American Baptist—became major players in the religious landscape.[8] While each of these groups has its own spirituality, all were viewed as "mainline" in the sense that the majority of Protestants of the successive periods belonged to them. These denominations were identified with the social and political establishments of the time.[9]

As my introduction indicates, although much has changed, these groups continue to be called "mainline," even though they represent today only about 9 percent of the religious marketplace.[10] I will now

---

8. McKinney, "Mainline Protestantism 2000."

9. Wade Clark Roof and William McKinney, *American Mainline Religion: Its Changing Shape and Future* (New Brunswick, N.J.: Rutgers University Press, 1992), 72–105.

10. The Association of Religion Data Archives (ARDA), "U.S. Membership Report: Denominational Groups, 2000," www.thearda.com/mapsReports/reports/US_2000.asp (accessed November 21, 2010). ARDA's "mainline Protestant denominations" include, in addition to the seven denominations listed in the text, such groups as Friends (Quakers), Latvian Evangelical Lutheran Church in America, International Council of Community Churches, Universal Fellowship of Metropolitan Community Churches, National Association of Congregational Christian Churches, and various provinces of the Moravian Church in America.

identify selected key aspects of mainline Protestant spirituality and in the process further clarify the nature of the term. Where progressive stances can be detected within the mainline views, I will focus on them.

Commitment to Shared Witness and Mission through Ecumenical Cooperation

The first characteristic that shapes the lived experience of faith for mainline Protestants grows from the commitment to ecumenical cooperation. During the late nineteenth and early twentieth century, a number of Protestant groups found common cause for conversation. In 1908, the Federal Council of Churches, and later in 1950 the National Council of Churches, gave institutional expression to the optimism that conversations based on mutual respect might lead to shared witness and mission. During these years, evangelization programs in various countries of the world were given to specific denominations. For example, the Presbyterian Church in the United States sent missionaries to Korea, while the Christian Church (Disciples of Christ) evangelized the Congo in Africa. It soon became obvious that many of the ecclesiological and theological characteristics differentiating denominations with European origins were irrelevant in the various contexts in which missionaries from mainline churches were serving. Partly in response to this, many progressive leaders in mainline Protestant churches thought that Christian churches should unite to enhance their witness to the world.

The Consultation on Church Union, established in 1962, was committed to the theological belief that the church of Jesus Christ needs to overcome its own divisions so that the world may believe that Jesus is the Christ, the Son of God (see John 17:21). As long as the churches themselves were hostile to one another and divided in their witness, it would remain difficult to convince those outside the faith that the message of Jesus was truly good news. The nine communions that engaged these conversations included many of the denominations historically embraced by the term *mainline*—the United Presbyterian Church, the Episcopal Church, the Methodist Church, the United Church of Christ, the Christian Church (Disciples of Christ)—plus several historic black churches, such as the African Methodist Episcopal Church, African

Methodist Episcopal Zion Church, the Christian Methodist Episcopal Church, and the International Council of Community Churches.[11] The expression *mainline* continued to be used for denominational bodies seriously engaged in conversations about mission, faith and order.

A "Plan of Union for the Church of Christ Uniting," proposing an organic union, was brought to the churches in 1970, but it was clear within two years that there was a growing lack of theological consensus, especially around polity concerns. What these churches did share, however, was a commitment to maintain their ongoing dialogue in search of a covenant emphasizing not organic union but, among other things, mutual recognition of members, sacraments, and ministries, and a desire to overcome the injustices of racism.[12] In 2002, Churches Uniting in Christ became the successor organization to the Consultation on Church Union. "Christians in the pews know that we belong together because we all belong to the same Lord. Churches Uniting in Christ is a framework for showing to the world what we truly are — the one body of Jesus Christ."[13] The spirit of goodwill was so pervasive within mainline Protestant communities that within a few years not many within the organization felt the need to continue meeting.

While the ecumenical movement did not produce a large Protestant denomination or move nearly far enough in overcoming racial injustices, many smaller unions and mergers did occur, often restoring divisions that occurred between the North and South during the Civil War (though not limited to such divisions). The commitment to ecumenism by these mainline churches reflects an ecclesiology where no one church assumes that it offers the only path to salvation. The enthusiasm for ecumenical cooperation was grounded by the experience of living and working in communities where close proximity to Christians of other denominations results in a belief that "we are all going to the same place," even if the routes differ. While the ecumenical movement has often been criticized as an example of leadership "at the top" advocating

---

11. See John Briggs, Mercy Amba Oduyoye, and Georges Tsetsis, eds., *A History of the Ecumenical Movement, vol. 3: 1968-2000* (Geneva, Switzerland: World Council of Churches, 2004), 621.

12. Ibid., 623. See also Thomas E. Fitzgerald, *The Ecumenical Movement: An Introductory History* (Westport, Conn.: Praeger, 2004), 183.

13. Churches Uniting in Christ, www.cuicinfo.org/whatiscuic/cuic.html (accessed October 27, 2010). The Moravian Church Northern Province is also a member of CUIC.

a vision out of touch with the "grassroots," I think this underestimates the magnitude of goodwill that has been fostered by the ecumenical discussions throughout various levels of church life.

As a child in the 1950s, I have vivid memories of worshiping each Wednesday evening during Lent with other mainline churches in my community. This opportunity created an appreciation for the various ways each denomination worshiped and shared communion. The bond of goodwill helped us value the alternative paths on which others traveled on their faith journey. The spirituality of mainline Protestants has valued and continues to deeply value the community that exists among and between Christian people of goodwill.

Biblical Interpretation and Scholarly Inquiry

Mainline Protestant communities of faith have from their inception believed the religious life of both laity and clergy is enhanced through scholarship and learning. In the seventeenth century, as Puritans populated the northeastern colonies of America and Anglicans settled in the southern colonies, they began establishing colleges. Although the original names were often changed, the educational institutions begun in those early days of colonial life are a mainstay of the contemporary educational system in the United States. Congregationalists founded Harvard University (1636), Yale University (1701), Dartmouth University (1769), and the University of California (1868); Anglicans founded The College of William and Mary (1693), the University of Pennsylvania (1740), and Columbia University (1754). This commitment to advanced education was widespread in mainline Protestant circles, where educational institutions continued to be founded well into the nineteenth century. Presbyterians founded Princeton University (1746); Baptists founded Brown University (1764) and the University of Chicago (1892); Christian Church (Disciples of Christ) founded Transylvania University (1780); Methodists founded Vanderbilt University (1873); Lutherans founded St. Olaf College (1874).[14] Although by the twentieth century such ambitious educational ventures were over and financial support for these institutions from denominations had waned,

---

14. "Colonial Colleges," Wikipedia, http://en.wikipedia.org/wiki/Colonial_Colleges (accessed November 20, 2010).

the legacy of trained clergy continues through freestanding seminaries and university-affiliated divinity schools.

The religious values that fostered the creation of many of America's premier universities ensured that as theoretical and empirical advances were made in secular disciplines, the impact would eventually be felt in mainline Protestant churches. The theological implications of advances made in such fields as philosophy, literature, biology, geology, astronomy, and the social sciences came to the fore during the modernist controversies in the 1920s and 1930s. The impact of scientific discoveries on matters of faith and questions involving biblical interpretation divided those who espoused a fundamentalist understanding of the inerrancy of Scripture from the progressives or modernists. Denominational conflicts emerged over such issues as creationism and evolution. To a considerable degree, the spirituality of mainline Protestants continued to adapt its religious understanding to the modern worldview, seeing the methods of science as essential for describing the workings of the physical universe. Religious meaning, on the other hand, was increasingly in retreat as psychology and the other human sciences used their interpretive systems to "explain" religious phenomena, while modernist approaches to biblical interpretation drew increasingly from the textual methodology used in the academy for other types of literary analysis.

Early historical critics of biblical texts noted inconsistencies and contradictions not only among but within biblical books. For example, the differences between the creation stories of Genesis 1 and Genesis 2 led to an investigation of the sources and eventually to the belief that "the Pentateuch was composed of four sources of substantially different origins and outlooks (known as J, E, P, and D), originating from 850 to 450 BCE."[15] As textual studies developed, this type of source criticism was followed by "form criticism (study of popular genres), redaction criticism (study of editorial composition), and numerous others,"[16] including feminist interpretation (a critique of patriarchy), womanist interpretation (a critique by women of color of first-world assumptions), sociological interpretations (study of societal structures and systems), liberation and

---

15. R. Kendall Soulen, "Protestantism and the Bible," *Blackwell Companion to Protestantism*, 251–67.

16. Ibid.

postcolonial interpretations (critiques of various forms of power and heterosexist assumptions), and narrative interpretation (focused on biblical narratives as stories rather than repositories of historical "facts").

These interpretive tools exposed within the texts attitudes and biases that have more to do with the vested interests of the authors and the norms of their social locations than with divine aims of love and justice. With these interpretative frames of reference, the reader asks a series of questions: (1) What is happening behind this text? What are the issues, debates, and concerns of this particular social location that gives rise to the text? What is not said in the text? Why? (2) What is happening within the text? What is the point of the story as the author tells it? (3) What is happening in front of the text? What is happening in the readers' lives that shape their response to the passage? What is the reader seeking? How does the reader's social location impact the selection of the texts being studied or used devotionally?

Mainline Protestants have spent much of their religious education engaged in this style of Bible study. They have recognized that the Bible is a diverse collection of stories, poems, prose, histories, and parables written by a variety of authors from strikingly different social locations and across vast periods of time. By asking these interpretative questions, they have sought to understand how these texts address the contemporary needs, desires, and hopes of the community of faith. They believe that God is still speaking through the text and in everyday life to inform, surprise, and even transform both individual lives and the community of faith.[17] Such study is an integral element of mainline Protestant spirituality.

From God "Out There" to the God of Relationship

Progressive Protestants in the early and mid-twentieth century were profoundly influenced by the theological reflections of Karl Barth and Paul Tillich.[18] Barth's focus on God's transcendence prevented the

17. The United Church of Christ in 2004 adopted a branding campaign proclaiming that "no matter who you are, or where you are on life's journey, you're welcome here." A total of 2,500 churches have chosen to participate in the "God Is Still Speaking" program of the church, www.ucc.org/god-is-still-speaking/about/ (accessed January 2, 2011).

18. Karl Barth, *Church Dogmatics*, ed. G. W. Bromiley and T. F. Torrance (Peabody, Mass.: Hendrickson, 2010); Paul Tillich, *Systematic Theology* (Chicago: University of Chicago Press, 1967).

identification of any human point of view or understanding of God with the Godhead. Thus, God is beyond the greatest imaginings of humankind and is revealed primarily in Jesus Christ. Tillich's focus on God as "the ground of being" provided a foundation for all of life. God's primordial ground was the underpinning of all that is. In both instances God was a foundational source of life, yet a source that is far removed from daily life. As the creator and sustainer of all that is, God remained above the fray of daily existence. The God of the universe was considered by progressive Protestants to be much too busy to intervene in the commonplace happenstances of daily life.

This attitude toward God's involvement with the world was a source of some curiosity for me as a child. I remember a childhood friend from an evangelical church who used to speak of God's assistance with her daily activities. God would help her with any given task, no matter how mundane. For example, God would help her find the fastest-moving line when checking out of the grocery store. Even as a child I can remember thinking she held beliefs about God that my family did not share. In my family there was a great distance between God and daily life, except in matters of death and justice. At times of suffering, death, or the loss of a loved one, progressive Protestants still spoke of God's loving care and comfort. Here God was not remote or distant but was available for solace. Also, when dealing with injustices, progressives felt they were responding to an immediate mandate from God to respond with justice and compassion. The modern worldview was quite compatible with the more rational, distant God of my childhood. However, as the twentieth century moved onward, even the notion of a God "out there" or "underneath" also came to be questioned, as progressive Protestants continued to reconcile their faith with the modern worldview.

In 1963, Bishop John A. T. Robinson's book *Honest to God* created much debate as it challenged the idea of a God who is "out there."[19] Notions of heaven as "up there" or "out there" and hell as "down there" were fading rapidly in progressive mainline denominations by the mid-twentieth century. "You make your heaven or hell here on earth by the way you live" was a commonplace statement among progressives. The

---

19. John A. T. Robinson, *Honest to God* (London: SCM Press, 1963), 40th anniv. ed., with essays by Douglas John Hall and Rowan Williams (Louisville, Ky.: Westminster, 2002).

notion of a three-storied universe with heaven above and hell below had eroded with the continuing advance of the modern worldview. Progressives accepted the vastness of the universe as explored with high-powered telescopes and through space missions. If our understanding of "out there" was radically transformed by what we could now see—a universe beyond our previous imaginings—then the notion that God was somehow simply farther "out there" gradually became implausible.

How would this "faraway" God relate to the planet? God's interventions from "out there" came to be viewed as at best selective and at worst unethical. How could God "so love the world" and yet allow much of its population to starve? If God is "all-powerful," why does God allow genocide? Questions of theodicy, as well as the seeming randomness of "divine" interventions, begged the question: If God is all-powerful, then how can God be just? For many progressive Protestants the answer came with the affirmation that something was wrong with our theology, with our understanding of God and how God was at work in the world. The all-powerful, "out there" God of supernatural theism was inadequate to a progressive reading of the biblical witness to a God who is love, who is as near as our breath, and who is yearning to be in relationship with us.

Matthew Fox, a former Dominican priest and now Episcopal priest, became an early proponent of an understanding of God that offered an alternative to supernatural theism and that was widely influential with progressive Protestants. Fox's "creation spirituality" emphasizes God's original blessing instead of traditional doctrines of original sin and proposes a panentheistic view of God.[20] *Pan* means "all" or "everything"; *en* means "in"; *theism* comes from *theos*, "God." Thus, "rather than imagining God as a personlike being 'out there,' this concept imagines God as *the encompassing Spirit* in whom everything that is, is. The universe is not separate from God, but *in* God ... We are in God; we live in God, move in God, have our being in God."[21] This understanding of God provides for the immanence of God's love and closeness while maintaining the transcendent otherness of God's mystery. It offers an

---

20. Matthew Fox, *Original Blessing: A Primer in Creation Spirituality: Presented in Four Paths, Twenty-Six themes, and Two Questions* (1983; repr., New York: Tarcher/Putnam, 2000).

21. Marcus J. Borg, *The Heart of Christianity: Rediscovering a Life of Faith* (San Francisco: HarperSanFrancisco, 2004), 66.

understanding of God that progressives have increasingly embraced as the modern worldview has faded.

Who Is Jesus?

The response to this question is shaped by progressives' commitment to each succeeding advance in biblical interpretation and to their acceptance of the modern worldview's knowledge of the universe. Progressive Protestants in the twentieth century found especially problematic those aspects of Jesus' life that appeared to abrogate the laws of nature. The notion of the virgin birth and miracles such as the feeding of the five thousand and the healing of the blind man found many exegetes seeking rational explanations to account for biblical events that defied contemporary approaches to rationality.[22] Bible study groups in mainline Protestant congregations wrestled with the meaning of these passages, often using psychological insights to explain the healing stories.

For progressive Protestants, the heart and core of Jesus' life and teachings reside in the way he extends compassion and seeks justice for his contemporaries. These teachings became the cornerstone for attributions that Jesus is the Son of God. Jesus was understood as an inspired leader, committed to an ethic of love and forgiveness even in the face of martyrdom. The Christology of many progressive Protestants focused on the earthly Jesus, the great teacher, who invited his followers to a lifestyle necessitating love for God and love for neighbor. The divinity of the post-Easter Christ rested in the depth of his faithfulness to the will of God even unto death. "Jesus saves by making people more loving through the transforming power of his example. The beauty of Jesus' life and death moves people to actualize more fully their own potential to love, and his example guides people's action by modeling what love is."[23]

The resurrection is treasured as God's vindication of Jesus' earthly life and the powerful capacity of love to overcome death. The faith of many progressive Protestants rests not first and foremost in the resurrec-

---

22. See the works of Bishop John Shelby Spong for an extreme representative of this position. See, for example, *A New Christianity for a New World: Why Traditional Faith Is Dying and How a New Faith is Being Born* (San Francisco: HarperOne, 2002).

23. Don Schweitzer, *Contemporary Christologies: A Fortress Introduction* (Minneapolis: Fortress, 2010), 33.

tion as an historical event but in its symbolic power. The symbolic power of the resurrection gives inestimable meaning to life. Each day, countless numbers of people face racism, genocide, hate, starvation, and indifference. The symbolic power of the resurrection gives hope in the face of the worst defeats imaginable, love in the face of the horrors of evil, and light that will not be extinguished by the power of the darkness.

As the modern age, with its preoccupation with the rational, waned and the postmodern emerged, the fresh breeze of a renewed appreciation of the Spirit challenged the understanding of Jesus as "the only way to God." As progressive Protestants increasingly have a renewed awareness of the spiritual aspects of Jesus' life and teachings, so, too, they see the divine Spirit at work throughout the creation. Marcus Borg's biblical scholarship represents this increasingly accepted interpretation of Jesus: "Rather than being the exclusive revelation of God, [Jesus] is one of many mediators of the sacred ... There really are people like this—and Jesus was one of them. They really are experiences of the sacred, of the numinous, of God—and Jesus was one for whom God was an experiential reality."[24]

Thus have many progressive Protestants moved away from focusing on answering questions related to the role of "miracles" in a rational universe to affirmations of the movement of the sacred in all of life. With this affirmation comes the belief that God's transforming love works in many ways, in many faith traditions. While some mainline Christians may see this view as taking away from the uniqueness of Jesus, others find it liberating to recognize the depth of Jesus' humanity without having to affirm a type of uniqueness available to no other faith tradition. The path of Jesus is *a* way to God but not the *only* path. In a globalized, pluralistic world, the spirituality of progressive Protestants affirms the meaning of their own tradition(s) while respecting the religious traditions of other faithful people.

The Social Gospel, Justice, and Social Action

The lived faith experience of progressive Protestants in the twentieth century owed much to the prophetic voice of biblical faith embodied

---

24. Marcus J. Borg, *Meeting Jesus Again for the First Time: The Historical Jesus and the Heart of Contemporary Faith* (San Francisco: HarperSanFrancisco, 1994), 37.

in the largely Protestant social gospel movement of the late nineteenth and early twentieth centuries. Walter Rauschenbusch, a Baptist clergyperson who as a young man had focused on the saving of individual souls through personal repentance, came to believe that focusing on personal conversion and individual salvation was misguided. The coming of the kingdom of God required repentance for social sins. The endgame for believers required spreading the gospel of Jesus by living a Christlike life of mutual love and cooperation.

Rauschenbusch identified six social sins that he believed were responsible for the crucifixion of Jesus: religious bigotry, graft and political power, a corrupt legal system, mob spirit and action, militarism, and class contempt and divisions.[25] The antidote for these ills comes from love, service, and solidarity. Rauschenbusch and the movement worked for the betterment of society by addressing social ills with creative alternatives: "by challenging the philosophy of competitive individualism; by promoting humane customs and attitudes toward children, women and the poor; by supporting useful institutions, such as public education, public parks, profit sharing, and agencies of international cooperation."[26] The concern with social rather than personal sin and the focus on social justice remain aspects of the lived experience of faith for progressive Protestants.

Another late-nineteenth-century work that contributed to the concern for social justice of progressive Protestantism was Charles Monroe Sheldon's *In His Steps: What Would Jesus Do?*[27] Sheldon, a Congregational clergyperson from Kansas, found the question helpful for understanding Christian ethics. Rauschenbusch noted that Sheldon's work had influenced his own quest to alleviate social sin by stimulating his reflections on ways Jesus would deal with such issues. It is ironic that the question posed in the title was generally asked by generations in the later twentieth century to adjudicate individual moral acts rather than to address social circumstances.

---

25. See Rita Nakashima Brock and Rebecca Ann Parker, *Saving Paradise: How Christianity Traded Love of This World for Crucifixion and Empire* (Boston: Beacon, 2008), 401.

26. Douglas F. Ottati, "Social Gospel," in *New and Enlarged Handbook of Christian Theology*, ed. Donald W. Musser and Joseph L. Price (Nashville: Abingdon, 2003), 469.

27. Charles Monroe Sheldon, *In His Steps: What Would Jesus Do?* (Chicago: Advance, 1897).

Progressive Protestants continue to be committed to human flourishing by addressing social ills through activist responses. Two biblical texts that are privileged in progressive Protestant congregations are Micah 6:6–8 and Matthew 25:31–46. In the Micah passage (verse 8 NRSV), the faithful are required "to do justice, and to love kindness, and to walk humbly with your God." The passage continues by warning that the injustices of cheating and violence must be avoided. The Matthew passage, commonly called "the great judgment," commends feeding the hungry, giving drink to the thirsty, visiting those in prison, offering hospitality to the stranger, and caring for the sick. In both instances, ministries of justice and compassion are emphasized as actions favored in God's eyes. These teachings are considered priorities by progressive Protestants and touch the affective dimensions of faith that shape and guide their priorities.

Women in progressive mainline Protestant churches have since the mid-twentieth century been actively engaged in the feminist struggle to combat injustices associated with patriarchy. Within the church structure itself, this has involved opening positions of leadership to women,[28] as well as creating inclusive language liturgies, hymnbooks, educational curricula, and translations of the Bible. Many mainline Protestant churches have adopted inclusive language policies that guide the language of worship and study.[29] *An Inclusive-Language Lectionary* was published by the National Council of Churches in 1983 for "experimental and voluntary use" in churches.[30] The New

---

28. In 1976, the General Convention of the Episcopal Church, USA, regularized the ordinations of fifteen women priests. Barbara C. Harris became the first woman bishop in the Episcopal Church in 1989. Women began moving into ordained leadership positions (deaconate, in many instances, and in some cases, to word and sacrament) in what became the Presbyterian Church (U.S.A.), United Church of Christ, United Methodist Church, and Christian Church (Disciples of Christ) traditions by the late nineteenth century.

29. The Eleventh General Synod of the United Church of Christ (1977) called for the creation of a Book of Worship that would use inclusive language for both people and God. In 1980, the General Conference of the United Methodist Church formed a task force to eliminate sexist and racist language in the liturgy, hymns, and educational resources of the church. At the 1984 General Conference, their guidelines were adopted. For the inclusive language policy of the Evangelical Lutheran Church of America, visit www.elca.org/Growing-In-Faith/Worship/Learning-Center/FAQs/language.aspx (accessed January 19, 2011).

30. *An Inclusive Language Lectionary. Readings for Year A*, prepared for experimental and voluntary use in churches by the Inclusive Language Lectionary Committee appointed by the Division of Education and Ministry, National Council of the Churches of Christ in the USA (Philadelphia: Westminster, 1983).

Revised Standard Version of the Bible, which was published in 1989, was translated with an awareness of the growing importance of inclusive language.

In addition, women's voices calling for the elimination of domestic violence led theologians to consider ways in which the Christian emphasis on stories of "suffering" and "sacrifice" may contribute to violence in the home.[31] Given the number of men, including those from church families, who engage in physical and sexual violence against women and children in their homes, feminist theologians raised questions about how an exclusively male image of God as Father could be problematic for the abused. A loving God who nurtures and cares for women as well as for men could quite legitimately be approached through feminine as well as masculine metaphors. For example, God cares for God's creatures "as a hen gathers her brood under her wings" (Matthew 23:37 NRSV; Luke 13:34 NRSV) This God could be related to as a mother, as a wise and loving woman. The spirituality of progressive Protestant denominations has integrated many of the insights of feminist theologians. Public prayers, Bible readings, and the language of worship are to a considerable extent inclusive. Progressive Protestants are increasingly comfortable using gender-neutral language in reference to God or in using an address such as "Father and Mother God."

More recently, womanist literature from women of color has addressed the ills not only of sexism but also of racism and classism.[32] Women of color noted that many of the feminist critiques of patriarchy by economically and racially privileged white women failed to sufficiently recognize the injustices against those who are racially underrepresented or economically disadvantaged. In addition, the ecumenical conversations within Churches Uniting in Christ, where people of color and whites have conversed about the needs of the wider church and culture, identified the need to address structural racism in the United States. At the present time pro-reconciling, anti-racism work is a pri-

---

31. Marjorie Proctor-Smith and Janet R. Walton, eds., *Women at Worship: Interpretations of North American Diversity* (Louisville, Ky.: Westminster, 1993); for family violence and religious themes, see chapter 5 in *Women at Worship* (Sheila Redmond, "Remember the Good, Forget the Bad: Denial and Family Violence in a Christian Worship Service").

32. See Cynthia L. Rigby, "Protestantism and Feminism," in *Blackwell Companion to Protestantism*, 332–43.

ority on the agendas of several mainline churches, including but not limited to the United Methodist Church, the United Church of Christ, and the Christian Church (Disciples of Christ). Dismantling the structural racism present in the social order of the United States, as well as in churches themselves, continues to be a priority.

Care for the created order is increasingly on the agenda of progressive mainline churches. Sallie McFague's theological work on the earth as God's body has been influential in raising the theological implications of viewing the creation as the work of a loving God whose handiwork mediates the sacred.[33] Inasmuch as progressive Protestants' cosmology does not see the world as "evil" and some future paradise as "good," there is a growing commitment to care for the planet. The spirituality of progressive Protestants affirms an anthropology that sees the human person as profoundly a part of the created order, made of the "stuff" of creation. Faithfulness requires a deep and abiding concern for the environment, including being socially involved in such practical issues as reducing one's carbon footprint. Responding to the seriousness of global climate change by altering one's lifestyle to provide for a more sustainable future is not merely a helpful "action" but a matter of faithfulness. Rita Nakashima Brock and Rebecca Ann Parker warn that if "nature" is understood primarily as an idealized space useful for occasional escapes from the pressures of urban life, then not only does it lose its sacred nature; it becomes merely another commodity to be used up by our consumer society. The task of faithfulness is to see nature and all environments as arenas for God's creative love to express itself. Workplaces, homes, and cities need to be made humane and sustainable through forward-looking policies and actions.[34] Sustaining those ministries that rectify injustices and care for the created order are hallmarks of progressive Protestant spirituality.

The Church and Religious Authority

Mainline Protestants share a deep distrust of entrenched authority structures that dates from the sixteenth-century Reformation. Corrupt

---

33. Sallie McFague, *The Body of God: An Ecological Theology* (Minneapolis, Minn.: Fortress, 1993).

34. Brock and Parker, *Saving Paradise*, 388.

religious practices engaged in by dishonest religious leaders provided a major impetus for the Reformation. Reaction against the clerical class and the organizational structure of the church itself occurred in various regions of Europe, England, and Scotland. The intensity of these responses to abuses in the church resulted in a reorganization of its liturgical life and governance structures, as well as a diminishing of clerical authority. All of these factors continue to influence the spirituality of mainline Protestants today.

The notion of "the priesthood of all believers" expresses mainline Protestants' belief that they do not require the mediation of a priest or the church to approach God. Every believer by virtue of baptism not only is a member of the church but has direct access to God. The term has a variety of different nuanced meanings in differing Protestant denominations, but in all of them it makes clear that Protestants do not require an ordained priest to mediate their relationship with God or to absolve sin. The Protestant belief in justification by faith is understood as God's gracious gift of salvation, never earned, but given as a gift to those who have faith. It allows one to stand before God without fear, for God is a God of love, not retribution. "Each individual was to stand directly before God, to seek God's gracious forgiveness of sin, and to conduct life in accordance with the Bible and Christian conscience."[35]

The spirituality of progressive Protestants has been a relatively "guilt free" experience of faith. Confession is a personal matter, not a required sacramental action of the church, and in public worship, confession and the assurance of pardon are done collectively. One aspect of this experience is to view sin largely as an aspect of the human condition rather than a personal act of disobedience. Sin is viewed as "missing the mark" and, as such, requires correction but not ritualized absolution and penance. Today, this attitude is reflected in the worship services of many progressive congregations, where it is virtually anathema even to mention personal sin. The sins of racism, classism, sexism, and heterosexism remain a concern. But this work for justice and peace is primarily presented not as opposing personal sin but as opposing social, systemic injustices. And while progressive Protestants would acknowledge that

---

35. John Witte Jr., "Protestantism, Law and Legal Thought," in *Blackwell Companion to Protestantism*, 298–305.

they participate in these sins, they would also contend that corrective action, for example, transforming one's lifestyle rather than inducing guilt, is a more constructive response.

The church is viewed as a community of flawed saints, the gathering of the faithful. It is the place where the gospel is proclaimed, the sacraments are celebrated, and the ministries of justice and compassion are supported. Progressive Protestants value the opportunity to come together in true community and to be the hands and feet of Jesus in the world. The church as the body of Christ is called to be "a radiating centre of God's action within the whole world."[36] This community works to discern the places in the world in need of justice and compassion. As such, its members rely on "biblical norms for right living."[37] The church is "at heart a community of saints, not a corporation of law …"[38]

Church governance happens largely through elected councils, synods, presbyteries, assemblies, and boards or conventions. Constitutions, bylaws, guidelines, and terms of reference describe the various polities of mainline Protestant churches: e.g., Methodists have a Book of Discipline and Presbyterians a Book of Order. A centralized, highly developed canon law, as understood by the Roman Catholic Church, is nonexistent in Protestant denominations.[39]

While most progressive Protestants ordain clergy for the administration of Word and Sacrament, major leadership positions are also held by laypersons. Since much of the work is done through committees and councils, committed laypersons can expect, if they so wish, to serve in a variety of capacities. The distrust of clerical authority that resulted in governance structures being open to laypeople in progressive Protestant denominations has often given the laity voting power equal to or exceeding that of the ordained. The lived experience of faith affirms the presence of God's Spirit at work in democratic processes where men, women, and often youth have a voice in discerning where

---

36. Alister E. McGrath and Darren C. Marks, "Introduction: Protestantism—the Problem of Identity," in *Blackwell Companion to Protestantism*, 1–19.

37. Witte Jr., "Protestantism, Law and Legal Thought," 299.

38. Ibid.

39. Anglicans have a form of canon law, but it is specific to the various jurisdictions that comprise the Anglican Communion. For example, the Episcopal Church of the United States has its own unique canon law, which differs from Anglican canon law in the United Kingdom.

God's transforming love is at work. This opportunity to serve also gives the laity a deep sense that they are the people of God. They have not just influence but both power and authority in the church structure.

The Holy Spirit

The Spirit, *ruah* in Hebrew and *pneuma* in Greek, is a nonmaterial dimension of reality that blows where it will. The life force within, around, and beyond us is also the unseen which surprises, confounds, and transforms us. As such, the Spirit permeates all of life—all of the created order. Progressive Protestants reject the notion that spirituality is concerned with an otherworldly, holy realm distant from and superior to the physical, secular, or everyday plane of existence. "The experience of the Spirit does not release those who are touched by it from this earth and their own earthly bodies, so that their souls can soar into the realms of spirits. It fills them with a new vitality entirely and wholly, body and soul."[40] Progressive Protestants affirm that all of life is sacred and that because of the incarnation all of life has spiritual significance. Attempts to view the flesh as lower or evil and the spirit as higher or good are rejected. Jürgen Moltmann observes, "When I love God I love the beauty of bodies, the rhythm of movements, the shining of eyes, the embraces, the feelings, the scents, the sounds of all this protean creation."[41] This affirmation of the intimately enmeshed nature of flesh and Spirit in the world that God so loves, contributes to the progressives' emphasis on caring for the world by exercising ministries of justice and compassion.

For many progressive mainline Protestants of the mid- to late twentieth century, the primary way of relating to the Spirit was through Sunday morning worship. The Spirit of Christ, affirmed as the energy and dynamic that draws the community together, was believed in, yet increasingly seemed absent from, the experience of worship. In congregations that were predominantly white, much worship became predictable—hymns selected from a relatively limited canon, lengthy pastoral prayers, twenty-minute sermons, lengthy Scripture readings from both Testaments, concluding with ample time for socializing at postworship "coffee hours." While there was often a strong sense of community

---

40. Jürgen Moltmann, *The Spirit of Life: A Universal Affirmation* (Minneapolis, Minn.: Fortress, 2001), 274.
41. Ibid., 98.

among those attending, an experiential relationship with the sacred Spirit of life was missing. This focus was often expressed with metaphors of directionality. Progressives were said to sense the Spirit horizontally, in community, but only weakly in the vertical dimension, where a transcendent dimension of the Spirit is experienced. Without an experiential connection to the Spirit in worship, staleness and dryness replaced joy, energy, and life-giving vitality. Those who had grown up with this form of worship often continued to attend, but as the diminishing numbers indicate, younger generations were not attracted to these staid patterns.

Concurrently, the spirituality of congregations of color in mainline denominations was a source of energy, where a living faith fed the congregants. African-American services are filled with a sense of spiritual vitality through the use of gospel music and the genre of black preaching. Korean Americans vocalize spontaneous prayers to express the joy or concerns on their hearts. Hispanics draw on their rich cultural traditions expressed in music and art to celebrate a living faith. It was many years, however, before white congregations acknowledged that their underrepresented racial and cultural sisters and brothers offered their congregants something lacking in staid white worship services. The mainline patterns of worship throughout the later twentieth century in many white congregations continued to replicate the affirmations acceptable to participants shaped largely by the rationality of the modern worldview that ignored the role of the Spirit in worship and prayer.

Progressive Protestants do affirm the presence of the Spirit in their social life as a community of faith. However, this approach often identifies the Spirit with the sense of goodwill and well-being that occurs as any community of friends and associates gathers for fellowship. It tends to lack any surplus of meaning, any sense of awe or mystery. Yet so seriously do mainline Protestants value their commitment to fellowship with one another that it has lightheartedly been noted that during Lent while Roman Catholics fast, many progressive Protestant congregations add a midweek church potluck dinner for additional fellowship! While the observation can be considered flippant, it exposes the deep commitments that mainline Protestants have to their social time together. There are a number of progressive members who would readily share their serious doubts about a tenet of faith (e.g., the meaning of the resurrection), yet would affirm the importance of gathering with others in a community that values each member and reaches out to the world with ministries of compassion and justice. Fundamentally, there is a belief that "where two or three gather in my [Jesus'] name, there am I with them" (Matthew 18:20), but in my experience this phrase is used as often to justify the importance of small gatherings as to affirm a sense of the holy between and among people.

The lack of attention to a sense of mystery and awe in progressive Protestant church life was ably demonstrated in the mid-twentieth century or high modern period by the architecture of many neighborhood churches. Progressive Protestants wanted to be engaged in ministries that would serve a variety of community needs. Churches that were built in stages as the local congregation raised funds often started with a gymnasium where children and youth from the community could play basketball or engage in other athletic activities. This multipurpose space could be transformed when it was time for worship. Communion tables were brought out of storage closets and folding chairs set up for those attending worship. There was little sense of sacred space, for once the hour of worship had concluded, the room reverted to its function as a gym. No one questioned the absence of sacred space; it was taken for granted that it was more important to serve the fellowship needs of the youth in the community than to work at creating a sense of awe or mystery in worship. The lived experience of faith for progressive Protestants centered on the joy of being together in worship, with little thought of attending to an experience of the holy that transcends the pleasures of shared community. The Spirit was not intentionally neglected; it was so far from the collective awareness that it was not even missed.

Poet Donald Davie summarizes this omission in his poem "The Comforter." He notes that the Holy Spirit is the most neglected and misunderstood member of the Holy Trinity.

> St. Patrick bound unto himself
> the Trinity, but showed his practical sainthood
> by playing down the third
> member of the Triad. No
> anxious souls would be won by
> that vaporous Holy Ghost.[42]

---

42. Donald Davie, "The Comforter," in *Collected Poems* (Chicago: University of Chicago Press, 1990), 413.

Davie's poem not only identifies St. Patrick's lack of attention to the Holy Spirit but, by so doing, also calls attention to mainline Protestant's lack of attention to the Holy Spirit. Progressive Protestants spent little time teaching about the Holy Spirit and, until the last decades of the twentieth century, even less time teaching about the spiritual life. Many progressive Protestants in the mid- and late twentieth century viewed the emerging interest in spiritual practices negatively, as a turn to popular spirituality and individual piety. The centrality of justification by faith in mainline Protestantism in the spirituality of twentieth-century progressive Protestants resulted in a rejection of any act of piety. Spiritual practices were deemed as "working" for God's grace. As such, personal devotional acts were viewed as antithetical to a concern with the social justice agenda of the church. If faith rather than merit was the basis of salvation, progressive Protestants wanted to "get on with it," not by focusing on individual acts of piety, but by putting their energy into transforming the world. For them, "Protestant spirituality" was an oxymoron.

During the passing decades of the last half of the twentieth century, however, increasing numbers of mainline church members voted with their feet. They left. Those faithful members who stuck with the church and waited for their absent children to return to the fold found that the next generation of young adults did not return. Some quit the church altogether, while others sought more vital, Spirit-filled evangelical congregations. Mainline clergy seeking spiritual renewal discovered a variety of alternatives—programs at Roman Catholic retreat centers, Buddhist meditation practices, Jungian dream work, and workshops focused on New Age spiritual practices. By the concluding decades of the twentieth century there was a sustained interest in Christian spirituality, and increasing numbers of progressive Protestants recognized that the failure to attend adequately to the spiritual life had resulted in the experience of major negative consequences for their communities of faith. I now turn to this development.

Rediscovering Protestant Spiritual Practices

As the questions and issues of high modernity succumbed to the questions and concerns of postmodernity, there was renewed interest in spirituality not only in the culture but also in progressive Protestant churches. Clergy who had turned to other traditions to discover an experiential relationship with the holy began discovering the life-giving affective practices of their own mainline traditions. Dedicated, committed people who were working for the transformation of society were burning out. Seminaries found middle-aged individuals from secular professions (e.g., social workers and community organizers) returning to school in search of spiritual practices that could address their exhaustion. These professionals had taken on society's principalities and powers and needed more than a desire to help and a naive optimism to nourish them. As they turned to religion for spiritual sustenance, they needed not only more than what traditional, predictable mainline worship offered but also theological discourse offering an approach to reality that could not be reduced without remainder to insights from the human sciences.

The waning of modernity brought with it the demise of grand narratives whose "self-legitimating theories ... sought to explain the entirety of reality ... In postmodernity, Westerners have begun to realize that science and philosophy cannot be the self-appointed arbiters of ultimate truth that they had been throughout the modern period."[43] Theology is increasingly understood as a unique language transmitted by the Christian tradition itself. Engaging spiritual practices becomes one of the ways in which this reality is experienced and understood. Postmodernity's assumptions allow a deepened interest in narrative, in "seeing the truth as dependent upon the stories one tells about reality, and living one's life as a participant in the particular story of God's action through Israel, Christ, and the church."[44]

Progressive mainline denominations have since the late twentieth century been discovering the importance of spiritual practices for nurturing a vital and faithful relationship with God. The goal of the spiritual life is expressed in the first two commandments: to love God and to love neighbor. Spiritual practices provide avenues for deepening one's relationship with the Holy Spirit. An experiential relationship with God has as its goal love of God; such love draws the believer ever closer to living a life of faithfulness. A life lived with an awareness of the Holy One as its core is increasingly shaped by moral acts. Simply stated, spiritual practices have the potential to become habits. These habits create

---

43. Diana Butler Bass and Joseph Stewart-Sicking, "Christian Spirituality in Europe and North America since 1700," *Blackwell Companion to Christian Spirituality*, 151.

44. Ibid., 152.

patterns of living that shape character, and character results in a life of faithfulness. This is true for individuals and communities. Our experiential relationship with God is the foundation for the fruits of our labors.

There are a number of indications that progressive Protestants have recognized this insight, thus ending older attitudes that bifurcated prayer and action, spiritual practices and social action. Books by mainline authors on spiritual practices both for individuals or congregations include Marjorie Thompson, *Soul Feast*; Diana Butler Bass, *The Practicing Congregation*; Dorothy Bass, *Practicing Our Faith*; Janet Parachin, *Engaged Spirituality*; my book *Protestant Spiritual Exercises*; and numerous others being read and used in congregations and seminaries.[45] Programs focused on developing faithful lives of prayer and action (e.g., the Methodists' Academies of Spiritual Formation) have over the last twenty-five years become a staple of progressive denominational life. Increasingly, progressives who were skeptical about these developments have seen their importance for maintaining the spiritual grounding needed to continue working for societal and personal transformation. The principalities and powers that corrupt through policies that maintain the privileged status of the few at the expense of the many require more than goodwill and naive optimism to be transformed. The task is a crucial aspect of a life of faithfulness.

Progressive Protestants increasingly understand the links between spiritual practices and the moral life of faithfulness. They recognize that spiritual practices have the potential to transform ministries of justice and compassion. By reclaiming a sense of the holy in the midst of daily life, mainline Protestants are rediscovering the power of prayer and spiritual practices to transform their actions. Humans have the capacity for self-transcendence in the direction of their deepest values. By allowing time for a sense of the holy to infuse daily life, they make space for the working of God's transforming love in what may otherwise seem to be mundane existence. Spiritual practices have the potential

---

45. Marjorie Thompson, *Soul Feast: An Invitation to the Christian Spiritual Life* (Louisville, Ky.: Westminster, 2005); Diana Butler Bass, *The Practicing Congregation: Imagining a New Old Church* (Herndon, Va.: Alban, 2004); Dorothy Bass, *Practicing Our Faith: A Way of Life for a Searching People*, 2nd ed. (San Francisco: Jossey-Bass, 2010); Janet W. Parachin, *Engaged Spirituality: Ten Lives of Contemplation and Action* (St. Louis, Mo.: Chalice, 1999); Joseph D. Driskill, *Protestant Spiritual Exercises: Theology, History and Practice* (Harrisburg, Pa.: Morehouse, 1999).

to help people make space within their lives to hear more than their own subconscious self-interest speaking. Some would call this listening to their better selves. Others would call it listening to the Holy One. Allowing time for quiet discernment in the midst of decision making has the potential to alter an outcome for the better.

Other active forms of spiritual practices (e.g., walking with eyes of compassion in the midst of a decaying urban neighborhood) can help one read one's context and environment in more creative and constructive ways. Prayer, contemplation, and reflection permit perspective taking. By consciously affirming a wider horizon than one sees with "normal" vision, a person is able to better discern the injustices that need addressing. By releasing the imagination, options not previously considered arise unexpectedly. Being faithful requires this attention.

In this new environment, spirituality can be understood not as a privatized act of piety but as an integrating dynamic at the very heart of the creation. An experiential relationship with the Holy Spirit not only gives, motivates, and integrates life, but it also offers the possibility for transformation, individually and collectively. Donald Davie describes this unexpected gift of the Spirit:

> Invasion is His note:
> disintegration.
> A wind from the outside corners
> of the human map;
> disorienting;
>
> His strangeness for the comfort
> of those not at home in the grid[46]

The Spirit can destabilize the structures of the status quo, turning things on their head in much the same way that the Magnificat speaks of upsetting things as they are. The high and mighty are laid low:

> "[God] has brought down rulers from their thrones
> but has lifted up the humble.
> He has filled the hungry with good things,
> but has sent set the rich away empty."
> *Luke 1:52–53*

---

46. Davie, "The Comforter," *Collected Poems*, 413.

Affirming the significance of living in the tension between that which integrates and is life giving and that which disintegrates and invites us to start anew is at the heart of faith. Progressive Protestants have from the Reformation inherited an iconoclastic stance that is quick to expose the overidentification of any vessel that mediates the Spirit with the Spirit itself. The Bible, icon, creed, liturgy, or any other object, belief, or notion that reveals the Spirit is not itself the Spirit. Jürgen Moltmann notes that when we confuse the things that point to God for God, we become not only disappointed but also fearful and angry: "The soul that is in search of God divinizes things or powers which are not God, expects too much happiness and security of them, and by doing so destroys them."[47] Progressive Protestants would contend that many of the injustices and violent acts associated with irrational religious zeal arise from the misplaced identification of human vessels with the transcendent realities to which they point. Ultimately, this results when the human capacity for devotion is not appropriately shaped and nourished.

The Enduring Elements of Progressive Mainline Spirituality

We are witnessing a number of transitions in progressive mainline communities of faith at the national, regional, and congregational levels of church life. Many of its institutional and bureaucratic structures have been and continue to be dismantled. The loss of members, dwindling economic resources, and the changed context in which these churches find themselves offer so many challenges that, lacking clairvoyant powers, one is hard-pressed to imagine how their future lived experience of faith will be embodied. While strong and vital congregations from these traditions will continue to thrive in a postmodern world, the institutional structures that shape ministries of justice and compassion beyond the local congregation are yet unknown. What's more, within the internal life of congregations that embody combinations of these various markers we will find unique spiritual expressions. Certain changes are occurring, however, that, when understood within the richness of the tradition itself, portend some characteristics that will continue to thrive

---

47. Jürgen Moltmann, *The Source of Life: The Holy Spirit and the Theology of Life* (Minneapolis, Minn.: Fortress, 1997), 78.

as progressive mainline spirituality adapts to the needs of postmodern individuals and communities.

First, the world is hungry for authentic spiritual practices that integrate rationality with spiritual devotion. The rational and the affective are not opposed to one another. Progressive Protestants have in their tradition an approach to the spiritual life that honors both mind and heart in the service of faithful action. Even though the affective and experiential have been in need of attention, we see a new emphasis beginning to happen in congregations.

Second, the global and pluralistic world that defines our context stands in acute need of ministries of justice and compassion. The enduring commitment to ministries of compassion and justice that shapes progressives' spirituality makes care for others and care of the environment chief priorities. For a number of years, however, progressive denominations were making only small gains within their own structures to bring justice to their own ethnically and culturally underrepresented members. One critique that underrepresented people direct toward traditional, white progressives' spirituality is that their commitments to justice usually avoid surrendering little of the privilege they enjoy. There is a "cause of the month" for people of privilege who have the luxury of remaining a step removed from the personal commitment needed to transform the world, especially if it involves changing their lifestyles. While I think this critique is frequently accurate, I also think that progressives stand under the judgment of their own claims and that these claims, when understood as religious commitments, offer the possibility for changing those who glimpse only dimly the self-implicating nature of what they profess and believe.

For example, the racism that pervades life in the United States was minimized and ignored by many white progressive Protestants whose racial and economic privilege resulted in their devoting more resources for international missions than for racial justice at home. While there is yet much to be done, programs that address structural racism are on the agendas of many progressive mainline congregations and denominations. When white progressives are at their best, they recognize that justice requires being willing to yield some of their economic, racial, and class privilege so that all may be treated equitably. While this commitment has yet to be tested widely, the rhetoric of progressives suggests that they are going to need to walk the walk if they talk the talk. Given the magnitude of transformation needed to overcome racism, those who are its victims and those who work to transform it are often sustained by an experiential relationship with God. Transcending the cynicism, hopelessness, and exhaustion that can accompany working for justice and peace in the world will require a grounded spirituality sustained by an actively involved community of faith.

Third, in an increasingly dangerous world where humans have the capacity to bring mass destruction, a Christian faith that is open to dialogue with other traditions is vital for human flourishing. Progressive Protestants have a tradition of profound respect for human flourishing through respecting the beliefs of those whose views differ from their own. The century of dialogue they enjoyed has given their communities of faith a predisposition to be respectful and open to the insights of others, even those who differ profoundly from them. This is not to say that mainline Protestants have avoided their own forms of prejudice toward others, including in the early and mid-twentieth century, Roman Catholics and Protestant evangelicals. However, their century of dialogue has given them tools for engaging in dialogue that can serve well in the multifaith, multiethnic context of the world. As technology and global trade make the world increasingly interconnected, voices from the world's major faith traditions calling for mutual respect and human flourishing will be necessary for world peace. Progressives generally share a "big tent" attitude toward diversity and may well contribute to the mutual respect and tolerance needed for a just sharing of the world's space and resources.

Fourth, the Christian tradition needs voices that both value and celebrate its aesthetic traditions and symbolic power. Progressives approach their own Scriptures with a hermeneutic of both suspicion and appreciation. That is, they recognize the fully human nature of the text as well as its divine invitations. The symbolic, linguistic universe of poetry, metaphor, and narrative is appreciated. The critical tools of textual criticism are engaged not to diminish holy texts but to more deeply understand the contexts in which they were produced as well as the enlightenment they can shed on meaning making in the contemporary context. Notions of textual inerrancy and interpreting the Bible literally are rejected in favor of more textually diverse ways to understand and value the recorded witness of earlier Hebrew and Christian communities of faith. This approach to texts offers members of other religious traditions a table at which they can share their insights and learn from the Christian tradition.

As we encounter those grounded in other communities of faith with their own distinct spiritualities, progressives see this as an opportunity not only to know others better but also to explore and celebrate the depths of their own spirituality. They recognize that the journey toward justice and peace for all citizens of the world is long and arduous. Everyone sees through a glass darkly. But love of God and love of neighbor give the hope, courage, and endurance to remain faithful to the path, even when the night is dark and the vision obscured.

RESPONSE TO JOSEPH DRISKILL

BRADLEY NASSIF

The strength of Joseph Driskill's presentation of mainline Protestant spirituality was memorably impressed on me this semester through the testimony of one of my students. As soon as I heard her speak, I instantly thought of his essay. A class I teach, titled Christian Spirituality, is composed of a diverse group of about thirty-five college students. Their denominational backgrounds include Evangelical Covenant, Lutheran, Roman Catholic, Independent, Baptist, charismatic, Presbyterian, and others. The topic during that memorable week focused on the role of the church in spiritual formation. To get their engines started, I asked these eighteen- to twenty-three-year-olds two provocative questions: What was church like for you during your growing-up years? How do you think your childhood experiences affected your present attitudes toward church? The young lady's answer affirmed the positive value of mainline Protestant spirituality. Here's what she said:

> I grew up in a conservative church. But during those years I felt very judged. The people talked alike and acted alike. They went to church every Sunday morning, Sunday evening, and Wednesday night. If I missed a service now and then, I felt condemned for not living up to the people's standards. I guess you might say the place was kind of legalistic. But a few years ago, I started going to a different church. The pastor there made me feel loved and welcomed. She didn't condemn me at all or make me feel like less of a Christian for my personal beliefs or church life. She just listened to what I had to say and loved me as I was, without telling me what to do or making me feel guilty for something I shouldn't have felt guilty about in the first place. The pastor and people loved and accepted me as I am. [Then sheepishly she added] Boy, if the people at my old church knew about me now, they wouldn't have a thing to do

with me! I know it's a liberal community, but to be honest, that pastor's love is what keeps me in church now.

This story illustrates what is good and right in mainline Protestant spirituality today. Always more than a progressive religious movement, mainline spirituality offers an alternative vision of the church's mission. For this woman, its mission saved her faith. At no time did the student say she had changed her conservative theology. On the contrary, she kept it but placed her spirituality in a radically new social environment of love and acceptance. Her new pastor embodied the core convictions of the social gospel—love of God and love of neighbor. These are the spiritual qualities that gave this student the hope, courage, and endurance to remain faithful to Christ even when her former conservative church obscured the greatest commandments of Jesus.

Definition and Key Emphases of Mainline Protestant Spirituality

A number of years ago, my doctoral mentor, the late Fr. John Meyendorff, impressed on me that any truly "Orthodox" approach to ecumenical dialogue must reflect the church's vision of "catholicity." This catholicity requires us to embrace all that is holy and right and good, wherever it may be found—even in a religious tradition that is almost completely at odds with the Orthodox faith. Indeed, Joe Driskill's definition of spirituality is one to which an Orthodox Christian can agree in principle: "My definition maintains that spirituality is concerned with the lived experience of faith, the communities that shape the experience, the practices that sustain it, and the moral life that embodies it."

In principle, the Orthodox tradition shares this definition of Christianity as a "lived experience of faith." We would agree that one's "lived experience" is best understood within the communities that shape and sustain it, and within the moral life it embodies. However, we have vast differences that lie not in the affirmation of a "lived experience" but in the *source and content of it*. It seems to me that the solution to our differences lies largely in the area of ecclesiology (the nature of the church). In other words, we need to ask, "What is the source of our understanding of the ecclesial community that shapes and sustains an authentic 'lived experience of faith'?" Will it come from communities whose thinking rests on the conclusions of individual Christians and

Bible scholars? Or will our communities rely on the collective experience of *historic Christianity?*" These questions seem to lie at the heart of our differing theological epistemologies.

The Role of the Church, Christ, and the Spirit in Spirituality

In the Orthodox experience, the nature of the church is experienced on the basis of Scripture and the wider tradition of the undivided church in roughly the first millennium of Christian history (before the "Great Schism" between the Roman Catholic and Orthodox communions). Following St. Irenaeus's response to the Gnostics of the second century, the Orthodox still rely on the "rule of faith" (*regula fidei*) as the community's guide to the apostolic tradition. Christian truth is inseparable from the Christian community, understood as the eucharistic gathering. Truth is known communally, not secretly or privately. This was also the point of St. Ignatius of Antioch a generation earlier than Irenaeus: "Let that be considered a valid Eucharist over which the bishop presides, or one to whom he commits it. Wherever the bishop appears, there let the people be, just as, wherever Christ Jesus is, there is the Catholic Church."[48] This is not to say that Orthodoxy naively relies on only two church fathers; Irenaeus and Ignatius are simply two representatives of Orthodox ecclesiology.

This ecclesial hermeneutic — still considered valid by the Orthodox Church — is the very principle that has kept the church united around the core teachings of the gospel over the past two thousand years. Without it, biblical interpretation turns into interpretive anarchy. Truth becomes relative. Each interpreter does what is right in their own eyes based on the quality of their scholarship and learning. Jesus' teachings about the kingdom of God can then easily be reduced to a single idea — social justice. Ultimately, this sort of reductionism changes the very nature of the church from a kingdom community gathered around the Eucharist in obedience to Christ's divine rule to a secular institution whose main mission is to create human fellowship and a just society. As a result, there is little difference between the church as a divine organism and social clubs such as the Veterans of Foreign Wars, Fraternal Order of Police, and similar groups. As Driskill pointed out, in

---

48. Ignatius, *Letter to the Smyrneans*, 8:2.

the history of progressive Protestantism, the Holy Spirit eventually gets defined as the bond of fellowship in any community of friends:

> However, this approach [by progressive Protestants] often identifies the Spirit with the sense of goodwill and well-being that occurs as any community of friends and associates gathers for fellowship. It tends to lack any surplus of meaning, any sense of awe or mystery. Yet so seriously do mainline Protestants value their commitment to fellowship with one another that it has lightheartedly been noted that during Lent while Roman Catholics fast, many progressive Protestant congregations add a midweek church potluck dinner for additional fellowship!

The Function of the Institutional Church

My concern over the secularization of the church by mainline Protestantism does not mean that Orthodox Christianity is the opposite of that. It would be unfair to say, "The church is so heavenly minded it is of no earthly good," or that the eucharistic nature of the church minimizes social justice and concern for the poor. On the contrary, the deepest aspirations of liberal Protestantism for social justice at all levels of society are, paradoxically, *fulfilled* in Orthodoxy's vision of the Eucharist. The Eucharist is, in fact, the most *social* of all sacraments. The divine aims of love and justice—so central to mainline Protestantism—are most fully carried out in the church's weekly celebration of the Eucharist.

To cite but one example from the church fathers, the teachings of St. John Chrysostom (fourth century) grounded the church's social theory in the Eucharist and shows how the quests of mainline Protestant spirituality can find their greatest fulfillment in the Christian liturgy. How so? By seeing the connection between philanthropy, the incarnation, and worship. Chrysostom's stress on Christian philanthropy is rooted in the church's liturgy, the incarnation, and the gospel's emphasis on love for others. Like many who hold to the Protestant spirituality described in Driskill's essay, John Chrysostom was convinced that people find their fulfillment by loving others. As we love and serve one another—especially the poor—we grow in the image and likeness of Christ. But it's important to realize that the context for these views is the church's liturgy. "You honor the altar at church," Chrysostom says, "because the body of Christ rests upon it. But those who are themselves the very body of Christ you treat with contempt and you remain indifferent when you see them perishing."[49] Thus the inner transformation of the individual and the outer transformation of society go hand in hand.

In light of Chrysostom's teaching and Driskill's insightful analysis of mainline Protestant spirituality, there is every reason for Orthodox Christians to cooperate with mainline Christians in doing good works where such cooperation for the good of human beings is possible (such as feeding the hungry, aiding the poor, and settling refugees). At the same time, theological integrity requires the Orthodox to speak the truth in love (Ephesians 4:15) by humbly warning against the errors of "progressive" Protestantism. Although Driskill has skillfully composed a brilliant historical narrative of the tenets of liberal Protestantism, he described it for what it actually is, namely, a religious movement that knowingly rejects the very heart of the historic Christian gospel. Its adherents self-consciously substitute a "social gospel" for the saving realities of the Trinity and the person and work of Christ confessed in sacred Scripture, the church's liturgy, and the ecumenical councils from 325 to 787. Although liberal Protestants see this as a desirable improvement over a Christianity that is rooted in an unenlightened past, Orthodoxy would view it as a digressive heresy—if not an entirely different religion (see 1 John 2:21–23).

Nothing, of course, would be more wrong than to believe that the gospel has no social relevance or is concerned only with so-called "spiritual" matters. The Orthodox have always maintained that the church can only be "the salt of the earth" and "the light of the world" if she remains true to her nature—to be the kingdom of God, to provide an experience of divine freedom and justice that goes above and beyond human sociology, and to witness to the joy of Christ's resurrection and eternal life. In that context, we are grateful for the unselfish example of progressive Protestantism, which continually reminds us to not only love God but also love our neighbor as ourselves.

---

49. John Chrysostom, *On Wealth and Poverty* (Crestwood, N.Y.: St. Vladimir's Seminary Press), 27, 33.

SCOTT HAHN

Joseph Driskill demonstrates indeed that "the progressive face of mainline Protestant spirituality" is "still here." I recognize it well and with great fondness for the people I knew in our family's Presbyterian Church (USA) community as I was growing up. I can put names and faces to all the lovely qualities that Driskill describes. My fellow Presbyterians cared about humanity, but they also took care of people. They thought globally, and they acted locally. They were good, polite, and generous neighbors and friends.

They gave our congregation a strong sense of community, which was based somewhat on shared values. If you tried to pin us down on what those values were, however, you would probably end in bafflement. We didn't talk much about doctrine, and perhaps we could not have agreed on much if we had started such a conversation. Ours was a church large enough to employ several different pastors, and they themselves represented a spectrum of belief and unbelief. One would talk up Barth and neoorthodoxy, while another openly doubted the resurrection and encouraged teens to experiment with Ouija boards.

Like most of the mainline churches in town, ours harbored a certain love of pluralism. That was a value most of our members could affirm in the abstract. Yet when we met on Sunday, we sat among a congregation that was almost entirely white, of northern European extraction, and upper middle class. And shrinking. Driskill discusses this as a current problem, but even back in the 1960s and 1970s, we were looking at six-figure membership declines in almost every denominational census. Looking back, I can identify several reasons for our diminishment.

One was elected infertility. There were fewer young Presbyterians born, though we kept dying at a constant rate. Planned Parenthood was not only a favored philanthropy of our people but also a basic principle of family life. Another factor was religious competition. Some members left when evangelical megachurches offered warmer worship, singles programs, or intensive Bible study. Other congregants left when their lives got too busy and forced them to make choices among many civic and community duties. The church was one among many—and once those commitments grew to be *too* many, something had to give. Presbyterianism claimed no privileged place over Rotary or Kiwanis in their lives.

As a church member, I was often active, but I can't say I ever felt a sense of momentum or energy—about our congregation or our denomination. No one ever spoke as if we had a ghost of a chance of growing or stanching the outward flow of members. We tried things—youth programs, adult education—and the usual folks would usually attend. But I can't recall a time when we had serious expectations that we might attract new members. There was a constant sense of resignation about the inevitability of our decline.

I got the same sense as I read Joe Driskill's essay. He established the expectation in his opening pages, describing the dying of the light in mainline Protestant denominations: "survival ... decline ... loss ... reduced ... smaller ... shadow of an earlier existence ... shrinkage." These are not terms that suggest vitality or inspire hope for the future. They are terms associated with decrepitude and obsolescence.

It pains me to say that this essay reads like the sort of draft obituaries that newspapers keep on file for long-ago celebrities who are now on life support. It pains me because I know that the impulse at the heart of mainline spirituality is a good and holy one. It is the desire to imitate God, who in his incarnation in Jesus Christ has accommodated himself to humanity. God has stooped down to accommodate our weakness and taken on our form. He has done all of this in order to lift us up and make us like himself.

The mainline denominations represent Christians' noble desire to stoop down to Western culture. They have taken on the form of Western culture. The problem is that there has been no consequent movement of elevation. Instead, the mainline denominations have simply taken up the causes of secular culture as their own. Their accommodation has ended in complete identification and capitulation.

The spirituality Driskill describes is simply what Robert Bellah called "American civil religion."[50] It is Christianity tamed by American

---

50. Robert Bellah, "Civil Religion in America," *Daedalus, Journal of the American Academy of Arts and Sciences* 96 (Winter 1967).

secular culture. How does this express itself? First of all, in disbelief. Since academic and cultural elites are uncomfortable with claims of the miraculous, the mainline accommodates their doubt, rendering optional the beliefs associated with historical Christianity. Driskill mentions, for example, the virgin birth, miraculous healings, and even the resurrection: "The resurrection is treasured" by progressive mainline Protestants "as God's vindication of Jesus' earthly life and the powerful capacity of love to overcome death. The faith of many progressive Protestants rests not first and foremost in the resurrection as an historical event but in its symbolic power."

To deny the historicity of the resurrection, however, is to empty it of all symbolic power. Very few people will give their tithe or an hour of their Sunday—never mind their life and death—for the sake of a metaphor. This should not arrive as news to anyone. St. Paul put it starkly in the first century: "If Christ has not been raised, our preaching is useless and so is your faith … If Christ has not been raised, your faith is futile; you are still in your sins … If only for life we have hope in Christ, we are of all people most to be pitied" (1 Corinthians 15:14, 17, 19). Yet if the progressive mainline is united by anything, it is by what its leaders no longer believe about historical Christianity and by what they affirm of contemporary Western (and specifically upper-class American) culture.

The mainline turns from the divine and otherworldly to the contemporary and this-worldly. It identifies with certain social concerns, and again these seem to match rather exactly the concerns of a very specific segment of American society—and even a specific political party. The mainline is concerned not so much about sin and salvation as about racism, sexism, and heterosexism.

If that is so, then it is the apotheosis of the Ivy League. Driskill is rightly proud of the mainline's long-ago achievement in establishing the Ivy League universities, though none of these schools have retained their Christian identity. I am inclined to think George Marsden was right when he said the Ivies' loss of faith foreshadowed a more general loss of faith that would come to afflict the American Protestant establishment.

And while we should admire the progressive mainline's desire to serve the underprivileged, it is abundantly clear that the underprivileged have taken no great interest in the "faith" of the mainline. While the liberationists have been opting for the poor, the poor have been opting for evangelicalism, Pentecostalism, and Catholicism.

People want transcendence, but the progressive mainline cannot seem to transcend the assumptions of its own elite, white, American neighborhoods. Thus, it finds God's Spirit at work, not in miracles and sacraments, but in "democratic processes," "councils," "boards," "bylaws," and "guidelines." The metaphors for church that come most readily to Driskill are not those of Christ's "body" or God's "family," but rather of the "marketplace" and "local government."

Most people want their markets to look and feel like markets. They want their government to look and feel like a government. Those who want a religion want a religion that can transcend, judge, and transform their markets, legislatures, and indeed all the things of culture and society. As G. K. Chesterton put it, "We do not want, as the newspapers say, a church that will move with the world. We want a church that will move the world."[51]

"If Christ has not been raised," it's hard to see how progressive mainline spirituality can ever be more interesting, relevant, or inspiring than actual direct participation in local government or civic philanthropic clubs.

---

51. Quoted in Maisie Ward, *Gilbert Keith Chesterton* (Lanham, Md.: Rowman and Littlefield, 2006), 398.

RESPONSE TO JOSEPH DRISKILL

EVAN HOWARD

It is a pleasure to respond to Joe Driskill's essay. Driskill has been a pioneer in the recovery of Protestant spiritual practices for some time now. Through his own recovery of Protestant spirituality, he has become the right man at the right time, drawing from the springs of the Protestant tradition to quench many mainline Protestants who were thirsty for just such waters. I found his essay to exhibit the very character he desires to promote in his ministry—"an integrated and transforming spirituality which informs and is informed by faith, justice, and compassion."[52]

As evangelicalism has for the past two centuries identified itself particularly in dialogue with—and at times in opposition to—progressive elements in Protestantism, my responses reflect the history of conversation between these two streams. I will use the terms *mainline* and *progressive* somewhat interchangeably. I will use *mainline* to draw attention to the denominations and to the overall ecclesial tradition identified by Driskill in his introduction, and *progressive* to point to the perspective held by many mainline Protestants.

My responses also reflect my own long history of dialogue between the progressive and evangelical streams of Protestantism. I was raised in a mainline Protestant church and attended a college of that denomination during one of its more progressive seasons. My training at a conservative evangelical seminary was particularly sensitive to issues dividing progressive and evangelical Protestants. My doctoral studies were completed in a progressive academic milieu (both Protestant and Roman Catholic). I have felt my share of animosity for—and, to be honest, animosity from—the "liberals." More recently, I have enjoyed nearly a decade of teaching spirituality periodically at a mainline Protestant

---

52. Quote from Joe Driskill on his bio page at Pacific School of Religion's website, www. psr.edu/joseph-d-driskill (accessed October 20, 2011).

seminary. Though as an evangelical my approach to relationship with God differs from a progressive approach in both foundation and style, I am grateful for what I have received from — and grateful that I have been warmly received by — representatives of mainline Protestantism.

Driskill's essay does not consider the spiritualities that are emerging out of recent developments within mainline Protestantism (such as postliberalism and radical orthodoxy). Limitations of space prevent my discussion of these schools of thought.

Key Emphases

Driskill identifies three "salient features" of mainline spirituality that are not directly related to the core issues listed in the introduction in this book: (1) ecumenical cooperation, (2) biblical interpretation and scholarly inquiry, and (3) sense of God.

As Driskill points out, mainline Protestants have maintained a solid commitment to *ecumenical cooperation*. He identifies the formation of the Federal Council of Churches in 1908 as a starting point for this cooperation. As my own essay suggests, however, the roots of Protestant cooperation go much deeper in evangelical history. Even in the mid-twentieth century, while mainline denominations were establishing formal alliances, many conservative evangelicals — perceiving themselves to be marginalized by "the liberals" — were establishing their own set of alliances. Ironically, ecumenical cooperation was pursued by both progressives and evangelicals, at times in opposition to one another. The important point for our purposes in this volume — various views of *spirituality* — is that these different alliances shaped Christian identity and in so doing channeled the energies out of which the Christian life was lived.

The importance of the *Bible* has been mentioned by all of the contributors to this volume. Of course the Bible is the sacred text of the Christian faith and as such is central to the spirituality of all Christians. Driskill has put his finger on a critical point, however, when he titles his section "Biblical *Interpretation* and Scholarly Inquiry" (italics added). Interpretation is a key question, and it is not simply a matter of theological debate but also a matter of lived spirituality. Orthodox and Roman Catholic writers tend to emphasize interpretations affirmed through hierarchical process. Anabaptists tend to emphasize the gathered local community as the primary interpretive context. Evangelicals tend to emphasize the ability of the ordinary individual believer to receive from the text. As Driskill mentions, progressive Protestantism emphasizes the role of scholarly inquiry in biblical interpretation. My suspicion is that the Reformation simply raised the important question of biblical interpretation, a question that remains unresolved. Yet no matter how we may imagine the hermeneutical functions of tradition, reason, and experience, what is most important for the evangelical is the *authority* of Scripture. Evangelicals read and meditate on Scripture, listen to expository preaching, sing Scripture songs, and open their Bibles when they need guidance because they find, in this book, God's authoritative word. This is a matter on which evangelicals differ from progressives — a matter that is debated in theological classrooms but is also visible in the rank and file of congregations.

Driskill also addresses the important issue of our *view of God*. Just as Nassif and Hahn acknowledge the importance of a Trinitarian perspective for their respective spiritualities, so Driskill, rightly, I believe, acknowledges the importance of the progressive view of God for mainline spirituality. He documents important changes in the mainline view of God, changes that have brought with them a new sense of the immediacy of the presence of God. Contrary to the earlier semi-Deist variety of mainline Christians, evangelicals consider God to be actively present in their lives. And whereas contemporary, more spiritual progressives might embrace a Spirit who is experienced, who is everywhere present, and who leaves more in history to human intervention, evangelicals tend to pray to a God who is personal, distinctive, and sovereign. Nevertheless, though we may understand the foundations of this intimacy differently, both evangelical and contemporary progressive Protestants share a sense of the importance of this intimacy.

The Role of Jesus and the Holy Spirit

The role of Jesus, along with our views of Scripture, has perhaps been the most significant dividing point between evangelicals and mainline Protestants over the past century. Evangelicals, along with the Roman Catholic and Orthodox traditions, have been insistent about affirming the Christological claims acknowledged in the early creeds, believing these creeds to be a faithful summary of the teachings of Holy Scripture —

the deity of Christ, the virgin birth, and the historical resurrection. In addition, we have emphasized the substitutionary function of Christ's work and the historicity of the miracles of Jesus. These are all traditional Christian claims with which progressive Protestants have struggled to one degree or another. They are important enough matters that, when some Protestant liberals at times plainly denied them, many evangelicals felt obliged to suggest that they had left the Christian faith. We evangelicals have at times been so focused on the historical resurrection that we have forgotten its symbolic power. At the same time, some evangelicals would say that some progressives lost the foundations of the symbolic power of the resurrection when they denied its historical nature.

Our lived spirituality often reflects how we navigate these issues. I like the way Driskill puts it. Who is Jesus? For the progressive Protestant, Jesus has often been a moral example, "making people more loving through the transforming power of his example." For the evangelical, Jesus has been the justifying Savior. For the Orthodox, Jesus has been the deifying Lord. Hahn describes the Catholic Jesus as a reconciling Son. We read our Bibles differently, pray differently, choose our callings differently, examine ourselves at the end of the day differently, when one or the other of these different "Jesuses" is in our mind. And each of these Jesuses emerges from the theological reflections of one of our theological ancestors — Athanasius, Anselm, Abelard, Scotus, and others. It is a blessed thing to enlarge our experience of Jesus by exploring the Jesus of another theologian or tradition. It is an unfortunate thing to truncate our experience of Jesus by denying, for example, that Jesus could be a justifying Savior. I am convinced that the Christian Scriptures — and even our own traditions at their best — confess a Jesus whose life and work encompasses infinitely more than we can comprehend.

Driskill suggests that for mainline Protestants of the mid- to late twentieth century, the Spirit of Christ was believed in, yet played only a minimal role in the lived experience of their communities of faith. My experience concurs. The charismatic movement of the 1960s and 70s affected this experience in some communities. Nevertheless, what one saw most commonly in the context of the mainline tradition has been, as Driskill describes, an identification of the Spirit with the sense of goodwill in the community. Indeed, this was one of my points of criticism against "liberal" churches in my youth: they were just social clubs.

And yet there has been a great deal of change between the semi-deism of early twentieth-century mainline Protestantism and the Spirit-conscious mainline Protestantism of today. Although there are important (though subtle) differences between some progressive understandings of Spirit and some evangelical understandings of the Holy Spirit, one need only read a sample of the influential works of mainline Protestant Marcus Borg or the early chapters of Driskill's own *Protestant Spiritual Exercises* to see how the Spirit has found an increasing place in mainline spirituality. I suspect that once again, whether consciously or not, we are learning from each other.

The Goal or Endgame of Spirituality

I noticed two places where Driskill speaks directly of the "goal" or "endgame" of spirituality. In his narration of the life and thought of Walter Rauchenbusch, which introduces his section "The Social Gospel, Justice, and Social Action," Driskill summarizes the gospel demands Rauchenbusch discovered as follows: "The kingdom of God required repentance for social sins. The endgame for believers required spreading the gospel of Jesus by living a Christlike life of mutual love and cooperation." The endgame of spirituality is the kingdom of God, a world in which people live out Christ's values of love and cooperation both personally and corporately. Later, in his treatment of the recovery of Protestant spiritual practices, Driskill links the pursuit of these practices with the goal of spirituality. He states, "The goal of the spiritual life is expressed in the first two commandments: to love God and to love neighbor." He then describes how spiritual practices foster the fulfillment of particularly the first of these commandments.

What I gather from Driskill's presentation is that mainline Christians uphold, as their goal of spirituality, both love of God and love of neighbor. Their strength has been the practice of living out the latter, particularly with regard to issues of justice and social action. Their weakness—the experiential dimension of love for God—is currently being addressed in part through a recovery of spiritual practice. Evangelicals also affirm this dual goal of loving God and neighbor. Our strength, however, has been our experiential relationship with God, while our weakness has been the love of neighbor, especially in areas of social justice. But this has not always been the case. The connection between revivalism and social reform is well documented. And just as mainline Christians are recovering their own spiritual practices, so evangelicals are recovering our own sense of social conscience.

As I see it, the challenge for both evangelicals and progressives as we seek to embody and to encourage the reign of God is to develop the right blend of conviction and humility. We are both rightly convinced that our faith demands not only personal piety but also social responsibility. Yet drawing the appropriate connections among biblical theology, social strategy, and political policy is not always easy. At times, we associate a particular political agenda with kingdom justice or biblical values without a careful hearing of our sisters and brothers. Spirituality and social justice both require a politics of humble care.

We have seen a number of goals presented in this volume — deification, perfection, holiness, sanctification, kingdom of God, love of God and neighbor. I applaud them all! My suspicion is that each goal is interconnected with the others such that our ability to receive from one another in humility is necessary for the fulfillment of any.

The Church and Religious Authority

Driskill describes mainline Christianity as struggling with authority. "Mainline Protestants share a deep distrust of entrenched authority structures," he states. He describes them as having an "iconoclastic stance that is quick to expose the overidentification of any vessel that mediates the Spirit with the Spirit itself." Driskill's list of vessels includes "Bible, icon, creed, liturgy, or any other object, belief, or notion." I think he would find it fair to include "institution" in this list as well. Evangelicals, like mainline Protestants, have inherited something of this character from our Reformation heritage. We know from church history — and from Bradley Nassif's essay — that it was the iconodules, rather than the iconoclasts, who won the day in the Second Council of Nicea (787). The iconoclasts were condemned as heretics. Are Protestants, therefore, in danger of heresy? My answer in brief is that it is one thing to believe that God can and does mediate the Spirit through material form and human creations, and to respect that mediation through the use of these material forms and human creations in our personal and corporate spirituality. It is quite another to trust that any *particular* material form or human creation *necessarily and normatively* mediates the Spirit of God.

Yet while evangelical Protestants might share caution with mainline Protestants regarding icons, liturgies, objects, and institutions, evangelicals are more willing to trust traditional statements of belief (Baptist distinctives, Reformed confessions, and so on) and historic creeds as recognized summaries of the teachings of the Bible. And here we are back to the issues of biblical interpretation and authority treated above.

Means, Disciplines, Regimens

Little needs to be said in response to Driskill's treatment of spiritual practices. Mainline Protestants, like evangelicals, are in the process of exploring spiritual practices that emerge from within—and are appropriate to—our respective traditions. Driskill does a fine job of showing how spiritual practices fit within an overall understanding of the nature and goal of spiritual life. For a treatment of the practices themselves, however, one must turn to his *Protestant Spiritual Exercises*, a wonderful introduction to practices that "either emerge from the Protestant tradition or are consonant with it."[53]

Finally, I want to affirm Driskill's suggestion that the Spirit works both to stabilize and to destabilize, and that our practices must foster both dimensions. Sometimes we are the "mainline" church or the moral "majority" that has voice to speak to the powers. At other times we feel like an oppressed minority in the midst of a sea of "secularism" or "fundamentalism." Evangelicalism has been keenly aware, in our opposition to the state religions of Europe and in our critiques of the mainline middle-class Protestantism of mid-twentieth-century America, of the ease with which the church drifts away from true religion when it possesses political power. May we all learn to discern our own level of influence in the larger world in an attitude (and in the spirit) of Christian care.

---

53. Joe Driskill, *Protestant Spiritual Exercises* (Harrisburg, Pa: Morehouse, 1999), 79.

EVANGELICAL SPIRITUALITY

EVAN HOWARD

Come, ye sinners, poor and needy,
Weak and wounded, sick and sore;
Jesus ready stands to save you,
Full of pity, love, and power.

Come, ye thirsty, come and welcome,
God's free bounty glorify;
True belief and true repentance;
Every grace that brings you nigh.

Chorus
I will arise and go to Jesus,
He will embrace me in His arms;
In the arms of my dear Savior,
O there are ten thousand charms.

These lines from the well-known hymn by Joseph Hart (1712–1768) invite us into the world of evangelical spirituality. Hart's journey of faith reached a turning point under the ministry of evangelist George Whitefield (1714–1770) in 1757, but not until he had passed through seasons of religious pride, libertine behavior, and paralyzing doubt of his salvation. He navigated what he later called the "two dangerous gulfs" of dead sloth and pharisaic pride into possession of "true belief and true repentance," an intimate relationship with Jesus, who stands ready to save and in whose arms are "ten thousand charms."[1]

---

1. On Joseph Hart, see Thomas Wright, *Joseph Hart* (London: Farncombe, 1910), www.ebooksread.com/authors-eng/thomas-wright/joseph-hart-ala/page-4-joseph-hart-ala.shtml (accessed November 4, 2010).

Evangelical spirituality focuses, subjectively, on the "with-God" life in all of its lived dimensions. It concerns the manner by which we live in communion with Christ in response to the Spirit in pursuit of holiness resulting in service to others. Objectively, Christian spirituality is that academic discipline that explores this "with-God" life. As a student and representative of evangelical spirituality, I purpose to share something of the ways in which evangelicalism distinctively approaches the "with-God" life, or vital spiritual relationship with God.

This brings us to the question of just what is an evangelical, a much-debated question.[2] Nevertheless, a consensus seems to be emerging for defining evangelicalism. This consensus sees evangelicalism as an historical religious movement characterized by a number of salient features. The evangelical movement has roots in the Protestant Reformation—and more so in the Puritan and Pietist movements—but emerges as a single transatlantic movement most clearly with the Awakenings of the early eighteenth century. Evangelicalism then expands in the nineteenth century to a place of dominance in the English-speaking world, only to experience disruptions, reorganization, and a global diffusion in the twentieth century.

David Bebbington suggests that the centrality of Scripture, the cross, conversion, and active ministry (biblicism, crucicentrism, conversionism, activism) are the characteristic marks of evangelicalism.[3] More recently, Timothy Larsen has expanded the Bebbington quadrilateral into a pentagon, identifying orthodox Protestantism, association with a network of revival movements, Scripture, the atoning work of Jesus Christ, and the converting and empowering work of the Holy Spirit as the chief marks of evangelicalism.[4] Scholars are careful to balance the

---

2. Samples of this discussion include Bernard L. Ramm, *The Evangelical Heritage* (Waco, Tex.: Word, 1973), 89; Donald W. Dayton, *Discovering an Evangelical Heritage* (New York: Harper, 1976); Timothy R. Phillips and Dennis L. Okholm, *Welcome to the Family: An Introduction to Evangelical Christianity* (Wheaton, Ill: BridgePoint, 1996); Stanley J. Grenz, *Renewing the Center: Evangelical Theology in a Post-Theological Era*, 2nd ed. (Grand Rapids: Baker, 2006).

3. D. W. Bebbington, *Evangelicalism in Modern Britain: A History from the 1730s to the 1980s* (Grand Rapids: Baker, 1992); see also the multivolume History of Evangelicalism series published by InterVarsity Press (2003–).

4. Timothy Larsen, "Defining and Locating Evangelicalism," in *The Cambridge Companion to Evangelical Theology*, ed. Timothy Larsen and Daniel J. Trier (Cambridge: Cambridge University Press, 2007), 1–3.

unity with the diversity of evangelicalism, using terms like *mosaic* or *kaleidoscope* to describe this movement.[5]

Similarly, in this essay I will first explore various marks of evangelicalism as these illumine evangelicals' approach to relationship with God. Following this, I will consider the means and institutions through which evangelical relationship with God is experienced. Some of the core issues of Christian spirituality (key emphases, spiritual formation, role of Christ and the Spirit, goals or endgame) will be addressed within my discussion of the marks of evangelical spirituality, while other issues (means and disciplines, institutional church) will be treated in the second part of this essay.

Evangelical devotional manuals, sermon collections, treatises, tracts, magazine articles, autobiographies, memoirs, diaries, and letters are, as John Wolffe observed, a "rich and as yet little studied material."[6] Even the studies mentioned above, while locating evangelicalism as an ecclesial movement, are incomplete as descriptions of the lived spirituality of evangelicalism.[7] Consequently, I will also address evangelical *lay orientation* and *bounded ecumenicity*—valuable lenses through which to view evangelical spirituality. My hope is that this essay will stimulate a lively exploration of the spirituality of the evangelical tradition; my grief is that space permits only cursory treatment and illustrative documentation of the treasures to be mined.

Characteristic Marks of Evangelical Spirituality
Evangelical Spirituality Is Protestant

The formative roots of evangelical spirituality are in the Protestant Reformation, a definitive break with the Roman Catholicism of the

---

5. See Timothy L. Smith, "The Postfundamentalist Party," *Christian Century* (February 4, 1976), 125–27; "The Evangelical Kaleidoscope and the Call to Christian Unity," *Christian Scholar's Review* 15 (1986): 125–41.

6. John Wolffe, *The Expansion of Evangelicalism: The Age of Wilberforce, More, Chalmers and Finney* (A History of Evangelicalism; Downers Grove, Ill.: InterVarsity, 2007), 96.

7. For samples of research in evangelical spirituality, see James M. Gordon, *Evangelical Spirituality: From the Wesleys to John Stott* (London: SPCK Press, 1991); D. Bruce Hindmarsh, *The Evangelical Conversion Narrative: Spiritual Autobiography in Early Modern England* (Oxford: Oxford University Press, 2005); Richard F. Lovelace, "Evangelical Spirituality: A Church Historian's Perspective," *Journal of the Evangelical Theological Society* 31.1 (1988): 25–35; Ian M. Randall, "'Live Much under the Shadow of the Cross': Atonement and Evangelical Spirituality," in *The Atonement Debate*, ed. Derek Tidball, David Hilborn, and Justin Thacker (Grand Rapids: Zondervan, 2008), 293–310.

sixteenth century. The "Protest"-ants saw cause to distance themselves not just from the corruption of the Roman church or from doctrinal particulars; there were spiritual issues as well. The Protestants broke with the scholasticism of Catholic theology, the hierarchy of Catholic ecclesiology, the mechanics of late medieval spirituality, and the basic structure of late medieval Catholic ascetic and mystical consciousness.[8] The Ten Articles published in 1536 by Thomas Cranmer, serving as the first guidelines of the Church of England when it separated from Rome, specifically condemned Roman practice of the sacrament of penance, inappropriate use of images in devotion, and the invocation of saints, along with other rites and observances. Eighteenth-century Puritans and Pietists carried the memories of the Reformation as they sharply distinguished themselves from the "popery" they associated with the menacing French monarchy. Mid-nineteenth-century evangelicals in England distanced themselves from the Anglo-Catholic Tractarian Movement that sought to reintroduce Roman practices and perspectives, as did late nineteenth-century American evangelicals in light of rising Catholic immigration.[9] Though tensions have softened in the last half century, "Protestant" has been part of the self-image of evangelicalism, whether or not evangelicals understood the changing Catholicism that confronted them. Moreover, this Protestant identity has shaped the spirituality of evangelicals. We have been quick to affirm a spirituality of home and work and slower to affirm the specifically "religious" calling. We have been cautious about hierarchical authority structures and ready to permit a wide range of disconnected groups and meetings. In both obvious and subtle ways, evangelicalism has been shaped by its Protestant roots.

---

8. See my "What Did the Protestants Protest? Reflections on the Context of Reformation Spirituality as a 'Break' with Roman Catholicism," www.evangelicalspirituality.org/papers/otherpapers/protprot (accessed November 4, 2010).

9. See, e.g., Mark A. Noll, *The Rise of Evangelicalism: The Age of Edwards, Whitefield, and the Wesleys* (A History of Evangelicalism; Downers Grove, Ill.: InterVarsity, 2003), 143; John Wolffe, "The Evangelical Alliance in the 1840s: An Attempt to Institutionalize Christian Unity," in *Voluntary Religion*, ed. W. J. Sheils and Diana Wood (Oxford: Blackwell, 1986), 335–40; D. W. Bebbington, *The Dominance of Evangelicalism: The Age of Spurgeon and Moody* (A History of Evangelicalism; Downers Grove, Ill.: InterVarsity, 2005), 154–61. For more recent developments, see Donald W. Sweeting, "Changing American Evangelical Attitudes towards Roman Catholics: 1960–2000," *Southern Baptist Journal of Theology* 5.4 (2001): 20–34; William M. Shea, "Modernity as a Stimulus of Reconciliation between American Evangelicals and Catholics," *Horizons* 31.1 (2004): 150–59.

Evangelical Spirituality Is Orthodox

I refer, by the term *orthodox*, not to the historic tradition associated with Eastern Christianity (evangelical Christianity had little contact with the Eastern Church until the late nineteenth and twentieth centuries), but to the commitment of evangelicals to basic historic (Nicene) Christian belief. Evangelicalism has distinguished itself not only from Roman Catholicism but also from forms of Christianity that appeared to compromise the deity of Christ, the virgin birth, original sin, the bodily resurrection of Christ, the substitutionary function of Christ's atonement, and the authority of Scripture. Evangelicals—in contrast to Deists—believe in a God who intervened in history and is able to intervene in lives here and now. Evangelicals believe in the bodily resurrection of Christ and in a final restoration of the physical earth and human body, a belief that shapes our hope and the way we navigate our relationship with God in light of that blessed hope. Evangelicals are also grounded in Scripture. As we will see below, evangelical devotion is steeped in Scripture. Many evangelicals have composed biblical and theological treatises, as well as edifying spiritual literature as needed, though from the mid-nineteenth century forward, conflicts with modernism increasingly demanded the particular attention of some to the defense of Scripture and orthodox doctrine, while rising interest in the Holy Spirit, holiness, and victorious living drew the attention of others. The interests of both orthodox doctrine and spiritual life were intentionally combined in the landmark evangelical multivolume work *The Fundamentals*, published between 1910 and 1915. The integration of orthodox doctrine and spirituality was further explored as twentieth-century Asian evangelicals (such as Sadhu Sundar Singh, Watchman Nee, and Toyohiko Kagawa) sought to understand and express their relationship with God in a non-Western environment.

Basic to its orthodoxy is the fact that evangelical spirituality is about the *euangelion*, the evangel, the gospel, of Jesus Christ. The person and work of Jesus is replete in evangelical writings. Puritan divine Isaac Ambrose (1604–1664) wrote a popular meditation manual titled *Looking Unto Jesus*, which guided the reader through a practice of meditating on the birth, life, death, and return of Christ. Or consider, for example, this excerpt from the letters of Samuel Rutherford (c. 1600–1661), a Scottish Presbyterian divine imprisoned at the time of his writing:

Some have written to me, that I am possibly too joyful of the cross; but my joy overleapeth the cross, it is bounded and terminated upon Christ. I know that the sun will overcloud and eclipse, and that I shall again be put to walk in the shadow: but Christ must be welcome to come and go, as He thinketh meet. Yet He would be more welcome to me, I trow, to come, than to go. And I hope He pitieth and pardoneth me, in casting apples to me at such a fainting time as this. Holy and blessed is His name! It was not my flattering of Christ that drew a kiss from His mouth. But He would send me as a spy into this wilderness of suffering, to see the land and try the ford; and I cannot make a lie of Christ's cross. I can report nothing but good both of Him and it, lest others should faint.[10]

Similarly Charles Trumbull (1872–1941), editor of the *Sunday School Times* and prominent speaker at Keswick conferences promoting a higher Christian life, describes his own Christ-centered spirituality:

I had always known that Christ was my Savior; but I had looked upon Him as an external Savior, one who did a saving work *for* me from outside, as it were; ... But now I knew something better than that. At last I realized that Jesus Christ was actually and literally within me; and even more than that, He had made Himself my very life, taking me into union with Himself—my body, mind, and spirit—while I still had my own identity and free will and full moral responsibility.[11]

Some of the fiercest debates within nineteenth-century evangelicalism dealt with the character and extent of Christ's atonement. Evangelical prayer is directed particularly to Jesus. Evangelical spirituality ultimately is obtained *through* Christ and *into* Christ.

---

10. Andrew A. Rutherford and Samuel Bonar, eds., *Letters of Samuel Rutherford: With a Sketch of His Life and Biographical Notices of His Correspondents by the Rev. Andrew A. Bonar, D.D.* (Edinburgh: Banner of Truth, 1984), 239–40.

11. Charles Trumbull, *Victory in Christ* (1959; repr., Fort Washington, Pa.: CLC Publications, 2007), 34.

Evangelical Spirituality Is Lived Conversion

If Protestantism and orthodoxy—and even the emphases on Scripture and Christ—were the only characteristics of evangelical spirituality, there would be little to separate it from the Lutheran or Reformed orthodoxy of the late sixteenth and early seventeenth centuries. Yet there is more—this *more* being the feature that distinguishes evangelical spirituality from other forms of Protestant spirituality. Evangelicalism comprehends relationship with God in terms of "conversion": a radical turning to Christ and transformation by the Spirit of God. Jonathan Edwards called Christian conversion "a divine and supernatural light" wherein the Spirit of God awakens a sense of the excellency of God in the convert. John Wesley spoke of the new birth as a "great work which God does *in us*, renewing our fallen nature." No matter how it is described, conversion is arguably the most significant element in evangelical spirituality, for through authentic conversion, religion— *true religion*—is found and maintained.

Evangelical emphasis on conversion cannot be understood apart from a sympathetic grasp of the socioreligious context of its development. Post-Reformation links between state and church, along with the effects of doctrinal and political "individuation" of European countries, had created a society in which nearly everyone was baptized (therefore "Christian") and wherein religious self-understanding and citizenship rights were attached to profession of faith (Lutheran, Anglican, Reformed, Roman Catholic, or, in colonial Massachusetts, Congregationalist). Needless to say, residential location, doctrinal profession, and baptismal documentation did not necessarily result in transformed individuals or societies. Ecclesiastical officials would communicate smug confidence in their salvation while living nominally religious or even dissolute lives. Ordinary Protestant citizens would assume their salvation was mediated through baptism, justification, and perfunctory observance. Others, longing for immediate experience of the Spirit, would join with "enthusiasts" whose faithfulness to Scripture was often less than orthodox. Baptism, profession of faith, spiritual experience, and moral behavior—were these guarantees, or even sure signs, of authentic relationship with God? Or could they be stumbling blocks to real Christianity? Just what was *true religion*?

Anabaptist leader Menno Simons (1496–1561) sensed this issue when he proclaimed in 1536 the need for a "spiritual resurrection" from sin and death to a new life and a change of heart. Johann Arndt (1555–1621) also responded to this concern as he penned his defense of true Christianity, which "does not consist in words or in mere learning, but in a living, loving, gracious, powerful consolation in which through grace one tastes the sweetness, joyousness, loveliness, and graciousness of God in his heart." Jonathan Edwards introduced his monumental *Treatise Concerning Religious Affections* (1748) with the importance of establishing "wherein true religion does consist." John Wesley made "real Christianity" an important theme of his ministry and writings. The influential work *A Practical View* (first published in 1797), written by British politician and writer William Wilberforce, compared the "prevailing religious system" to "real Christianity." More recently, Anglican clergyman John R. W. Stott has contrasted inadequate understandings of faith with what he calls "basic Christianity."[12]

Examples of this theme in evangelical writings are ubiquitous. Scottish theologian Henry Scougal (1650–1678) addressed the question of true religion with exceptional clarity in his oft-reprinted *The Life of God in the Soul of Man*, which was influential in the conversion of George Whitefield. Scougal began his treatise with a discussion of common "mistakes about religion": placing religion in "orthodox notions and opinions," in "external duties," or yet "in the affections, in rapturous heats and ecstatic devotion." All these have a "resemblance of piety and at the best are but means of obtaining it, or particular exercises of it." "But certainly religion is quite another thing," proclaimed Scougal. True religion is "a union of the soul with God, a real participation of the divine nature, the very image of God drawn upon the soul; or, in the Apostle's phrase, *it is Christ formed within us*. Briefly, I know not how the nature of religion can be more fully expressed, than by calling

---

12. See Menno Simons, *The Complete Writings of Menno Simons: c. 1496–1561*, ed. J. C. Wenger (1956; repr., Scottdale, Pa.: Herald, 1984), 53–62; Johann Arndt, *True Christianity*, ed. Peter C. Erb (The Classics of Western Spirituality; New York: Paulist, 1979), 69; Jonathan Edwards, *Religious Affections*, ed. John E. Smith (The Works of Jonathan Edwards; New Haven: Yale University Press, 1959), 2:89; Kenneth J. Collins, *The Scripture Way of Salvation: The Heart of John Wesley's Theology* (Nashville: Abingdon, 1997), 148–52; William Wilberforce, *A Practical View of the Prevailing Religious System in the Higher and Middle Classes of Society, Contrasted with Real Christianity* (1797; repr., Eugene, Ore.: Wipf and Stock, 2003); John R. W. Stott, *Basic Christianity*, 2nd ed. (Downers Grove, Ill.: InterVarsity, 1971), 7–9.

it *a divine life.*[13] What this means is that evangelicalism is essentially mystical; to use the words of D. Bruce Hindmarsh, evangelicalism "is, above all, *a form of spirituality.*"[14]

Which brings us back to conversion, for conversion is the mechanism through which union with God is established and maintained. The unconverted have no union with God. They are lost—lost in vanities, wantonness, heresy, or nominal religiosity. Conversion, for the evangelical, is the entrance into life with God. While many have understood evangelical conversion to refer simply to a brief moment of decision or experience, study of the history of evangelicalism uncovers a much greater diversity and subtlety. The goals or endgame of evangelical spirituality are the components of conversion to Christ. Conversion involves our *justification* by faith, our reception of what Christ has done *for* us. It also involves our *regeneration* by the Holy Spirit, our experience of the work of Christ *in* us. Conversion effects a mystical *union* with God, a joining of God *with* us, which is not the fruit of purgation and illumination but rather the ontological and existential condition for the possibility of this fruit (and of an ever greater experience of union). Authentic conversion additionally plants the seeds of both *assurance* and *sanctification*, grounding our relationship with God in confidence and inclining that relationship toward maturity. Conversion is completed in *glorification.*[15]

Each of these components was a matter of intense controversy within evangelicalism as Calvinists debated Arminians, revivalists simplified Puritans, Methodists questioned Moravians, holiness Christians

---

13. Henry Scougal, *The Life of God in the Soul of Man* (Boston: Nichols and Noyes, 1868), 4–7.

14. D. Bruce Hindmarsh, "Contours of Evangelical Spirituality," in *Dictionary of Christian Spirituality*, ed. Glen G. Scorgie (Grand Rapids: Zondervan, 2010), 147.

15. The wealth of literature regarding these components can be explored by connecting keywords (e.g., sanctif*, regenerat*, justif* and so on) to primary figures of evangelicalism. A few interesting examples of such literature are Floyd T. Cunningham, "'Justification by Faith': Richard Baxter's Influence Upon John Wesley," *Asbury Journal* 64.1 (2009): 55–66; Joel R. Beeke, *The Quest for Full Assurance: The Legacy of Calvin and His Successors* (Edinburgh: Banner of Truth, 1999); Melvin E. Dieter, "The Development of Nineteenth-Century Holiness Theology," *Wesleyan Theological Journal* 20.1 (1985): 61–77. See also the indices of the InterVarsity Press's A History of Evangelicalism series; George M. Marsden, *Fundamentalism and American Culture: The Shaping of Twentieth-Century Evangelicalism, 1870–1925* (New York: Oxford University Press, 1980); Joel A. Carpenter, *Revive Us Again: The Reawakening of American Fundamentalism* (New York: Oxford University Press, 1997).

argued with Pentecostal Christians, and postmillennial and premillennial evangelicals crossed swords. What is striking is the evangelical consensus regarding the basic character and importance of conversion, given the widely different sociopolitical contexts wherein conversion was experienced, the various functions it served within evangelical communities, the range of procedures or experiences considered normative for conversion, and the diversity of doctrinal frameworks involved. Again, to use the words of Hindmarsh, "the heated debates that evangelicals had about conversion bore witness to the importance of the experience in their lives."[16]

Mention should be made here of the role of the Holy Spirit in evangelical spirituality. In an 1844 report regarding American religion, Scottish clergyman Robert Baird observed, "I know of no one idea that has been so dominant in American churches for the last hundred years as that of the office and work of the Holy Spirit."[17] Nor did the importance of the Holy Spirit diminish in the decades which followed. Indeed, Presbyterian pastor and author Arthur T. Pierson, in a 1900 account of the "forward movements of the last half century," wrote that "of all the important spiritual movements of the half century not one compares in importance with the revival of interest in the person, functions, and offices, the in-working and out-working of the Spirit of God."[18] And all this before Azusa Street, the charismatic movement, and the Third Wave!

Evangelical interest in the work of the Spirit emerged from Anabaptist and Puritan roots, roots that flowered in the context of the Great Awakening of the eighteenth century. Yet the flowers of interest in the Holy Spirit's work in believers — and in matters of Christian maturity

---

16. Hindmarsh, *Evangelical Conversion Narrative*, 325. See also Anthony N. S. Lane, "Conversion: A Comparison of Calvin and Spener," *Themelios* 13.1 (1987): 19–21; Jerald C. Brauer, "Conversion: From Puritanism to Revivalism," *The Journal of Religion* 58.3 (1978): 227–43; David Laurence, "Jonathan Edwards, Solomon Stoddard, and the Preparationist Model of Conversion," *Harvard Theological Review* 72 (1979): 267–83; Bebbington, *Dominance of Evangelicalism*, 31–36; Carpenter, *Revive Us Again*, 76–80.

17. Quoted in Bruce M. Stephens, "Changing Conceptions of the Holy Spirit in American Protestant Theology from Jonathan Edwards to Charles G. Finney," *Saint Luke's Journal of Theology* 33.3 (1990): 209.

18. Arthur T. Pierson, *Forward Movements of the Last Half Century* (New York: Funk and Wagnalls, 1900), 137.

more generally—withered a little in some early nineteenth-century evangelical circles as initial conversion took center stage.

In a letter dated January 30, 1839, published in the new periodical *The Oberlin Evangelist*, Charles Finney looked back on his earlier single-minded emphasis on converting sinners and confessed that he had "overlooked in a great measure the fact that converts would not make one step of progress" without being guided into "sanctification and growth in grace."[19]

Charles Hambrick-Stowe, in his Finney biography, quoted the evangelist's description of the significant change he had undergone in his understanding of the role(s) of Christ in spirituality:

"I found that I knew comparatively little about Christ ... What I did know of Christ was almost exclusively as an atoning and justifying Savior. But as a JESUS to save men from sin, or as a sanctifying Savior, I knew very little about Him." Charles Finney came to know this sanctifying Jesus. He recorded in his *Memoirs*, "After a season of great searching of heart [God] brought me, as he has often done, into a large place, and gave me much of that divine sweetness of soul of which President Edwards speaks as an experience of his own soul. That winter I had a thorough breaking up, so much so that sometimes for a considerable period I could not refrain from loud weeping in view of my own sins and of the love of God in Christ.[20]

This transformation also stimulated a development in Finney's sense of the role(s) of the Holy Spirit in spirituality. On August 14 of the same year, he published a lecture in *The Oberlin Evangelist* titled "The Holy Spirit of Promise," specifically identifying the Abrahamic promise to the Gentiles with the Holy Spirit received through faith as "Parakletos, Comforter, Guide, Instructor." Finney was concerned that many Christians, including himself, had not received this promised Holy Spirit either through ignorance or unbelief.[21] Finney's interest in

---

19. Henry Cowles and Asa Mahan, *The Oberlin Evangelist*, vol. 1 (Oberlin, Ohio: R. E. Gillett, 1839), 25.

20. Charles E. Hambrick-Stowe, *Charles G. Finney and the Spirit of American Evangelicalism* (Library of Religious Biography; Grand Rapids: Eerdmans, 1996), 183.

21. See "Professor Finney's Lectures, Lecture XIV: The Holy Spirit of Promise," www.gospeltruth.net/1839OE/390814_hs_of_promise.htm (accessed November 11, 2010).

sanctification and the baptism of the Holy Spirit became central to his thought and ministry from this point on.

In 1843, Methodist Phoebe Palmer published *The Way of Holiness*, an inspirational account of her own entrance into sanctification. Palmer's influential little book was quite sensitive to the workings of the Spirit.

In 1858, Presbyterian minister William E. Boardman (1810–1886) published *The Higher Christian Life*, which drew together even more closely the themes of holiness, faith, the Holy Spirit, and power. He wrote, "Faith in the power and presence of Jesus as the risen Saviour with us and within us by the Holy Spirit, to emancipate us from the bondage of sin, and guide us into all truth and righteousness, is the means by which freedom is obtained, and the soul made to walk at liberty in abiding unison with the sweet will of God."[22] From these beginnings emerge the Holiness, the Higher Christian Life, and the Pentecostal movements.[23]

By the first quarter of the twentieth century, every sort of evangelical was involved in a lively discussion — and exploration — of the role(s) of the Holy Spirit, a valuable exploration that was short-circuited by the modernist controversies and the First World War, only to reemerge tentatively with the charismatic movement and, more significantly for evangelicals, with the "Third Wave" movement since 1980.[24]

Evangelical Spirituality Is Active

Historian Mark Noll writes, "To be evangelical inevitably meant a great stress on conversion, but from the start it also meant a great interest in

---

22. William E. Boardman, *The Higher Christian Life* (Boston: Hoyt, 1871), 94.

23. See Melvin E. Dieter, *The Holiness Revival of the Nineteenth Century*, 2nd ed. (Studies in Evangelicalism; Lanham, Md.: Scarecrow, 1996); D. W. Bebbington, *Holiness in Nineteenth-Century England* (Carlisle: Paternoster, 2000); Steven Barabas, *So Great Salvation: The History and Message of the Keswick Convention* (1952; repr., Eugene, Ore.: Wipf & Stock, 2005); Vinson Synan, *The Holiness-Pentecostal Tradition: Charismatic Movements in the Twentieth Century* (Grand Rapids: Eerdmans, 1977); Ian M. Randall, "Old Time Power: Relationships between Pentecostalism and Evangelical Spirituality in England," *Pneuma* 19.1 (1997): 53–80.

24. See C. Peter Wagner, *The Third Wave of the Holy Spirit: Encountering the Power of Signs and Wonders Today* (Ann Arbor, Mich.: Servant, 1988); Gordon D. Fee, "On Getting the Spirit Back into Spirituality," in *Life in the Spirit: Spiritual Formation in Theological Perspective*, ed. George Kalantzis and Jeffrey P. Greenman (Downers Grove: InterVarsity, 2010), 36–44.

what the converted should be doing."[25] True, there have been examples of evangelical contemplatives: Isaac Ambrose, who spent a month each year in private retreat; Jonathan Edwards, who spent thirteen hours a day in his study; E. M. Bounds (1835–1913), who devoted the first three hours of each morning (4:00 a.m. to 7:00 a.m.) to fervent prayer. Nevertheless, evangelicals (with Jesuits, Deists, and many Orthodox bishops) have, for the most part, lived out their relationship with God through action. Martin Luther emphasized the sanctity of ordinary vocations in life. Puritans identified a spectrum of "duties" to God and others through which spirituality was embodied. Anglicans and Moravians pursued cross-cultural missionary enterprises. The American and Foreign Anti-Slavery Society crusaded for the end of slavery. Evangelicals pursued urban planning and economic collectives as ways of embodying Christian values. Drinking establishments were closed and soup kitchens opened as evangelicals acted out their compassionate concerns.

Although the expressions of evangelicalism's active spirituality varied, the essential character remained the same. A few illustrations must suffice. The original title of Boston pastor Cotton Mather's popular *Essays to Do Good* (1710) was as follows: "Bonifacius: An Essay upon the Good that is to be devised and designed, by those who desire to answer the Great end of Life, and to Do Good while they live. A Book offered, first, in general, unto all Christians, in a Personal Capacity, or in a Relative: Then more particularly unto Magistrates, Ministers, Physicians, Lawyers, School-masters, Gentlemen, Officers, Churches, and unto all Societies of a religious character and intention: with humble Proposals of unexceptionable methods to *Do Good* in the world."

Mather's pattern of self-examination in the mornings was to propose a different question each day of the week:

> "*Sabbath morning.* What shall I do, as a pastor of a church, for the good of the flock under my charge?
> *Monday.* What shall I do in my family, and for the good of it? . . .
> *Thursday.* What good may I do in the several societies to which I belong?

---

25. Noll, *Rise of Evangelicalism*, 234.

Friday. What special subjects of affliction, and objects of compassion, may I take under my personal care, and what shall I do for them?"[26]

Mather saw himself, *as a Christian*, in the context of a network of relational spheres, each with its own particular virtues, responsibilities, and demands. Christian spirituality meant, at least in part, "doing good" within one's various spheres of life. Nor was Mather's approach unique. Richard Allestree's *The Whole Duty of Man* (1657), Henry Venn's *The Complete Duty of Man* (1763), and other manuals addressed the ordinary Christian's desire to serve God in the particulars of their circumstances, to transform ordinary vocations into "religious life."

Evangelical action was also an expression of compassionate mission. Pietist university teacher August Herman Francke (1663–1727), for example, found himself faced with the needs of uneducated, poor, and unbelieving children. It was the custom in the town of Halle for the poor to go from door to door begging for alms on a given day of the week. After a season of distributing bread in this manner, Francke decided to invite a few beggars in and attempted to give them some education along with their alms. Then he gave money for the weekly school tuition but discovered that the funds seldom made it to school. "I felt deeply the needs of these poor creatures who came every week to my house to get their customary alms," Francke reminisced. Eventually he started a little school in his house, supported by money collected in a box near his office at the university. The school grew, and he was forced to secure a meeting space. Then he began receiving orphans and finding them housing, and then building new housing. In the end, Francke developed the largest orphanage of his time. He saw this work as an experiment of faith, trusting God to provide the financial support for the ministry. Indeed, Francke titled the story of this orphanage "The Most Blessed Footsteps of the Living and Reigning, the Loving and Faithful God for the Shaming of the Unbelieving, and the Strengthening of the Believing, Disclosed through the True and Circumstantial History of the Orphan House in Halle."[27] George Whitefield — and

---

26. Cotton Mather, *Essays to Do Good* (Dover: Stevens, 1826), 4–5.
27. August Hermann Francke, *Faith's Work Perfected: Or Francke's Orphan House at Halle*, trans. William L. Gage (New York: Randolph, 1867).

later the evangelist George Müller (1805–1898)—followed Francke's example, founding orphanages in the American colonies and England. The orphanage work of Amy Carmichael (1867–1951) in India displayed a similar combination of compassion and mission.

One of the most distinctive activities of evangelical Christianity has been evangelism, although this has not always been the case. Many seventeenth-century Christians saw conversion as a slower process. Solomon Stoddard (1643–1729), grandfather of Jonathan Edwards and pastor of the church at Northampton, Massachusetts, prior to his grandson's installation published a little guide for young ministers and such to assist them in helping others through the dynamics of the conversion process. Stoddard's book is not a manual of evangelistic technique but rather a nuanced introduction to Puritan spiritual direction.[28]

Everything changed, however, with the outpouring of the Spirit in the Great Awakening during the first half of the eighteenth century. Jonathan Edwards himself, narrating events in Northampton and the surrounding region, describes how "a great and earnest concern about the great things of religion became universal in all parts of the town, and among persons of all degrees and all ages ... Other discourse than of the things of religion would be scarcely tolerated in any company ... And the work of conversion was carried on in a most astonishing manner, and increased more and more; souls did as it were come by flocks to Jesus Christ."[29]

The Great Awakening brought with it both a loosening of expectations regarding conversion and a new interest in the gatherings where conversion was often secured. The United States in particular was founded on religious freedom and equal "competition" between churches for members, presenting Americans with a unique context for the development of evangelical activity.

These factors led to a lively discussion regarding the techniques used in evangelistic ministry. Nineteenth-century revivalists such as Charles Finney employed a variety of "new measures" for the winning of souls,

---

28. Solomon Stoddard, *A Guide to Christ: Or the Way of Directing Souls That Are under the Work of Conversion* (Princeton, N.J.: William D'Hart, 1827).

29. Jonathan Edwards, "A Faithful Narrative of the Surprising Work of God in the Conversion of Many Hundred Souls ...," in *The Great Awakening*, ed. C. C. Goen (The Works of Jonathan Edwards; New Haven: Yale University Press, 1972), 4:149–50.

including organized prayer, youth ministry, use of the "anxious bench," and the efforts of laypersons within their own social circles, just as John Wesley and George Whitefield had pioneered open-air preaching and class meetings in the eighteenth century. Concern with modernist social agendas, de-emphasis of religious duties or "means of grace," and pre-millennial expectations all combined in the early twentieth century to create an environment in which appropriate evangelical activity often became singularly identified with evangelism. Hence, while fundamentalist culture, for example, was "fleeing the world," it was also winning the world to Christ through radio broadcasts, small groups, Bible colleges, independent church plants, and person-to-person communication.[30]

Evangelical Spirituality Is Lay Oriented

Having addressed Bebbington's four primary marks of evangelicalism (biblicism, crucicentrism, conversionism, and activism), it is appropriate to briefly touch on a couple of other features that illumine the character of evangelical spirituality. The first is evangelicalism's lay orientation. The priesthood of all believers was a foundational doctrine of the Protestant Reformation, a doctrine that was applied more thoroughly by Luther's associate Andreas Karlstadt (1486–1541) and later Anabaptist movements. This place of lay leadership was also central both ecclesiastically and politically during the Reformation in the British Isles.[31] The Bible was translated into the vernacular, and worship was organized through a Book of *Common* Prayer. Hymns and catechisms were composed with the laity in mind. Pietist "conventicles" (small Bible study groups) and Puritan "prophesying" meetings (sermon and dialogue gatherings) permitted even greater lay involvement. With the Awakenings of the eighteenth century, evangelical religion was not only designed *for* the laity but also was led *by* the laity. Through the nineteenth and into the twentieth century, the hymns, journals, and guidebooks of evangelical spirituality were increasingly

---

30. For a sensitive presentation of these dynamics, see Carpenter, *Revive Us Again.*

31. See Calvin Augustine Pater, *Karlstadt as the Father of the Baptist Movements: The Emergence of Lay Protestantism* (Toronto: University of Toronto Press, 1984); W. J. Torrance Kirby, "Lay Supremacy: Reform of the Canon Law of England from Henry VIII to Elizabeth I (1529–1571)," *Reformation and Renaissance Review: Journal of the Society for Reformation Studies* 8.3 (2006): 349–70.

the products of lay initiative. Furthermore, if we consider not merely "texts" but also societies, initiatives, and actions as evidence of evangelical spirituality, we see laity even more clearly not only as beneficiaries but also as primary shapers of the forms of lived relationship with God.

In this sense, evangelicalism may be best interpreted less as an ecclesiastical tradition or institution and more as a loosely connected movement of popular spirituality, much as scholars have explored networks of apocalyptic interest, informal religious community, and modern devotion in the thirteenth and fourteenth centuries. Evangelical spirituality, like many popular religious movements, exhibits both a strength (breadth) and a weakness (depth). It is dangerous indeed to reduce the gospel to "four spiritual laws." Yet when these four laws provide millions of people appropriate entrance into relationship with God, this weakness becomes a strength.

A critic of popular evangelical hymn writer Fanny Crosby described—with tongue in cheek—her well-known "Blessed Assurance" as follows:

> The music is ... easily remembered even by a backward member of the Jukes family after one hearing. It has a syrupy quality about it, with the added advantage that it lends itself to loud and raucous congregational singing—a combination which is difficult to come by in a hymn and hard to beat for purposes of public worship. Belted out by a church-full of enthusiastic Christians, with everyone unleashing a few extra decibels on the refrain, it will lift even the most stolid clod in the congregation out of his grubby, materialistic, unimaginative, uninspiring, everyday concerns and transport him to the Elysian fields of spiritual bliss.[32]

Bernard Ruffin, Crosby's biographer, makes an appropriate response to this critic:

> Although the author ridicules the tune, he is nevertheless right about its purpose. The tune served to furnish a musical setting for the words so simple that even the most backward and unmusical

---

32. Quoted in Bernard Ruffin, *Fanny Crosby* (Philadelphia: United Church Press, 1976), 155–56.

could readily remember it ... Even in her own day, Fanny's hymns were criticized as being substandard as poetry as well as music, but this did not trouble her for she was writing not for the critics but for common people.[33]

Evangelical Spirituality Strives for Bounded Ecumenicity

In his article on evangelicalism, Timothy Larsen speaks specifically of "the global Christian networks arising from the eighteenth-century revival movements associated with John Wesley and George White-field."[34] In this sense, ecumenical "networks" are part of the essential character of evangelicalism. True religion is not the preserve of a particular tradition or sect. When George Whitefield was attacked in Boston for his associations with Presbyterians, Baptists, and Methodists, he responded, "It was best to preach the new birth, and the power of godliness, and not to insist so much on the form: for people would never be brought to one mind as to that; nor did Jesus Christ ever intend it."[35] Whitefield's comments well summarize evangelical sentiment toward ecumenical relations.

Evangelical networks are the product of a lengthy history. Indeed, the revival networks mentioned by Larsen were preceded by a "religious refugee network" wherein Anabaptists, Nonconformists, and other undesirables found themselves traveling from Strasbourg to England to Scotland to the Netherlands and around again, sharing perspectives, experiences, and ideas. This religious refugee network was further preceded by a "Reformers network" wherein Bucer, Calvin, Knox, Melanchthon, and others found themselves guests in Geneva, Wittenberg, portions of England, and other welcome locations. Cotton Mather carried on a significant correspondence with August Herman Francke. John Wesley visited Nikolaus Ludwig Zinzendorf in Germany and Zinzendorf visited Gilbert Tennent in New Jersey.

British devotional classics inspired the evangelicals of the American Great Awakening, just as Edwards's narrative of the events at Northampton inspired revivalists in Scotland and England. By 1747, mutual inter-

---

33. Ibid., 156.
34. Larsen, "Defining and Locating Evangelicalism," 1.
35. Quoted in Noll, *Rise of Evangelicalism*, 15.

est united Christians from the English-speaking world twice weekly to intercede on behalf of the revival of religion. Camp meetings drew attendees from every denomination. A wide range of volunteer societies joined evangelicals of various stripes around common causes. Thus, "in its final phase, between 1837 and 1844, the Second Great Awakening came closer than at any earlier date to becoming a genuinely international movement across the English-speaking world."[36] In 1846, the Evangelical Alliance was established in London, formally uniting evangelicals in common agreement. Bible, mission, millennial, and Keswick (a form of holiness teaching) conferences linked evangelicals from both sides of the Atlantic in study and action. Ecumenical union experienced something of a disruption from around 1927 to 1943, but with the creation of the National Association of Evangelicals in 1943, a new period of evangelical agreement began.

It would, however, be amiss to give the impression that evangelical unity is all about formal organizations and meetings. Quite the contrary, evangelical ecumenicity is rooted more in an intuitive spirituality. Evangelical Christians often bond with kindred spirits more significantly than they do with formal associations. When evangelicals move from town to town, their interest is not in finding a congregation of the same denomination they were part of in their previous location but rather in identifying communities where "real Christians" gather: those who exhibit authentic conversion, orthodox faith, and a living relationship with Jesus through the Holy Spirit.

Many other features of evangelical spirituality could be explored. We could trace the theme of surrender from Lutheran faith and Anabaptist *Gelassenheit* through Holiness altar prayers to Keswick surrender. We could explore the "victorious life" from Anglican William Law through Puritan, Methodist, and Higher Christian Life expressions. We could explore the distinctions between Puritans who expected more, Lutherans who expected less, and Methodists who divided these up into different groups. Nonetheless, what is presented here supplies at least a taste of the primary features of evangelical spirituality as it developed through the centuries.

---

36. Wolffe, *Expansion of Evangelicalism*, 87.

The Institutions and Practices of Evangelical Spirituality

A few questions remain to be addressed. One regards the role and function of the institutional church in spirituality. Another is the question of the means, disciplines, or regimens by which spirituality is achieved. Although a few hints have been suggested thus far, it is fitting to address these issues more directly. And perhaps there is a third question that needs further treatment: the relation of spirituality to spiritual formation. My treatment of formation will serve as a transition between the other two questions.

The Institutions of Evangelical Spirituality

This question is better understood by speaking of the *functions* of the institutional church in evangelical *spiritualities*, for as we have seen, evangelicalism is a network of Christians associated with a wide diversity of liturgical and institutional forms and divergent ecclesiologies. Evangelical Anglicans wrote devotional manuals assisting the churchgoer to prepare for regular Eucharist. The wild camp meetings of the southern United States had origins in the Presbyterian practice of making their periodic celebrations of Communion a special affair.[37] Others viewed the Lord's Supper as a simple remembrance of Christ's death. Some evangelicals believe in a baptismal regeneration that is realized in personal conversion. Others see infant baptism as a means by which a child joins the covenant community. Still other evangelicals treat baptism as an insignificant addendum to the real work of spiritual transformation. Anglican congregations are informed by archbishops, while independent fundamentalists are *independent*. Some evangelicals are tightly connected with their local congregation, experiencing the institutional church as a lifeline to God. Others are only loosely tied to a local congregation, finding their primary ties in Bible studies, fellowship groups, or voluntary societies disconnected from their local congregation. It is simply impossible to speak of "the evangelical" approach to ecclesial spirituality.

Furthermore, evangelical identity and spirituality have often been comprehended in terms of a nested set of institutions. First, there was

---

37. See ibid., 56–59.

the closet, the life one lived in solitude with God. Second, there was the family, with its own set of responsibilities and devotional practices. Next, there was one's local congregation, and with it a number of gatherings. And finally there was the town, with its days of prayer and its duties of propriety. Alongside town life were the various societies with which one might associate. Many devotional manuals of the seventeenth through the nineteenth centuries were written with this structure in mind.[38] Consequently, the institutional church functioned in the context of a wide spectrum of vital relationships. As we will see, Sabbath keeping was an important practice of many evangelicals even into the twentieth century. Sabbath celebration linked both congregational life (sermon, fellowship, sacrament, song, public prayers) and private reflection (Bible reading, self-examination, closet prayer) to create a virtual weekly retreat.

Finally, the functions of the institutional church within evangelical spirituality must be understood in terms of evangelicalism's view of the invisible church. Taking hints from Augustine (and later from Wycliffe), Ulrich Zwingli, John Calvin, and others distinguished "the catholic or universal church which is invisible" and which "consists of the whole number of the elect" from "the visible church," which "consists of all those throughout the world that profess true religion." Christ entrusts this visible church, also catholic and universal, with ministry, proclamation, and ordinances or sacraments "for the gathering and perfecting of the saints ... and doth by his own presence and Spirit, according to his promise, make them effectual thereunto." This catholic church, both visible and invisible, was further distinguished from "particular churches" which are "more or less pure."[39] These distinctions shaped the spirituality of evangelicalism throughout its history. They formed the context around which church membership requirements in early New England churches were discussed. They were used to correct those who neglected congregational participation. Ultimately, they formed a foundation for evangelicalism's bounded ecumenicity. The

---

38. See, e.g., Charles E. Hambrick-Stowe, *The Practice of Piety: Puritan Devotional Disciplines in Seventeenth-Century New England* (Chapel Hill: University of North Carolina Press, 1982), 91–193.

39. See the Westminster Confession of Faith, chapter XXV. The term *catholic* here refers not to the Roman Catholic Church but to the universal Christian body.

church—visible and particular, though not identified with any given institution—is the body of Christ, the family of God, and the home within which spiritual formation was fostered.[40]

Spirituality and Spiritual Formation

Although evangelicalism did not speak explicitly of *spiritual formation*, the goal of increasing conformity to Christ in heart and life (described as piety, godliness, sanctification, holiness, perfection, and such) was central to evangelical spirituality. As Whitefield's summary of the gospel message cited above affirms, the chief themes of evangelical spirituality were "the new birth and the power of godliness." Later, similar aims were promoted as "the victorious Christian life." Whatever the terms used, evangelicals sought to be formed into Christ.

Yet while evangelicals were essentially united in their affirmation of the basic task of spiritual formation, they differed widely in their understanding of the primary aims, agents, and means of spiritual formation.[41] Is sinless perfection possible, or even a reasonable aim of the Christian walk? Is maturity about a purity of love as defined in the intention of the will toward God underneath human activity, or is it a general conformity of behavior with the law of God or Christ? What is the relationship between process and crisis in Christian spiritual formation? Is the ordinary ministerial office of itself a divinely appointed agent of grace, or are there serious dangers involved in association with an unconverted ministry? What is the relationship between the Spirit's role and our role in sanctification? Are sacraments, spiritual disciplines, and such appropriate means of grace, or are they mere "works" through which we bolster our egos and further separate ourselves from God? These are some of the questions that have haunted—and still haunt—evangelicals.[42] As can be imagined, a host of biblical issues surround

---

40. See, e.g., Baird Tipson, "Invisible Saints: The 'Judgment of Charity' in the Early New England Churches," *Church History* 44.4 (1975): 460–71; G. S. Barrett, "The Visible Church," *The Puritan: an illustrated magazine for free churchmen*, vols. 1–2 (February-December 1899), 867–69.

41. On these categories, see Evan B. Howard, *The Brazos Introduction to Christian Spirituality* (Grand Rapids: Brazos, 2008), 267–97.

42. Some of these questions are addressed from the perspective of the evangelical doctrine of sanctification in Stanley N. Gundry, ed., *Five Views on Sanctification* (Grand Rapids: Zondervan, 1987). The five contributors are Melvin E. Dieter, Anthony A. Hoekema, Stanley M. Horton, J. Robertson McQuilkin, and John F. Walvoord.

issues such as the nature of Paul's "old man," the function of the Sermon on the Mount, the meaning of "baptism in the Holy Spirit," and many others. How do evangelicals understand the relationship between spirituality and spiritual formation? For some, like Hannah Whitall Smith (1832–1911), Keswick speaker and author of the popular *Christian's Secret of a Happy Life*, the divine life is not an "attainment" but an "obtainment." Keswick spirituality resembled an "evangelical quietism" wherein agents and means of grace play a minimal role in light of the centrality of interior surrender. For evangelical Anglican bishop J. C. Ryle (1816–1900), a contemporary of Smith and author of *Holiness* and *Practical Religion*, this approach was of grave concern.

The Practices of Evangelical Spirituality

This brings us to a discussion of the means, disciplines, or regimens of evangelical spirituality. Obviously, there is no single way of addressing this issue. For some in the late nineteenth and early twentieth centuries, surrender of self was *the* means of grace. Many fundamentalists of the twentieth century appeared to communicate that it wasn't the "dos" but the "don'ts" that characterized one's practice (a kind of evangelical discipline of abstinence). One feature of evangelicalism since 1970 has been the happy discovery of a number of spiritual disciplines from nonevangelical traditions. Nonetheless, whether consciously acknowledged as such or not, evangelicals have nourished and expressed their relationship with God through a number of practices characteristic of the evangelical tradition.[43]

1. Reading, Studying, and Meditating on Scripture

Bible study is *the* discipline of evangelical Protestantism. Pietist conventicles were designed especially for lay exploration of Scripture. Puritan diaries document their intense study of and meditation on sacred text. John Wesley encouraged Methodists to examine their practice of searching the Scriptures:

---

43. Lists of these practices can be found in John Wesley's accounts of the "instituted" and "prudential" means of grace, in Lewis Bayly's outline of the practice of piety, and in other manuals of the eighteenth and nineteenth centuries. On the use of early Puritan classics in later evangelical devotion, see Charles Hambrick-Stowe, "The Spirit of the Old Writers: The Great Awakening and the Persistence of Puritan Piety," in *Puritanism: Transatlantic Perspectives on a Seventeenth-Century Anglo-American Faith*, ed. Francis J. Bremer (Boston: Massachusetts Historical Society, 1993), 277–91.

Searching the Scriptures by, (i) Reading: Constantly, some part of every day; regularly, all the Bible in order; carefully, with the Notes; seriously, with prayer before and after; fruitfully, immediately practicing what you learn there? (ii) Meditating: At set times? by any rule? (iii) Hearing: Every morning? carefully; with prayer before, at, after; immediately putting in practice? Have you a New Testament always about you?[44]

British evangelical Edward Bickersteth published in 1812 a much-reprinted guide titled *Scripture Help* in which he takes pains to equip his readers "to study constantly, with fervent prayer, the Sacred Volume itself."[45] Similarly, Princeton theologian Charles Hodge (1797–1878) proclaimed the following:

> We cannot make progress in holiness unless we devote much time to the reading, hearing, meditating upon the word of God, which is the truth whereby we are sanctified. The more this truth is brought before the mind; the more we commune with it, entering into its import, applying it to our own case, appropriating its principles, appreciating its motives, rejoicing in its promises, trembling at its threatenings, rising by its influence from what is seen and temporal to what is unseen and eternal; the more we may expect to be transformed by the renewing of our mind so as to approve and love whatever is holy, just, and good.[46]

Many other examples could be given. One can recognize in the above quotations the well-known elements of reading, meditating, praying, and contemplating (and obeying). Perhaps it is time we acknowledge the *lectio divina evangelica* that pervades evangelical literature.[47]

---

44. John Wesley, "Minutes of Several Conversations between the Rev. Mr. Wesley and Others, from the Year 1744 to 1789," in *The Works of John Wesley* (Peabody, Mass.: Hendrickson, 1984), 8:323.

45. Edward Bickersteth, *Scripture Help: Designed to Assist in Reading the Bible Profitably*, 21st ed. (1812; repr., London: Seeleys, 1852), iii-iv.

46. Charles Hodge, *The Way of Life* (Philadelphia: American Sunday School Union, 1841), 376–77.

47. See Evan B. Howard, "'*Lectio divina*' in the Evangelical Tradition," *Journal of Spiritual Formation and Soul Care* (Spring 2012, forthcoming).

2. Preaching, Hearing, and Reading Sermons

Martin Luther avowed that "one thing and one only is necessary for Christian life, righteousness, and freedom. That one thing is the most holy Word of God, the gospel of Christ." He concluded that "to preach Christ means to feed the soul, to make it righteous, to set it free, and to save it, provided it believes the preaching."[48] From this point on, preaching became a central means of grace for Protestant—and particularly for evangelical—Christians. George Whitefield preached to crowds of ten thousand. Methodist itinerant Francis Asbury (1745–1816) traveled on horseback over five thousand miles a year, preaching virtually every day. At times, significant movements of God were accompanied by changes in the practice of preaching. The discipline of hearing sermons was explicitly developed by evangelicals in manuals of spiritual life, describing how to prepare, to listen, and to respond. The art of preaching sermons was similarly developed, with guides to the composition of sermons appearing throughout evangelical history.[49] With the advent of publishing, the practice of reading sermons became a popular discipline, and many evangelical devotional classics were (and are today) edited collections of sermons.

3. Family Worship

Another discipline that has been strong in the evangelical tradition is that of family devotions. Once again, from the time of Luther's Small Catechism (written for the instruction of children), Protestants—and particularly evangelical Protestants—have emphasized the importance of family worship. Puritan classics such as Benjamin Jenks's *Prayers and Offices for Children* and James Janeway's *A Token for Children* were popular in later evangelical awakenings. Many revivals (e.g., the Great Awakening in Northampton and the Welsh revival of 1904) were stimulated by God's work among young people. This fact was not lost among those who wished to foster the spread of God's kingdom. One cannot read accounts of revivals without hearing about the rekindling of family

---

48. Martin Luther, *On Christian Liberty*, ed. Harold Grimm (1520; repr., Minneapolis: Fortress, 2003), 5, 7.

49. See, e.g., Charles Simeon, *Evangelical Preaching* (Classics of Faith and Devotion; Portland, Ore.: Multnomah, 1986); Charles H. Spurgeon, *Lectures to My Students* (Grand Rapids: Zondervan, 1954).

devotions as a consequence of the work of God. Edward Bickersteth, author of *Scripture Help*, also published a guide to family devotions in 1842. Evangelical guides to family devotions continue to be published, although the discipline is often neglected in contemporary practice.[50]

4. Song

It is odd that song is not more often identified as an intentional spiritual discipline, especially among evangelicals. In the late medieval Roman church, music was primarily the preserve of those who led the service of worship or the monks who sang in choirs. As Protestants made worship available in the vernacular, song became an important part of their worship. Luther himself wrote music for worship. The first book published in the New World was the *Bay Psalm Book*, printed within twenty years of the pilgrims' landing at Plymouth in 1620. Evangelical Isaac Watts (1674–1748) pioneered hymn writing in England, composing over seven hundred hymns. Charles Wesley published thousands of hymns, and John Wesley's *Collection of Psalms and Hymns* was the first "hymnbook" published in the United States (1739). Presbyterian leader Philip Doddridge (1702–1751) wrote more than four hundred hymns, as well as publishing *The Rise and Progress of Religion in the Soul*—a work that was to prove influential in the conversion of William Wilberforce. Camp songs and revival tunes provided a common language that united evangelicals from various denominational streams in the midst of mass meetings and global awakenings such as the prayer meeting revival of 1857–58. We have already heard about hymn writer Fanny Crosby, composer of over nine thousand hymns, who often wrote for Dwight L. Moody's revival meetings. Then there is the phenomenal impact of African-American music.

More recently, we can simply recall the impact of the Maranatha Scripture songs, Vineyard Music, and the phenomenon of Contemporary Christian Music. Cynthia Pearl Maus said it well: "The songs of a people keep alive their spiritual aspirations ... They furnish the atmosphere and wings by which mortals can, for a little time at least,

---

50. For a discussion of Puritan family life, see Edmund F. Morgan, *The Puritan Family: Religion and Domestic Relations in Seventeenth-Century New England* (New York: Harper and Row, 1966). For an example of a contemporary evangelical guide, see Rosalind Rinker, *How to Have Family Prayers* (Grand Rapids: Zondervan, 1977).

get almost free of matter, and rise as on wings to the realm of pure beauty.... Thus by the aid of music they may be lifted ... nearer to God."[51]

5. Intercessory Prayer

Whereas other Christian traditions have modeled fixed-hour prayer, the Jesus Prayer, or the simple deist prayer of thanksgiving, evangelicals have specialized in intercessory prayer. Martin Luther's treatment of prayer, offered to his barber, welcomes a simple petitionary approach to prayer. As mentioned earlier, August Herman Francke's orphanage was an experiment in intercessory prayer. The move of God in the Herrnhut community (1727) gave birth to a hundred-year-long 24/7 prayer session and a vast missionary movement. Evangelicals on both sides of the Atlantic in 1747 joined for an ecumenical concert of intercessory prayer for the outpouring of the Spirit of God—a call that was renewed in the worldwide revival prayer movement of the twentieth century. Prayer meetings have been a fixture of evangelical spiritual life, and manuals were written to instruct leaders how to conduct these meetings. Andrew Murray, E. M. Bounds, Thomas Payne, and Rees Howells all taught and modeled intercessory prayer. While not neglecting mystical intimacy with God,[52] evangelical spirituality is characterized by its confidence to pursue God for saving intervention in human life.

The above are only a few samples of the practices of evangelical spirituality. Space does not permit discussion of small groups, revivals, testimony, Sabbath keeping, journal writing, and more. Nevertheless, from this presentation one can begin to get a feel for the rich heritage of evangelical spiritual practice—a wealth that has only begun to be explored.

---

51. Quoted in Melva Wilson Costen, "African-American Liturgical Music in a Global Context," *Journal of the Interdenominational Theological Center* 27.1–2 (2000): 66; see also D. Bruce Hindmarsh, "End of Faith as Its Beginning: Models of Spiritual Progress in Early Evangelical Devotional Hymns," *Spiritus: A Journal of Christian Spirituality* 10.1 (2010): 1–21.

52. Treatises like William Dyer's (1632–1696), which discussed the happiness of drawing near to God (*The Strait Way to Heaven*), and Thomas Gouge's (1605–1681), which provided insights into walking with God throughout the day (*Christian Directions: Shewing How to Walk with God All the Day Long*), as well as William Law's *The Spirit of Prayer*, were standard fare. A collection such as *The Christian's Companion in Solitude* (Glasgow, 1827) brought together evangelical mystical writings into a single, edifying volume.

Conclusion

Some claim that since 1943 evangelicalism has once again come into its own after decades of cultural retreat and shallow moralism.[53] If so, one component of evangelical vibrancy—especially since 1978—has been the explosion of interest in spirituality. Yet, if such is the case, this evangelical "coming into its own" has also involved an appreciative coming into sympathetic appreciation for the spirituality of nonevangelical traditions. The renewal of the Roman Catholic community initiated by the Second Vatican Council fed an already active recovery of the various charisms, schools, and movements of Roman Catholic spirituality. This in turn nourished a hunger among evangelicals for spiritual intimacy and intentional Christian practice. Catholic recovery and evangelical hunger were further served by the exile of Orthodox spiritual masters from Russia to the West, who brought with them spices from the East. More recently still, in the wake of postliberalism, emerging/emergent Christianity, and other trends, evangelicals and progressive Protestants are eyeing one another with interest. An historic dialogue is building within the exploration of Christian spirituality—one that will shape the future of true religion.[54]

Evangelicals have much to receive from engaging in such conversations at a time when we are ready to receive. Meanwhile, the world of evangelical spirituality has much to offer the wider Christian community, including varied means of growth in Christlikeness—the goal of true spirituality.

---

53. For one perspective on this history, see George M. Marsden, *Reforming Fundamentalism: Fuller Seminary and the New Evangelicalism* (Grand Rapids: Eerdmans, 1987).

54. For my own synthesis of this dialogue, see *The Brazos Introduction to Christian Spirituality*. For a more personal reflection, see "The Gift of Tears: Three Stories of Ecumenical Experience," www.evangelicalspirituality.org/newesletter/aug11.

RESPONSE TO EVAN HOWARD

BRADLEY NASSIF

"The intersection between Orthodoxy and evangelicalism in the area of Christian spirituality is very likely the most dynamic manifestation of their common ground." That was my assessment in a 2004 essay titled "The Evangelical Theology of the Eastern Orthodox Church."[55] It was a comparative analysis of Orthodox and evangelical theology that was based on the definition of evangelicalism given by David Bebbington, which Evan Howard has also used in his essay. My article did not address the specific characteristics of evangelical *spirituality* that have been given by Howard, so I'm glad for the opportunity to touch on it here.

Definition and Goal of Evangelical Spirituality

Howard follows Bebbington's definition of evangelicalism, which identifies four main lines of thought: Scripture, the cross, conversion, and active ministry. In his section titled "Evangelical Spirituality Is Orthodox," Howard writes, "I refer, by the term *orthodox*, not to the historic tradition associated with Eastern Christianity ..., but to the commitment of evangelicals to basic historic (Nicene) Christian belief." As an Orthodox Christian, I find this statement difficult to comprehend. As much as we agree on many points in the Nicene Creed, I still wonder how evangelicals can maintain allegiance to "historic" Christian belief by embracing the *faith* of Nicea but not the *church* to which that faith belongs. "History" itself makes no such separation. The Great Tradition of historic Christian belief is inseparable from the Great Church that articulated it. When the Nicene Creed affirms, "I

---

55. Bradley Nassif, "The Evangelical Theology of the Eastern Orthodox Church," in *Three Views on Eastern Orthodoxy and Evangelicalism*, ed. James Stamoolis (Zondervan, 2004), 74, n. 49.

believe one holy catholic and apostolic church," it was not confessing trust in an invisible group of believers in the universal body of Christ. Rather, the Fathers of Nicea were saying that *their* churches are "one holy catholic and apostolic." Those same churches at the Council of Nicea have their historic continuity in the main body of Christians in Western Europe and the former Byzantine Empire, i.e., in what is now known (after the Great Schism of the eleventh to thirteenth centuries) as the Roman Catholic and Eastern Orthodox Churches. So when we refer to the faith of Nicea, it is these historic churches that we have in mind. And the claim of Orthodoxy is that their church is in fact the same historic community that produced the Nicene Creed and remains faithful to it.

Aside from the question of history, Howard's discussion of spirituality as "lived conversion" encapsulates the very heart of evangelical spirituality. That is what makes evangelicalism *evangelical.* He explains: "Evangelicalism comprehends relationship with God in terms of conversion: a radical turning to Christ and transformation by the Spirit of God ... No matter how it is described, conversion is arguably the most significant element in evangelical spirituality, for through authentic conversion, religion — *true religion* — is found and maintained." Simply stated, the unconverted are lost and have no union with God. Over and over again, Howard cites examples of this theme in evangelical authors, beginning with the Protestant Reformation and on to the present day. Henry Scougal (1650–1678) summarizes it best when stating that true religion is "a union of the soul with God, a real participation of the divine nature, the very image of God drawn upon the soul; or, in the Apostle's phrase, *it is Christ formed with us.* Briefly, I know not how the nature of religion can be more fully expressed, than by calling it *a divine life.*"[56]

Is this not also the theology of the great church fathers? St. Irenaeus in the second century described the Christian life in terms that were later articulated by St. Athanasius and the entire Greek patristic tradition: "God became humanized so that humans might become divinized." Christ's nature becomes our nature. By God's grace, his deified

---

56. Henry Scougal, *The Life of God in the Soul of Man* (Boston: Nichols and Noyes, 1868), 4–7 (quoted by Howard in his essay, p. 166).

humanity becomes our deified humanity. We become what he is without losing our individual identities or becoming additional members of the Trinity. The heart of Orthodoxy is also the heart of evangelicalism. So let's rejoice in that and affirm our common faith. The Christian life is the very image of God drawn within the soul. It is, as Scougal says, "Christ formed with us."

Readers may be surprised to learn that Orthodox and evangelical spirituality share a deeply held conviction that it is possible to be "religious, but lost." Howard points out that "John Wesley made 'real Christianity' an important theme of his ministry and writings." Yet the mystical theology of the Orthodox Church stressed this very theme long before Wesley and other evangelical children of the Reformation. Monastic theologians such as Sts. Makarios of Egypt (300–390), Mark the Ascetic (c. 430), and Symeon the New Theologian (949–1022) emphasized in their writings and teachings the need for having a direct, personal experience of Jesus Christ in the heart. Makarios of Egypt exhorted Christians to have "full certitude of heart" in their relationship with God—a spiritual doctrine that later influenced John Wesley's own thinking on the need for personal assurance. Mark the Ascetic stressed the need for "conscious assurance" of God's grace in the heart. And Symeon the New Theologian strongly cautioned the clergy against substituting barren ritualism for authentic faith. And so he preached the absolute necessity of having a "baptism in the Holy Spirit."

Having affirmed our common convictions that true spirituality is "lived conversion," it is important to add that for the Orthodox, this genuine turning to Christ takes place within the context of the church. In all cases, the mystical theologians of the Orthodox faith understood spiritual experience to be a direct outgrowth of the sacramental life of the church. In particular, baptism and the Eucharist are the source and content of a lifetime of "lived conversion." For St. Symeon, it was not enough to rest on the laurels of one's baptism for salvation. But neither was baptism unrelated to one's conscious "baptism in the Spirit." Rather, baptism is the sacrament of "new birth" that is consciously experienced in adulthood when a person surrenders to the Lord through repentance and faith. Thus there is no separation between the church's "spiritual" and "sacramental" ministries. Both go hand in hand.

Diverse Emphases in Evangelical Spirituality

A problem arises, however, when Howard moves beyond the common goal of the new birth and Christlikeness in evangelical spirituality. He acknowledges that "evangelicalism is a network of Christians associated with a wide diversity of liturgical and institutional forms and divergent ecclesiologies." Different groups have different beliefs about the nature of the church and the sacramental, or nonsacramental, character of the church: "It is simply impossible to speak of 'the evangelical' approach to ecclesial spirituality ... Yet while evangelicals were essentially united in their affirmation of the basic task of spiritual formation, they differed widely in their understanding of the primary aims, agents, and means of spiritual formation."

Issues that have divided evangelicals center on the questions of sinless perfection, the relationship between process and crisis in spiritual formation, whether ordained ministerial office is a divinely appointed agent of grace, the relationship between the Spirit's role and our role in sanctification, whether the sacraments are a means of grace or mere "works" that feed our pride, and similar issues.

The Orthodox Church has answered several of these ecclesial and sacramental questions, but it has not attempted to resolve other debated issues in a definitive way. Accordingly, we must not look for answers in the Orthodox Church that are not there. Yet, the most fundamental question we should be asking in order to discover answers is the *ecclesial* one: "What *ecclesial context* should we place ourselves in for finding the answers that we seek?" In order to answer that, Orthodox and evangelicals need to engage in serious ecumenical dialogue about which of our Christian *communities* (not individuals) have been the most faithful to the faith of the undivided church in the first millennium of Christian history? Theology and spirituality must be connected to the life of the worshiping church. That is how many Orthodox would think about resolving these and other evangelical divisions. Our ecclesial context is absolutely essential for doing theology in a way that can be faithful to the canon and community of historic Christianity, even if such answers are ultimately a matter of opinion or not discoverable. Otherwise, interpretive anarchy reigns, and the church is visibly divided — a reality that no doubt accounts for the thirty thousand denominations that have proliferated since the Protestant Reformation.

The Orientation of Evangelical Spirituality

Another feature of evangelical spirituality is its lay orientation. Howard observes, "With the Awakenings of the eighteenth century, evangelical religion was not only designed *for* the laity but also was led *by* the laity." Ecumenical networks have also united around common causes such as evangelical campaigns and social services. These lay and ecumenical endeavors express practical obedience to the gospel. I was surprised, however, to observe Howard's omission of Billy Graham's ecumenical approach to evangelism. When Billy Graham held evangelistic campaigns in Russia, where Orthodox Christians are the majority, Graham's philosophy was to work with the Orthodox clergy by directing the Orthodox converts in his meetings back into their own church. This approach can better unite us in furthering the cause of Christ.

The Orthodox Church would applaud the involvement, energy, and commitment of the laity; however, it would caution the almost dismissive attitude toward the clergy. Especially true today, with the creation of every conceivable belief system, the role of the clergy in the Orthodox Church is seen as essential for protecting the integrity and transmission of Christian truth.

The Practices of Evangelical Spirituality

Howard tells us that "Bible study is *the* discipline of evangelical Protestantism." This is an area in which the Orthodox and evangelicals have much to celebrate in principle (see pp. 47–52), though not in practice (evangelicals know the Bible much better than average Orthodox parishioners, though the situation is slowly improving). Family devotions are another discipline that has been strong in evangelicalism as well as in Orthodoxy, but in a different form. In devout Orthodox homes, family devotions take place through daily prayers that are said around a family altar on which rests a Bible, a cross, icons of Christ and Mary, and a prayer book. This approach is more holistic and ecclesial than Bible reading alone, though personal study and prayer are also encouraged.

Howard has done a commendable survey of evangelical spirituality from the Reformation to the present. By its biblical focus and Spirit-filled example, evangelicalism challenges Orthodox Christians to take our own mystical theology more seriously. Our saints—such as Makarios of Egypt, Mark the Ascetic, Symeon the New Theologian, and others—show us the Orthodox way to communion with God. They tell us that the ABCs of the gospel must be proclaimed in various ways within the church's life. We today must be honest enough to admit that even though the gospel is *in* the Orthodox Church, it does not mean our parishioners have always *understood and appropriated* it for themselves. To that end, may we engage in an aggressive "internal mission" of renewing or converting nominal Orthodox people to faith in Jesus Christ.

SCOTT HAHN

Evan Howard describes so many of the great qualities that drew me to Protestant evangelicalism when I was very young. I was raised in a mainline Protestant denomination whose beliefs were vague, whose worship was staid, and whose congregations were pretty homogeneous. We lacked vigor, and we were not reproducing ourselves in any way. The whole project felt fatigued, exhausted.

When I first encountered evangelical parachurch movements, I was in high school. Nothing could have stood in starker contrast to my earlier experience of religion. I met young people who were on fire for their faith, who prayed, who knew what they believed and believed it with all their heart, who expected miracles, who wanted my conversion because they cared about me deeply.

Reading Howard's essay moved me to gratitude for all these qualities that evangelicals first shared with me. I am just as grateful that evangelicals continue to share that witness on a vast, cultural scale — through media ministries, think tanks, political activism, and many other means. I shudder to think what the moral landscape of my country would look like if not for the witness of evangelical Christians over the last half century. How good it is to live at a time when one of the most vibrant and powerful Christian voices emerges from a movement called "Evangelicals and Catholics Together," founded by Richard John Neuhaus and Charles Colson. How good it is to be a Roman Catholic (especially one formed by the evangelical tradition) during the pontificate of Benedict XVI, who has been summoning the whole church to the way of "evangelical Catholicism."

Evangelicalism has indeed distinguished itself by strong faith, boldly expressed and deeply felt. Against a rising tide of secularism and materialism, evangelicals stand firm in their belief in "the deity of Christ, the virgin birth, original sin, the bodily resurrection of Christ

... and the authority of Scripture." Howard mentions also the belief in an eschatological "final restoration." These are indeed foundation stones of historic, orthodox Christianity, and it is good that evangelicals and Catholics can together build on these.

But it is at least questionable whether those doctrines are sustainable apart from the visible church, which for the first millennium was visibly united in sacramental and doctrinal life. Indeed, already in the first century and in every century afterward, enthusiastic movements arose and evanesced, and heretics already had denied each and every one of the doctrines affirmed in Howard's brief list. It was the church—one, holy, catholic, apostolic, and orthodox—that preserved, developed, and defended those doctrines.

While evangelicalism has admirably stood by some "core beliefs" of Nicene orthodoxy, it is a minimal core, and it is ever shrinking, especially in America, as evangelicals seek to accommodate new theologies and even lifestyles consistently condemned by the historic church.

As Howard acknowledges, evangelicalism is an uneasy alliance of mutually incompatible and even contradictory systems of Christian thought. Within a single movement, we must include Calvinists and Arminians, revivalists and Puritans, Methodists and Moravians, holiness and Pentecostal, postmillennials and premillennials. The issues that divide these groups are not insignificant. They are profoundly theological and doctrinal, and by all accounts they deal with matters essential to salvation. If that were not so, the movements would not exist. Most of them arose in opposition not to Roman Catholicism but to other forms of evangelicalism.

That fact calls into question the centrality of "conversion" as a hallmark of evangelicalism, because conversion must be *from* something and *to* something—but from what to what? Evangelicalism as a whole cannot sustain a unified answer to those questions. Indeed, many evangelicals will see most other evangelicals as standing in need of such conversion. Evangelicalism may speak of "true religion" and "real Christianity," but it cannot present a coherent sense of what that might be. If what is "real" and "true" is embodied only in the shrinking set of core beliefs expressed in Bible study, preaching, family devotion, music, and intercession, then evangelicalism becomes just a diluted form of classic Christianity.

This leads to a key question: Does the need for renewal and reform necessitate and justify more and more protests and splits based on this sort of "lowest common denominator" approach to a list of "fundamentals" that seems to be ever shrinking and under debate among an amorphous body of "true believers"?

Catholicism can and does affirm all those beliefs and practices. Do Catholics need to be (re-)evangelized and converted? Yes, continually—at least this one does. But Howard habitually sets evangelicalism in contrast to Catholicism and presents it as a reaction against catholicizing movements. I wish he had instead, or in addition, looked into the great evangelicals' efforts to recover elements of Catholic tradition and devotional life. It is impossible to understand John and Charles Wesley, for example, apart from their intense interest in the Catholic faith of the patristic era. It is the warmth of this faith that they sought to retrieve. The early English Puritans had no trouble whatsoever adapting continental Devotion to the Sacred Heart for their own purposes. Jonathan Edwards explored mystical and typological matters in ways that set him apart from mainstream evangelicalism but closely align him with the scholastics and the Fathers. Billy Graham's devotion to the angels differs little from what we would expect to find in a Catholic church. Such background can surely help us to understand "the emergent church," "the new monasticism," and other recent missional movements in evangelicalism—movements that borrow freely from the liturgical, devotional, and artistic heritage of the church.

It is increasingly common to find churches whose worship incorporates incense, icons, vestments, and candles, and they still consider themselves "evangelical." On the other hand, I teach at a Catholic university noted for its "evangelical" zeal and "charismatic" worship—with vibrant music, fervent preaching, hands-in-the-air worship, and small prayer groups. And this is not an isolated phenomenon. Most Catholics, I think, would be surprised by Howard's oil-and-water presentation of evangelicalism in relation to Catholicism. John Wesley, too, perhaps would be surprised.

I think this prejudice gives Howard a distorted view of Christian history, especially of the years leading up to the Reformation. While histories in the English-speaking world once portrayed the conflict as pitting Protestant good guys with noble motives against Catholic villains driven by greed and lust, no reputable historian would do so today. It was not simply a "protest against corruption." Politics had a role to play, and there was murderous cruelty and power-mongering on all sides. Protestants forced it on Protestants as well.

Recent histories by Eamon Duffy, Anne Winston-Allen, J. J. Scarisbrick, Richard Rex, Christopher Haigh, and many others show us a quite different picture of the years leading up to the Reformation. They present a time when reform was already well under way, though not in the church-dividing ways initiated by Luther, Calvin, and Zwingli. There were giants on the earth already about the business of reform, men such as Thomas à Kempis, Cardinal Cisneros, Erasmus, and Thomas More. Their efforts would soon be richly developed by holy and zealous Catholics as diverse as Pope Pius V, Teresa of Avila, Francis de Sales, Ignatius of Loyola, Francis Xavier, John of the Cross, Charles Borromeo, Blaise Pascal, Bartolomé de Las Casas, Peter Claver, Philip Neri, Juan Diego Cuauhtlatoatzin, and a cast of thousands. Indeed, the Reformation spawned more than a Counter-Reformation; Protestantism's rise was matched by an unprecedented explosion of missions and saints — a veritable springtime of renewal and repentance for the Catholic Church.

I became a Roman Catholic more than a quarter century ago, but I never felt I left the good things of my evangelical heritage behind. Nobody asked me to do so. I found so many of those good things alive and well in the Catholic Church, as they have been since the beginning. Indeed, I am more grateful for my evangelical formation and roots today than on the day of my ordination as an evangelical Protestant pastor.

I am also grateful to Evan Howard for bringing these qualities into relief in his essay. I am pleased to live in a day when evangelicals and Catholics can stand together in common witness. I delight in the "evangelical Catholicism" preached today by a pope who labored for many years on an ecumenical faculty of theology among many evangelical friends.

JOSEPH DRISKILL

Evangelical spirituality as presented in Evan Howard's essay anchors the tradition solidly in the wider stream of Protestant church history. Throughout his presentation he turns to historical sources — including figures such as Luther, Calvin, Wesley, and Whitefield, and movements such as Puritans and Pietists — to trace the origins of evangelical spirituality. He also differentiates the pre-Reformation spiritual path of vowed religious from that of evangelical Christians. Instead of purgation and illumination leading to mystical union with God, evangelical spirituality believes conversion itself establishes the ontological and existential condition for mystical union with God. Through conversion God is joined with humankind; with assurance and sanctification each Christian grows toward maturity in Christ. Thus, evangelical Protestantism is anchored in the theological reforms of the sixteenth century.

In addition, by placing Puritans' and Pietists' spiritualities in the evangelical canon, Howard fosters a recovery of Protestant spiritual practices and traditions in the ensuing post-Reformation centuries, where attention to the inner life, the devotional life of followers, was a primary characteristic of faith.

Key Emphases of Spirituality

Howard introduces David Bebbington's quadrilateral and then uses Timothy Larsen's work to transform it into a pentagon for the purpose of introducing the primary markers or characteristics of evangelical spirituality. Two related themes — the search for "true faith" and sanctification — emerge as the characteristics to be developed. These themes both enrich the dialogue between mainline Protestant spirituality and evangelical Protestant spirituality and highlight their differences. I begin by using two additional quadrilaterals to engage the frameworks, which differentiate evangelical spirituality from mainline spirituality.

Following this, I turn first to sanctification, then to "true faith," and lastly to the evangelical understanding of an "active faith."

In 1870, William Reed Huntington introduced the Lambeth quadrilateral to highlight four characteristics of Anglicanism that had the potential to provide fruitful ecumenical discussions between themselves and the Orthodox and Roman Catholic traditions. These four characteristics were (1) Holy Scripture as the foundation of faith; (2) the Apostles' and Nicene Creeds as statements of belief; (3) the celebration of two sacraments, Eucharist and baptism; and (4) ministry through the historic episcopate. In 1964, Albert Outler, a Methodist scholar from the United States, used the quadrilateral framework to identify four sources that John Wesley used to reach his theological positions. These included Scripture, church tradition, reason, and experience. Wesley, an avid reader whose thirst for church history included extensive reading of the early church fathers and mothers from East and West, was ordained and died an Anglican priest. While for Wesley the Old and New Testaments are the foundation of faith, the other three dimensions of the quadrilateral (tradition, reason, and experience) provide the various vantage points for interpreting Scripture. Outler sees this Anglican "founder" of Methodism as a man of his time, living in a world in which reason and experience were increasingly valued. Thus, while the four aspects of the Lambeth quadrilateral relate to the historic church, those of Wesley reflect a growing awareness of the human subject as an interpreter of the Scriptures. Little imagination is needed to see how eighteenth-century understandings of "reason" and "experience" contributed to the mainline Protestants' ongoing history of interpretation.

Howard identifies five major characteristics of evangelical spirituality using Bebbington's quadrilateral, augmented by Larsen: (1) Scripture, (2) orthodox belief, (3) the atoning work of Jesus Christ, (4) conversion, and (5) the empowering work of the Holy Spirit (activism). While it appears at first blush that these five characteristics share considerable common ground with the other spiritualities in this volume, when the five notions are elaborated and nuanced, it is clear that they help define the differences among the four Christian spiritualities discussed in this book. I turn now to exploring the themes of sanctification and true religion.

The Role of Christ in Spirituality

Howard points out that evangelical spirituality views conversion as "a radical turning to Christ and transformation by the Spirit of God." In a letter from 1839, Charles Finney wrote about the importance of "sanctification and growth in grace." Finney saw this as an essential correction of an earlier error in which evangelical Christians emphasized the importance of conversion at the expense of continuing to guide converts toward a life conformed to Christ. Howard notes that although there was little agreement among evangelicals as to the "aim, agents, or means" of spiritual formation, there was an interest in many evangelical quarters to engage this task. He situates contemporary evangelical spirituality in a historical line that includes nineteenth-century figures Phoebe Palmer, a Methodist whose autobiographical *The Way of Holiness* tells her journey of sanctification, and William E. Boardman, a Presbyterian clergyperson whose *The Higher Christian Life* suggests that the risen Savior is not only with us but also within us. This attention to sanctification makes common cause with Orthodox spirituality's theological understanding of deification and the Roman Catholic focus on divine sonship.

Throughout much of the twentieth century, progressive Protestants identified spiritual practices associated with sanctification as "works" made superfluous by "justification by faith." Reclaiming the value of spiritual practices, including selected ones from Puritans and Pietists, is important to progressive Protestants. There is an increasing awareness in progressive traditions that an experiential relationship with the divine is a necessary aspect of faith development. Here progressive Protestants have much to learn from evangelical spirituality.

The Goal of Spirituality

The issue of seeking "true faith" highlights a major difference between progressive Protestant spirituality and evangelical spirituality. Evangelicals believe that it is important to find the "true faith." By this they mean an expression of faith that includes an internal, experiential relationship with God. Howard observes that a forensic understanding of "justification by faith" — the theological affirmation that Christ has done something *for* humankind without an accompanying internal experience of Christ—is merely a perfunctory form of faith. At the other extreme, Howard posits "enthusiasts" who emphasize an immediate experience of the Spirit at the expense of orthodox doctrine. Evangelical spirituality finds "true religion" between the extremes of dry, perfunctory observance and overzealous, yet unorthodox religious expressions.

From quite diverse social locations and varied epochs, Howard finds evidence of the quest for true religion: Menno Simons's need for a "spiritual resurrection," Johann Arndt's "true Christianity," Jonathan Edwards's signs of "true religion," John Wesley's "real Christianity," William Wilberforce's "real Christianity," and John R. W. Stott's "basic Christianity." Though a diversity of theological opinions emerges from this list, Howard notes that contemporary expressions of this quest for true religion is found not in denominational loyalties but in specific markers—"communities where 'real Christians' gather: those who exhibit authentic conversion, orthodox faith, and a living relationship with Jesus through the Holy Spirit." Evangelical spirituality's understanding of orthodoxy includes a belief in the virgin birth, the bodily resurrection of Christ, substitutionary atonement, original sin, and the authority of Scripture. Progressive Protestants' lived experience of faith differs considerably from that of evangelicals. Progressive Protestants have not been interested in defining the nature of "real Christians"; in general, progressive Protestants have recognized the diversity of beliefs within their memberships and have been open to tolerating a wide spectrum of theological beliefs.

The Means for Implementing Spirituality

The conflicts over modernism at the beginning of the twentieth century established the divide between mainline Protestants and evangelical Protestants that exists today. "The authority of Scripture" means something quite different to most evangelicals and progressives. One of the major differences between evangelical spirituality and progressive Protestant spirituality resides in their respective approaches to Scripture. While Howard notes that biblicism is a characteristic of evangelical spirituality and that *The Fundamentals* is a landmark multivolume work defining some key principles of evangelical spirituality, he does not distinguish fundamentalist spirituality from evangelical spirituality.

I associate a literal interpretation of biblical texts, often accompanied by a concept of biblical inerrancy, as a characteristic of fundamentalism rather than evangelicalism. As a progressive Protestant, I have thought that while most fundamentalists are evangelicals, there are a number of evangelicals who do not subscribe to a fundamentalist interpretation of the biblical texts. Howard does not address this issue directly. However, he leaves the impression that either all evangelical spirituality includes a fundamentalist approach to the Bible or that the distinction I am making is insignificant. Either way, mainline Protestant spirituality views this form of textual interpretation as, at best, uninformed and, at worst, an interpretive method that results in a misrepresentation of the biblical witness.

Both evangelical and mainline Christians would affirm that there is an important "active" dimension that is constituent to and involved in implementing their respective spiritualities. Howard begins his discussion of the "active" component with two engaging historical cases that increasingly progressive Protestants would also want to claim as antecedents of their social involvements. Cotton Mather, in his *Essays to Do Good* (1710), provides a pattern for morning self-examination that demonstrates his concern for his family, church, and society. By asking himself a different focus question on each morning of the week, Mather demonstrates the breadth and depth of his concerns. Howard provides an example: on Mondays, Mather would consider what good he might do for his family; on Thursdays, he would reflect on the good he might do for the societies of which he is a member.

Mather's German contemporary August Herman Francke, a key figure of the Pietist movement at Halle, was so moved by the needs of the poor as they begged each week for alms, that he eventually started a school in his house to provide them not only with food but also with an education. The university at Halle was one of the first educational institutions in which the wealthier classes sat in classrooms with the poorer classes. In the search to find housing for his students, Francke later founded the largest orphanage of his time. Howard points out that over time, Francke's influence resulted in other evangelists founding orphanages in England and the American colonies. Clearly, as Francke encountered the poor of his social location, he recognized the social implications of his deeply held religious convictions. Francke's actions move beyond what from a contemporary vantage point might be described as acts of charity and begin the lost quest to transform the structures of his social location.

At this point, one might assume that the spiritualities of evangelical Protestants and progressive Protestants would share a wide common ground, since they both identify with an "active" approach to faith. However, after providing these late seventeenth- and early eighteenth-century examples, Howard moves his discussion of the "active" nature of evangelical spirituality to evangelism itself. He identifies the Great Awakening during the early eighteenth century as a watershed for the activity of evangelicals. The process of converting others, bringing them to Christ, "winning souls" through a series of evangelical techniques or steps becomes the focus of evangelical spirituality. This turn, as a particular response to the enthusiasm of the Great Awakening, sets the groundwork for what in the twentieth century becomes the path not taken by progressive Protestants—the identification of an active faith with a focus on personal conversion.

Howard observes, interestingly enough, that although fundamentalist culture was "fleeing the world" by virtue of its lack of concern for modernist social agendas and its continued attention to "the means of grace," it was also increasing its ranks by using strategies that attracted new members—radio broadcasts, church plants, a focus on small groups, and Bible colleges. Concurrently, in the twentieth century, progressive mainline Protestants were decreasing their funding for colleges and universities, surrendering their influence on both college and seminary curricula, and allocating only modest funds for audiovisual materials and even less for radio or television broadcasts. After decades of declining membership, mainline denominations at the end of the twentieth century ultimately began to acknowledge the need for evangelism and church growth. For example, the "20/20 Vision" program of the Christian Church (Disciples of Christ) adopted in 1999 calls both for an antiracist/pro-reconciling faith and for 1,000 new congregations and 1,000 transformed congregations by 2020; and the "God Is Still Speaking" program of the United Church of Christ provides an inclusive welcome, accompanied by the desire to invite others to share their faith journeys.

Howard concludes by noting that evangelical spirituality not only has much to contribute to the wider Christian community but also is open to receiving from others. I judge that mainline Protestant spirituality is also open to both contributing and receiving from others. These discussions are happening in a variety of settings. For example, Christian Churches Together, founded in 2001, brings together participants from Orthodox, Roman Catholic, progressive Protestant, and evangelical Protestant faith communities. This highly inclusive and strikingly diverse group engages in sharing and missions on a regular basis. As this book demonstrates, by using a lens of spirituality, we can come to understand and appreciate the religious diversity of the planet. If our goal is not to convince others that we are "right," but to understand ourselves more deeply by being enriched from those who differ from us, then the world that God loves will be the beneficiary.

CONCLUSION ▰▰▰▰▰▰▰▰▰▰▰

BRUCE DEMAREST

This concluding chapter of the volume attempts a brief integrative exposition of Christian spirituality. I highlight insights from the four position papers and responses, as well as share additional perspectives drawn from Scripture, church tradition, and Spirit-led experience.

Definition and Key Issues of Christian Spirituality

Christian spirituality represents the affectively experienced reality of faith union with Christ, rooted in the biblically revealed story of the Savior's life, death, and resurrection. Essential thereto is the Spirit-empowered integration of intellect, affections, relationships, and behaviors. Since Christian spirituality is about life in the Spirit (Romans 8:5–6), it represents the preeminent goal of the church. Authentically spiritual persons don't withdraw from life in some "rapturous dream-land" (Evelyn Underhill), but join relationship with Christ and practical action on behalf of others. Spiritually maturing disciples discover wisdom for living, words for speaking, and courage for persevering.

The four traditions of spirituality explored here suggest ways in which the Spirit has been at work among God's people through the centuries. Differences among Christian spiritualities emerge in part by virtue of diverse historical and cultural settings. As Simon Chan points out, "Different spiritualities may appeal to Christians of different temperaments or even to the same person at different times."[1]

Disciplines That Nurture Spirituality

Mature Christian spirituality develops through spiritual practices involving the synergy of the divine initiative and our human responses (Philippians 2:12–13; 2 Peter 1:3–9). Henri Nouwen observes, "We cannot plan, organize, or manipulate God. But without careful discipline we

---

1. Simon Chan, *Spiritual Theology* (Downers Grove, Ill.: InterVarsity), 20.

cannot receive him either."[2] Christian spirituality is enhanced by practicing a rule of life or spiritual *askesis* (cf. Greek, a*skeô*, "train" or "exercise"). The Eastern desert father John Cassian (360–435) noted, "There is no arrival unless there is a plan to go."[3] Chan rightly observes that "living by rule (Latin, *regula*) is what turns one into a regular Christian."[4]

Bradley Nassif identifies Orthodox practices that facilitate spiritual union with the triune God as participation in Eucharist (liturgy), asceticism (systematic discipline), continual supplication (the Jesus Prayer), silent contemplation (hesychasm), veneration of icons (windows into eternity), spiritual direction (guidance under an *abba*, *starets*, or *geron*), and service to the world.

Scott Hahn would agree that Catholicism commends a range of disciplines for enhancing spiritual life—*lectio divina*, contemplative prayer, reciting the Rosary, making retreats, journaling, and receiving spiritual direction. Catholic ascetic disciplines, however, are more commonly practiced by priests and religious than by the laity. Protestants have incorporated selected Catholic (as well as Orthodox) disciplines into their protocols of spiritual maturation.

Progressive Protestant exercises, as noted by Joseph Driskill, focus on studying the Bible (albeit interpreted more critically and figuratively rather than literally), prayer for Christian unity, interreligious dialogue, and schemes of social and political praxis. Driskill's *Protestant Spiritual Exercises* helpfully outlines classical patterns for spiritual formation.[5]

Evan Howard points out that typical evangelical spiritual practices include worship, Bible study, prayer, and service in the church and world. Underscoring the centrality of prayer, John Calvin's chapter on prayer (3.20) is the longest in his *Institutes of the Christian Religion*. Evangelicals commonly emphasize petitionary and intercessory prayer rather than nonverbal prayer such as "practicing the Presence" (Brother Lawrence) and contemplation (Basil Pennington). As Scott Hahn notes, evangelicalism tends to minimize the role of the physical body and its senses as routes to spirituality.

---

2. Henri Nouwen, *Reaching Out* (Garden City, N.Y.: Doubleday, 1975), 89.

3. John Cassian, *Conferences*, 2.26.

4. Chan, *Spiritual Theology*, 137.

5. Joseph D. Driskill, *Protestant Spiritual Exercises: Theology, History, and Practice* (Harrisburg, Pa.: Morehouse, 1999).

The Role of Christ and the Spirit in Spirituality

Christian spirituality is thoroughly Trinitarian, nurtured by the living God who is three distinct persons in one infinite spirit being. God as unity graciously brings humans to wholeness by countering dark forces of disintegration. God as three facilitates newness of life, as the Father plans salvation, the Son provides salvation, and the Spirit applies salvation to all who put their faith in Christ as Savior and Lord. Believers partake of the Trinitarian life as they are caught up into dynamic, relational life of the three-in-one God.

Christian spirituality is rigorously Christological in that the "with-God" life is grounded in the sinless life, atoning death, and glorious resurrection of Jesus Christ (2 Corinthians 5:21; 1 John 3:5; Romans 5:8; 6:5 – 10). The pathway to authentic spirituality begins with renunciation of sinful ways and faith in Christ's reconciling work on Calvary. Spiritual maturation involves deepening participation in Christ's death on the cross and his victorious resurrection life (Romans 6:5).

Both Orthodoxy and Catholicism emphasize Christ's saving death — Catholicism affirming that Christ was made sin for us.[6] Regarding Christ as a model for ethical conduct or liberator of the politically and economically oppressed, progressive Protestantism selectively mutes Christ's divinity and substitutionary death for sin. Evangelicalism consistently upholds Christ's atoning sacrifice (Mark 14:23 – 24), insisting that God grants to those who trust his resurrected Son forgiveness of sin, perfect righteousness, and restored relationship.

Christian spirituality is robustly *pneumatic* or *charismatic* in that living the "with-God" life is totally Spirit enabled. In the pursuit of mature spirituality, followers of Jesus seek the empowerment and direction of the Holy Spirit. The fruit of the Spirit (Galatians 5:22 – 23) represents the outworking of a maturing spirituality.

Both Orthodoxy and Catholicism emphasize Holy Spirit incorporation into the life of the Trinity. Through the Catholic charismatic renewal, rightly celebrated by Scott Hahn, God has wrought renewed participation in the "with-God" life, although half a century later, the charismatic renewal needs reenergizing by the same Spirit.

---

6. *Catechism of the Catholic Church* (New York: Doubleday, 1995), pars. 602 – 3, p. 171.

Evangelicalism insists that the Spirit effects conversion, new birth, sanctification, assurance of salvation, and (for the most part) perseverance in the faith. A maturing spirituality involves being led by the Spirit, empowered by the Spirit, and manifesting the fruit of the Spirit. As noted by Evan Howard, an essential feature of evangelicalism is its rejection of nominal Christianity in favor of personal appropriation of the good news that launches spiritual life.

The Role of the Church

Christian spirituality is nurtured in the Christ-centered body of believers in which Scripture is taught and preached, the sacraments observed, and biblical discipline exercised. In a local evangelical Presbyterian church, the Spirit brought me as a teenager to faith in Christ and later challenged my wife and me to forty years of discipleship in overseas missions and seminary teaching. Citing another example, a young Chinese woman student of mine, filled with the Spirit, planted and nurtured thirty house churches in the People's Republic of China in the face of considerable persecution. In these and other cases, leadership was provided by qualified, Spirit-filled Christ-followers raised up from local congregations. Since God works in many and diverse ways, I also honor the formative role played by overseers and bishops in spiritual nurture.

Orthodoxy invests authority in the Bible, tradition, and the ecumenical councils, whereas Catholic spiritual authority resides in Scripture, tradition, and the magisterium. Both affirm questionable postulates of interaction between living and deceased saints with participation in each other's prayers and good works. Orthodoxy's reverence for saints is reflected in veneration of icons that allegedly facilitate communion with the Deity. Evangelical spirituality would be enriched by greater engagement with the historical experience of the visible church through the centuries, errors excepted.

Biblically tenuous is the Orthodox and Roman Catholic cult of Mary wherein prayers are offered, devotion directed, and protection sought from the ever-virgin "Mother of God." Protestants dissent from the Catholic conviction that "by her manifold intercession [Mary] continues to bring us the gifts of eternal salvation."[7] The nineteenth-

---

7. *Catechism of the Catholic Church*, par. 969, p. 275.

century doctrine of Mary's heavenly assumption likewise lacks biblical foundation.

Orthodoxy and Catholicism both uphold baptismal regeneration wherein the baptized allegedly receive spiritual life and heavenly inheritance. Lacking scriptural support, such a position leads to a false sense of spiritual security. Many raised in strongly sacramental traditions who later converted to Protestant evangelicalism testify that their baptism as infants failed to impart the "with-God" life. Evangelicalism, however, does well to recapture a legitimate sacramentalism that fosters holistic spirituality involving the physical body and its created senses.

Related Theological Issues

Sin

Fundamental to robust spiritual life in Christ is overcoming the effects of original sin. Tending toward Semipelagianism, Orthodoxy asserts that pre-Christians are morally weak rather than spiritually dead, focusing more on specific sins than fallen human nature. Rome judges that because the fall allegedly left the natural human endowments untarnished, sinners retain the power to attain virtue through ascetical practices. Theologian Richard McBrien acknowledges that the doctrine of original sin doesn't play a large part in contemporary Catholic theology.[8] Recent Catholic "new morality" teaching involves a radical reinterpretation of sexual ethics, including validation of homosexuality and same-sex marriage. The traditional moral code rooted in Scripture is replaced by a situational ethic governed by "love."[9]

Minimizing the classical doctrine of original sin, progressive Protestantism traces sin to evolutionary anomalies or social and cultural forces. The tradition holds out hope of human perfectibility through right judgments and compassionate deeds. Evangelicalism, on the other hand, insists that sin has corrupted all human faculties, both in Adam and his descendants.[10] Alienated from God, sinners are "dead in ... transgressions and

---

8. Richard P. McBrien, *Catholicism* (Minneapolis: Winston, 1981), 162.

9. See Charles Curran and Richard McCormick, eds., *Dialogue about Catholic Sexual Teaching* (New York: Paulist, 1993); Vincent Genovesi, *In Pursuit of Love: Catholic Morality and Human Sexuality*, 2nd ed. (Collegeville, Minn.: Liturgical Press, 1996).

10. See, e.g., John Calvin, *Institutes of the Christian Religion*, ed. John T. McNeill (Philadelphia: Westminster, 1960), 2.2.

sins" (Ephesians 2:1; cf. v. 5; Romans 3:9–18), or holistically depraved. Authentic spirituality requires radical renovation of the heart by God's saving grace. All four traditions correctly insist that specific sins (e.g., Romans 1:29–31; Colossians 3:5–9) must be put to death.

Grace

According to Orthodoxy, the weak human will is upheld by divine power. Humans pursue the good, whereupon God responds with assisting grace without destroying freedom. John Chrysostom writes, "We must first select good, and then God adds what pertains to his office; he does not act antecedently to our will, so as not to destroy our liberty."[11] Eastern and Western monasticism judge that effectual grace would undermine ascetic discipline and encourage spiritual sloth.

Catholicism claims that God responds to human spiritual longing by bestowing sanctifying grace through baptism. Cooperating with said grace, the faithful perform meritorious works such as praying the Rosary, fasting, and performing charitable deeds.[12] Additional grace is supplied by Mary's sinless life and intercessions, together with the surplus of merits of exceptional saints. Vatican II and leading theologians (e.g., Karl Rahner) interpret grace as God's self-communication that orients persons toward God such that all are spiritually transformed by it. Those who follow this "supernatural existential" knowingly or unknowingly are judged to be oriented to the immediacy of God and new life.

In agreement with Scripture, evangelicalism identifies grace both as God's unmerited favor to undeserving sinners (2 Timothy 1:9) and his power operative in the soul to transform believers into Christlikeness (2 Peter 3:18). Throughout the Christian life, God graciously forms believers into the image of his beloved Son. Spiritual disciples exercised in faith represent important means of grace. Both initial salvation and increase of spiritual life are gifts of God's grace.

Justification

Minimizing juridical themes, Orthodoxy emphasizes Christ's conquest of death leading to divinization. Daniel Clendenin observes, "In the

---

11. John Chrysostom, "Sermon 12 on Hebrews," quoted in *Exploring Christian Spirituality*, ed. Kenneth J. Collins (Grand Rapids: Baker, 2000), 110.

12. See *Catechism of the Catholic Church*, pars. 2006–11, pp. 541–42.

history of Orthodox theology ... it is startling to observe the near total absence of any mention of the idea of justification by faith."[13] Closer examination reveals the real issue to be "a difference of emphasis — the East emphasizing mystical union through theosis, the West emphasizing judicial categories."[14]

Catholicism judges that "justification is conferred in Baptism, the sacrament of faith."[15] Thereafter, the baptized strive for eternal life by obedience to God and the church, together with love-inspired works. The merits of Mary and the saints contribute to the advancement of justification, the latter judged to be identical with sanctification. Insofar as Vatican II and many contemporary thinkers envision grace as a universal bestowal, justification is said to embrace all people. Evangelicals dissent from universalist statements such as, "Every human, by reason of birth and God's universal offer of grace, is already called to be a child of God and an heir of heaven."[16]

Evangelicals interpret justification as God's judicial declaration whereby on the basis of Christ's atoning death he freely pardons sins, reconciles repentant sinners to himself, and bestows eternal life (Romans 3:21–26). "Justified by faith is he who, excluded from the righteousness of works, grasps the righteousness of Christ, through faith, and clothed in it, appears in God's sight not as a sinner but as a righteous man."[17] Evangelicals envision justification and sanctification as two sides of the same coin: "You cannot possess him [Christ] without being made partaker in his sanctification, because he cannot be divided into pieces (1 Corinthians 1:13)."[18] The justified normally possess assurance of peace with God — objectively on the basis of scriptural teaching (1 John 5:13) and subjectively via the witness of the Spirit in the heart (Galatians 4:6–7).

---

13. Daniel B. Clendenin, *Eastern Orthodox Christianity*, 2nd ed. (Grand Rapids: Baker, 2003), 123.

14. Ibid., 124.

15. *Catechism of the Catholic Church*, par. 1992, p. 536. Stimulated by the colloquium Evangelicals and Catholics Together, other Catholic authorities acknowledge that justification is by faith (together with charity).

16. McBrien, *Catholicism*, 738.

17. Calvin, *Institutes*, 3.11.2.

18. Ibid, 3.16.1.

Goals or Endgame of Spirituality

The goal of spirituality according to Orthodoxy is divinization—a profound sharing in the divine life such that the baptized "participate in the divine nature" (2 Peter 1:4). Given this incorporation into the relational life of the Trinity, Christians live out the Great Commandment centered on perfection in love. As noted by Bradley Nassif, Orthodoxy consistently posits incorporation into the dynamic life of the Trinity.

Catholicism historically identifies the goal of spirituality, following purgation and illumination, as union with God. Analogous to the consummation of human marriage, union is said to represent the highest possible state of spirituality. Post–Vatican II Catholicism adds the humanization of the world[19] or, as expressed by Pope Benedict XVI, "a unification in view of human values, a unification of the spirit and of what is highest in the human spirit, its relationship to God."[20]

A primary goal of spirituality according to progressive Protestantism is love of God and neighbor evidenced in acts of mercy and justice. As noted by the other three contributors, such goals are commendable, although the endgame of spirituality cannot be limited to pursuit of social justice.

Evangelicalism avers that the primary goal of spiritual life is glorifying God by attaining loving union with the God wherein the *imago Dei* is restored and the *homo viator* conformed to the likeness of Christ (Romans 8:29; 2 Corinthians 3:18). As such, brokenness gives way to healing (Malachi 4:2), weakness to strength (Philippians 4:13), and bondage to freedom (Galatians 5:1). A new wholeness is achieved whereby believers become "fully mature in Christ" (Colossians 1:28; cf. Ephesians 4:13). In evangelicalism, as with the other traditions, spiritual persons manifest the fruit of the Spirit and fulfill the Great Commandment. Evangelicalism today affirms the classical view that the baptized are caught up into the relational life of the Trinity.

Orthodox, Catholic, and Progressive Protestant Spirituality

As Bradley Nassif points out, Orthodox spirituality embraces mystery (apophaticism), beauty (liturgy and icons), Scripture and tradition

---

19. See, e.g., James J. Bacik, *Catholic Spirituality, Its History and Challenge* (New York: Paulist, 2002), 41–42, 59.

20. Joseph Ratzinger, *Theological Highlights of Vatican II* (New York: Paulist, 1966), 248.

(Bible, writings, and seven ecumenical councils), and mystical union culminating in *theosis*. Orthodoxy's fidelity to the gospel, Trinitarian focus, and aesthetically rich liturgy enhance Christian spirituality. The same may be said for its disciplines of contemplative quiet, fasting, spiritual reading (particularly *The Philokalia*, the collection of Orthodox texts from the fourth to the fifteenth centuries), and spiritual direction. Orthodoxy has much to teach Western Christians about the discipline of suffering, particularly under atheistic Communism and radical Islam.

Although theologically and liturgically orthodox, does Eastern Christianity's subscription to baptismal regeneration marginalize faith appropriation of Christ? Nassif laments that many Orthodox have become sacramentalized rather than evangelized. "Parishioners are coming and going in and out of church with little visible change in their lives. In short, they do not know the core content of the gospel or how to integrate its meaning in their everyday lives." He adds, "Without the centrality of the gospel we end up imposing on our people the evil of religious formalism and barren ritualism."[21] Often perceiving their identity ethnically and culturally, Orthodoxy embraces many cultural adherents.[22] While acknowledging positive features of tradition, icons, the ministry of guardian angels, and *theosis* in spirituality, Orthodoxy places undue emphasis on these.[23] Certain idiosyncrasies might also be cited, such as forbidding women on Mount Athos (Orthodoxy's holy mountain) and instances of monks refusing to attend the funeral of a family member lest their prayer life be interrupted.[24]

Protesting Rome's system of indulgences, ecclesiastical opulence, and role of works for salvation, the Protestant Reformers regarded the Catholic Church as requiring major reform. Evangelicals take issue

---

21. Bradley, Nassif, "Reclaiming the Gospel," www.orthodoxytoday.org/articles6/Nassif-Gospel.php (accessed June 28, 2011); see also Clendenin, *Eastern Orthodox Christianity*, 150: "A related danger is that love for liturgy can turn into rote ritualism."

22. Matthew D. LaPlante ("Growing in the Word: What the Ethiopian Orthodox Have Learned from the Expansion of Evangelicals," *Christianity Today* 55 [September 2011]: 17–19) chronicles the lack of biblical teaching and evangelism in the world's largest Oriental Orthodox church and the positive impact that rapidly growing evangelical churches are having on the indigenous church.

23. Daniel Clendenin's generally positive appraisal of Eastern Orthodoxy also highlights deficiencies in these areas (*Eastern Orthodox Christianity*, 154–58).

24. As portrayed in an October 23, 2011, CBS television documentary featuring Mount Athos in Greece.

with the parity of Scripture and tradition, papal infallibility, Mariolatry, and sacramental salvation. Catholic theologian Lawrence Cunningham acknowledges:

> Not everything in the Catholic spiritual tradition is above reproach. Indeed, some elements that run like a thread in the tradition need correction or, better, benign neglect. One must also be on guard against an overblown Platonism and even Gnosticism within certain historical circles. Some devotional works and practices barely escape the charge of magic, while others seem rather undernourished in their theology of grace.[25]

Notwithstanding many edifying spiritual practices, does Catholicism obscure entry to the spiritual journey? Minimizing definitive decisions for Christ as Savior and Lord produces what appears to be many "cradle" or nominal Catholics. A common refrain offered by converts to evangelical faith reads thusly. I "regularly attended Catholic church and my weekly catechism. My faith was important, but I did not have a personal, intimate relationship with God."[26] An acquaintance of mine recently asked a priest if he could be certain of heaven, to which the priest replied, "Anyone who lives the Golden Rule can be assured of going to heaven." A friend evidenced no interest in Christ and the church throughout his life. At his funeral Mass, the priest announced that the angels were joyously welcoming him into heaven. Mark Noll and Carolyn Nystrom rightly highlight "the problem of nominal belief and nominal practice that evangelicals and even converts to Catholicism see whenever they look at Catholicism as a whole."[27]

A recent Barna survey of 876 Catholics highlights the spiritual downside of nominal faith:

---

25. Lawrence S. Cunningham, "The Way and Ways: Reflections on Catholic Spirituality," in *Life in the Spirit: Spiritual Formation in Theological Perspective*, ed. Jeffrey P. Greenman and George Kalantzis (Downers Grove, Ill.: InterVarsity, 2010), 96.

26. Mark W. Sheehan, MD, *Healing Prayer on Holy Ground* (Lake Mary, Fla.: Creation House, 2010), 8. Another convert testifies, "I grew up in a Catholic home with a mother and grandmother who were steeped in Catholic practices and rituals and a father who silently attended. We faithfully attended weekly Mass but with very little growth or relationship with the living God."

27. Mark A. Noll and Carolyn Nystrom, *Is the Reformation Over?* (Grand Rapids: Baker, 2005), 239. For further criticism from this source generally sympathetic to Catholicism, see ibid., 250.

The typical Catholic person ... was 38 percent less likely than the average American to read the Bible; 67 percent less likely to attend a Sunday school class; 20 percent less likely to share their faith in Christ with someone who had different beliefs; 24 percent less likely to say their religious faith had greatly transformed their life; and were 36 percent less likely to have an "active faith."[28]

Barna concludes, "The survey data portray Catholics as people whose lifestyles and thought patterns are more influenced by the social mainstream than by the core principles of the Christian faith."[29] On the positive side, reform impulses enrich Catholic spirituality — the charismatic renewal, for example, underscoring personal commitment to Christ, Bible study, and evangelism. For this we are thankful.

While appreciative of progressive Protestantism's intellectual rigor and peace and justice emphases, the tradition's ambivalence vis-à-vis biblical authority, Christ's redemptive sacrifice and bodily resurrection, the uniqueness of Christianity, and positive embrace of gay and lesbian agendas undercuts spiritual life. Marching to the drumbeat of the secular culture, the tradition marginalizes the good news — the heart of authentic spirituality. Nassif and Hahn rightly lament much of progressive Protestantism's forfeiture of the historic gospel.

The 2011 *Yearbook of American and Canadian Churches* chronicles membership declines within the mainline denominations. During the past decade, membership in the United Methodist Church has dropped more than 7 percent. From 1965 to 2010, membership rolls in the Presbyterian Church (USA) have shrunk from 4.25 million to 2.07 million.[30] Sociologist Rodney Stark attributes such declines to "the rise of modernist theology and the transformation of mainline churches into centers for progressive political action.[31] Research by the Barna Group indicates that "only half of all mainline adults say that they are on a

---

28. Barna Group, "Catholics Have Become Mainstream America," www.barna.org/faith-spirituality/100-catholics-have-become-mainstream-america (accessed December 12, 2011).

29. Ibid.

30. "PCUSA gives up," *American Family Association Journal* (July/August, 2011), 10, www.onenewsnow.com/Journal/editorial.aspx?id=1385134 (accessed December 12, 2011).

31. Cited in Timothy Dalrymple, "Mainline Rides the Pine," *World* 26 (March 26, 2011): 86, www.worldmag.com/articles/17774 (accessed December 12, 2011).

personal quest for spiritual truth."[32] Joseph Driskill cites "the discomfort mainline Protestants have with things identified as 'spiritual,' for example, a personal relationship with God."[33] He attributes spiritual indifference among progressive Protestants to a quasi-deistical view of Deity and "lack of attention to spiritual practices."[34]

Evangelical Spirituality

Evangelicalism is a vital spiritual movement claiming 90 percent of the fastest-growing churches in the United States. Bradley Nassif and Scott Hahn, particularly, both express their indebtedness to evangelical faith and life. Evangelicals insist that personal relationship with Christ—the necessary foundation for spiritual life—is launched by personal conversion (Acts 11:21; 15:3) and, according to Jesus, a "born again" experience (John 3:3).

As Evan Howard and others[35] correctly point out, historic evangelicalism—represented by Martin Luther, John Calvin, the Puritans, John Wesley, Jonathan Edwards, Billy Graham, etc.—drew on biblically sound patristic and medieval protocols for nurturing spiritual life. A robust recapturing of historic regimens for enhancing the "with-God" life has occurred in recent decades within evangelicalism led by James Houston, Eugene Peterson, Dallas Willard, Richard Foster, and others. Evangelical parachurch organizations, colleges and seminaries, journals, and publishing houses actively promote classical protocols for enhancing spiritual life and ministry. The latter include silence and solitude, contemplation, reading spiritual classics, making retreats, keeping a spiritual journal, and spiritual companionship.

Many evangelicals are rediscovering the richness of liturgical worship that involves reading Scripture, sharing in biblical responses (e.g., the *Magnificat, Benedictus,* and *Nunc dimittis*), singing psalms, reciting ancient creeds, and celebrating the sacraments—all of which rehearse the faith of God's people. Reformation worship built on the structure

---

32. Barna Group, "Report Examines the State of Mainline Churches," www.barna.org/barna-update/article/17-leadership/323-report-examin (accessed December 12, 2011).

33. Driskill, *Protestant Spiritual Exercises*, xii.

34. Ibid., xiii. Driskill notes that "mainline Protestants ... continue in significant numbers to lack an appreciation for the importance of spiritual nurture per se" (ibid., xvii).

35. Robert E. Webber (*Common Roots* [Grand Rapids: Zondervan, 1978], 219) describes the revival of spirituality within evangelicalism as a "restoration of historic spirituality."

of the Catholic liturgy found in the Mass.[36] John Calvin's worship protocol included the *Kyrie, eleison* ("Lord, have mercy"), the *Sursum corda* ("lift up your hearts"), and the *Nunc dimittis* ("dismiss us now") embedded in the Catholic liturgy.

Evangelicalism today is returning to its spiritual roots. Not all have fully embraced historic spiritual resources, not the least in overreaction to excesses of late medieval spirituality. I pray that overly cautious evangelicals will explore the spiritual practices inherent in their own tradition that will result in a more spiritually vital, historic evangelicalism.

What Is God Doing?

The revival of Christian spirituality represents the providentially directed impulse of God's Spirit for the renewal of Christ's church. Through biblically faithful spiritual resources, God is renewing disciples in the image of his Son. The Spirit is guiding evangelical Christians to supplement theological correctness and respectable behaviors with deepening relationship with Christ. A Doctor of Ministry student I supervised restructured his church along a spiritual formation model. When asked why he pursued this emphasis, he replied, "I long that my people become spiritually mature so that when Jesus returns they will not be shocked when they meet him face-to-face."

The spirituality revival is transforming believers into Christ-centered mystics, where relational mysticism—as opposed to Hindu and Buddhist metaphysical mysticism—involves intimate union with, and deepened love for, the Savior. Henri Nouwen helpfully identifies Christian mystics as godly men and women who "desire to dwell in God's presence, to listen to God's voice, to look at God's beauty, to touch God's incarnate Word, and to taste fully God's infinite goodness."[37] The mystical spirituality contained in many Orthodox and Catholic writings provide positive pointers in this direction.

As an outcome of the current spirituality revival, we are learning that considerable common ground exists between committed Christians in the four traditions. Thankfully, open dialogue, respect, and

---

36. See David G. Buttrick, "Liturgy, Reformed," in *Encyclopedia of the Reformed Faith*, ed. Donald K. McKim (Louisville: Westminster, 1992), 220.

37. Henri Nouwen, *In the Name of Jesus* (New York: Crossroad, 1989), 29–30.

mutual love among God's redeemed people are being forged. An egregious fault of Christendom has been its painful divisions in disobedience to Jesus' plain command in John 17:20–23. A healthy ecumenical spirituality is being cultivated, reflected in the Society for the Study of Eastern Orthodoxy, Evangelicals and Catholics Together, and other ventures. Richard Lovelace offers the provocative insight that "during almost every awakening, Catholics and Protestants have drawn closer to one another as they are doing now, because they have been moving toward one another's partial models of spirituality to recover scriptural balance."[38]

An important caution, however, needs to be sounded. As we wade into the life-giving waters of Christian spirituality, we must remain faithful to Christ and the gospel. We must hold fast to biblical truths and faithful traditions by which the Spirit forms us in Christlikeness. Let us humbly acknowledge that on this side of glory we all see imperfectly: "We don't yet see things clearly. We're squinting in a fog, peering through a mist" (1 Corinthians 13:12 MSG). Facing the future, we must modify perspectives as necessary to keep in step with the Spirit's redeeming and sanctifying work (Galatians 5:25). All four Christian traditions do well to heed this centuries-old dictum: "The church is reformed and always being reformed."

---

38. Richard F. Lovelace, "Evangelical Spirituality: A Church Historian's Perspective," *Journal of the Evangelical Theological Society* 31 (March 1988): 34.

SCRIPTURE INDEX

SUBJECT INDEX

ABOUT THE CONTRIBUTORS

Bruce Demarest (PhD, University of Manchester) taught theology and formation at Denver Seminary and currently is senior professor of Christian formation. He is the author of fifteen books, including *The Cross and Salvation*, *Satisfy Your Soul*, and *Seasons of the Soul*. He received the certificate in spiritual formation and direction from the Pecos (New Mexico) Benedictine monastery.

Bradley Nassif (PhD, Fordham University) is an Orthodox Christian, scholar, and trusted spokesperson for Orthodoxy, known especially for his ecumenical involvement and active role in Orthodox evangelism. Dr. Nassif is currently professor of biblical and theological studies at North Park University in Chicago, Illinois. He serves as a consultant for *Time* and *Christianity Today* magazines and is the author of *Holy Land, Holy People: The Desert Fathers and Mothers*.

Scott Hahn (PhD, Marquette University) is professor of theology at Franciscan University in Steubenville, Ohio. He is the founder, president, and chairman of the board of the Saint Paul Center for Biblical Theology and is one of the world's most successful Catholic authors and teachers. Dr. Hahn is the general editor of the *Ignatius Study Bible* and author of more than twenty books, including *Letter and Spirit*, *Understanding the Scriptures*, and *The Lamb's Supper*.

Joseph Driskill (PhD, Graduate Theological Union) served as professor of spirituality at Pacific School of Religion and dean of the Disciples Seminary Foundation at the Berkeley campus. As professor emeritus, Dr. Driskill leads students in exploring Protestant spiritualities, contemplative prayer, Disciples history, and the role of spirituality in pastoral care. His publications include *Protestant Spiritual Exercises*, *Spiritually Informed Pastoral Care*, and *Ethics and Spiritual Care*.

Evan Howard (PhD, Graduate Theological Union) is the founder and director of the Spirituality Shoppe, an evangelical center for the study of Christian spirituality. He is also a lecturer in philosophy and religion at Mesa State College in Grand Junction, Colorado. He is the author of *The Brazos Introduction to Christian Spirituality*, *Affirming the Touch of God*, and *Praying the Scriptures*.

Three Views on the Millennium and Beyond

*Stanley N. Gundry, Series Editor;
Darrell L. Bock, general editor*

Are these the last days? Could Jesus return at any time to establish his thousand-year reign on earth? What is the nature of Christ's millennial kingdom referred to in the book of Revelation? What must happen before Jesus returns, and what part does the church play?

Three predominant views held by evangelicals seek to answer these and related questions: premillennial, postmillennial, and amillennial. This book gives each view a forum for presentation, critique, and defense. Besides each contributor's personal perspective, various interpretations of the different positions are discussed in the essays.

Three Views on the Millennium and Beyond lets you compare and contrast three important eschatological viewpoints to gain a better understanding of how Christianity's great hope, the return of Jesus, is understood by the church.

The Counterpoints series provides a forum for comparison and critique of different views on issues important to Christians. Counterpoints books address two categories: Church Life and Bible and Theology. Complete your library with other books in the Counterpoints series.

Available in stores and online!

Three Views on the Rapture

Pretribulation, Prewrath, or Posttribulation

Craig Blaising, Alan Hultberg, and Douglas J. Moo; Alan Hultberg, General Editor; Stanley N. Gundry, Series Editor

The rapture, or the belief that, at some point, Jesus' living followers will join him forever while others do not, is an important but contested doctrine among evangelicals. Scholars generally hold one of three perspectives on the timing of and circumstances surrounding the rapture, all of which are presented in Three Views on the Rapture. The recent prominence of a Pre-Wrath understanding of the rapture calls for a fresh examination of this important but contested Christian belief.

Alan D. Hultberg (PhD, Trinity International University and professor of New Testament at Talbot School of Theology) explains the Pre-Wrath view; Craig Blaising (PhD, Dallas Theological Seminary and president of Southwestern Baptist Theological Seminary) defends the Pre-Tribulation view; and Douglas Moo (PhD, University of St. Andrews and professor of New Testament at Wheaton College) sets forth the Post-Tribulation view. Each author provides a substantive explanation of his position, which is critiqued by the other two authors. A thorough introduction gives a historical overview of the doctrine of the rapture and its effects on the church.

The interactive and fair-minded format of the Counterpoints series allows readers to consider the strengths and weaknesses of each view and draw informed, personal conclusions.

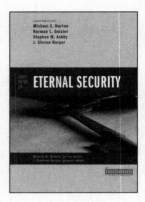

Three Views on the New Testament Use of the Old Testament

Stanley N. Gundry, Series Editor; Kenneth Berding and Jonathan Lunde, General Editors

To read the New Testament is to meet the Old Testament at every turn. But exactly how do Old Testament texts relate to their New Testament references and allusions? Moreover, what fruitful interpretive methods do New Testament texts demonstrate? Leading biblical scholars Walter Kaiser, Darrel Bock, and Peter Enns each present their answers to questions surrounding the use of the Old Testament in the New Testament.

Contributors address elements such as Divine and human authorial intent, the context of Old Testament references, and theological grounds for an interpretive method. Each author applies his framework to specific texts so that readers can see how their methods work out in practice. Each contributor also receives a thorough critique from the other two authors.

A one-stop reference for setting the scene and presenting approaches to the topic that respect the biblical text, *Three Views on the New Testament Use of Old Testament* gives readers the tools they need to develop their own views on this important subject.

Four Views on Moving Beyond the Bible to Theology

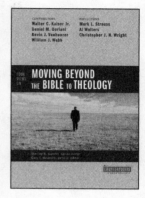

Stanley N. Gundry, Series Editor; Gary T. Meadors, General Editor

How can Bible teachers approach the same text and draw different applications for today's life of faith? How can Christians take opposing sides on contemporary issues, each side claiming their position best follows the biblical witness? Such questions drive the discussion in *Four Views on Moving Beyond the Bible to Theology.*

Scholars who affirm an inspired, relevant, and authoritative Bible each present an interpretive model they consider most faithful to biblical teaching:

- Walter C. Kaiser, Jr.: A Principlizing Model
- Daniel M. Doriani: A Redemptive-Historical Model
- Kevin J. Vanhoozer: A Drama-of-Redemption Model
- William J. Webb: A Redemptive-Movement Model

Each view receives three critiques, one from each proponent of the other positions.

Due to the far-reaching implications this topic holds for biblical studies, theology, and church teaching, *Four Views on Moving Beyond the Bible to Theology* includes three reflections from: Christopher J. H. Wright, Mark L. Strauss, and Al Wolters.

Available in stores and online!

Share Your Thoughts

With the Author: Your comments will be forwarded to
the author when you send them to *zauthor@zondervan.com*.

With Zondervan: Submit your review of this book
by writing to *zreview@zondervan.com*.

Free Online Resources at
www.zondervan.com

Zondervan AuthorTracker: Be notified whenever your favorite
authors publish new books, go on tour, or post an update
about what's happening in their lives at www.zondervan.com/
authortracker.

Daily Bible Verses and Devotions: Enrich your life with daily
Bible verses or devotions that help you start every morning
focused on God. Visit www.zondervan.com/newsletters.

Free Email Publications: Sign up for newsletters on Christian
living, academic resources, church ministry, fiction, children's
resources, and more. Visit www.zondervan.com/newsletters.

Zondervan Bible Search: Find and compare Bible passages in
a variety of translations at www.zondervanbiblesearch.com.

Other Benefits: Register to receive online benefits like
coupons and special offers, or to participate in research.

ZONDERVAN.com/
AUTHORTRACKER
follow your favorite authors